Copyright © 2021 by M.J.

The scanning, uploading (
without permission is a the   ...... author's property.
If you would like to use material from the book, please
contact lifteveryvoice20@yahoo.com

Editing of this work completed by Paul Kasselman
Cover design provided by Azarya Patterson of Wavy-A
Artz Studio
Cover created by Lynward Hunter Jr.
Photo provided by Xavier Patterson of Skipfrom41
Productions

ACKNOWLEDGMENTS

First and foremost, I give my thanks and praises to God Almighty for blessing me with the ability to complete this work. Without Him, none of this would be possible. My deepest gratitude goes to my loving and supportive husband, Jermaine, our two beautiful children, Xavier and Azarya, and our puppy Kobe. You were there to pick up the pieces when I was falling apart. You encouraged me to get back on my feet every time I fell. You supported me through the rough times and helped me celebrate my achievements. I couldn't have done this without you. Thank you my loves. I am extremely grateful to my parents, Sandra and Burleigh, for their love, support, sacrifices, and prayers over the years to ensure I had the best start to my future that they could give me. I would also like to thank my brothers and sisters Angela, Zahana, Kimberly, Jamiyl, Tremayne, LaToya and Antwine, who have been my constant friends throughout my life. A special word of thanks goes to my eldest sister, Angela Townsend-Wilson, who took time out of her busy schedule to be sure that my needs were being taken care of during my time of crisis, and to my little brother Antwine who constantly reminds me how much I am loved. I give my heartfelt thanks to all of you. I am Godly thankful for my Pastors, Lynward and Dora Hunter. Thank you for all of the love, prayers and support during this journey. I would like to thank my support team Kathy, Richard, Tyreasea, Mariame and Brooke. Finally, I would like to give a special thanks to those who have been there to support me in my times of need: Denise Esterlund, Cynthia Fish, Patricia Mayo, Davida and Amoke Wedington, Karen and Rosa Rivera, Michael Selby, Syreeta Scott, Amy Stranges, Kelly Gosik, Kathy Riddle, Allison Russell, Denise Voshell, Lorren, Jeanine, Megan, and Mia. Thank you. I love you all.

The completion of this work could not have been accomplished without the guidance of Mr. Paul Kasselman. It was a privilege and an honor to have him complete the editing of this work for me. He offered invaluable advice and continued to motivate me and inspired me to take my work to the next level. Thank you for your friendship, humor, and knowledge. I couldn't have completed this without you.

Table of Contents

All of Me

I never believed I mattered much to this world. I was too low on the scale of humanity to be of any significance. I had always felt like a tolerated nuisance, even to my family. So many times as a child I wondered if my parents had been given a choice, would they have even picked me to be their daughter. Then in my mind I am crushed by the realization that they most likely wouldn't. I held firmly to my truth that I was not created equal. Then, last year, my life took a dramatic shift; and I found myself on a journey of self-discovery, finally learning who I really am and who I have been pretending to be for over forty years. I realized I was not alone. There were other men and women, young and old, who had struggled with identifying with who they were and their sense of self. I had a story to tell, one that could help people like me. So this is me. My name is Esmene Munroe, nee Turner, a forty-three year old wife and mother of two, who lives in the small South Jersey town of Pennsauken. This is my story. My story is a love story: the story of how an innocent love morphed into a mixed stew of love and hate. It's a story of joy and pain, one full of misguided trust and cruel betrayal. It's the story of how I lost myself in the sea of mental illness and how I found my way to the lighthouse of sanity, still walking in its guiding light in a desperate attempt to save myself. This is a story of survival.

The first signs of my mental instability were evident as early as age nine, when I began to have visual hallucinations, seeing, touching, tasting or smelling things that were not actually there. These visual hallucinations were soon followed by auditory hallucinations. These are the perceptions of hearing voices that are not there. I developed other symptoms over the years which went unchecked, until they could be ignored no further. At the age of thirty, I received a correct diagnosis of Bipolar I Disorder with psychotic features. Bipolar I Disorder, formerly known as Manic-Depressive Disorder, is a mental illness defined by extreme emotional "highs" (mania) and "lows" (depression). A manic episode may include symptoms of being abnormally upbeat or wired, increased activity, euphoria, decreased need for sleep, being talkative, having racing thoughts, and poor decision making. A depressive episode may include signs of marked loss of interest in all or many activities, significant weight loss/gain, insomnia or sleeping too much, fatigue or loss of energy, decreased ability to think or concentrate, and suicidal ideation. Suicidal ideation can be passive or active. Passive suicidal ideation occurs when a person wishes he or she were dead or could die, but no plans for suicide have been made. Active suicidal ideation is having the intention to commit suicide, including a plan of how to do it. I should note that bipolar disorder is about eighty-five percent genetic. However, early childhood trauma and other life experiences have been shown to influence who will develop symptoms of bipolar disorder when there is a genetic link.

It's not unusual to be affected by multiple mental disorders or psychological impairments. I was diagnosed with several disorders and/or impairments after receiving my bipolar diagnosis. I was diagnosed with Complex Post Traumatic Stress Disorder. C-PTSD is caused by severe ongoing trauma or multiple types of trauma where the victim feels like he or she has no hope of escape. This differs from Post Traumatic Disorder, PTSD, which may be triggered by a brief, one time event such as a car crash. The symptoms of C-PTSD are severe enough to impair everyday functioning. They include visual, somatic, and emotional flashbacks, avoidance of triggers, chronic isolation, nightmares or night terrors, insomnia, severe dissociation, hypervigilance, difficulty with emotional regulation, depression, severe shame and guilt, and a distorted perception of a perpetrator. I developed a binge eating disorder as a child around the age of nine. I didn't know that I had a disorder and I carried it with me into adulthood. When I was twenty-nine, the effects of all those years of binge eating were taking a toll on my body. I was grossly overweight with high blood pressure, high cholesterol, and high blood sugar. I needed to lose weight. That is how I received my next diagnosis. In my efforts to lose weight, I developed Bulimia Nervosa, an eating disorder characterized by bouts of extreme overeating followed by extreme depression, guilt, and shame. The person who suffers from this engages in some form of purging to undo binge, either via purging which is vomiting, exercising, taking laxatives, or fasting. I am a purger.

So now you are probably wondering, what happened to bring this alphabet soup of mental illness into my life? My journey begins here.

Broken Crayons

One hot summer day, I was at my parents' house and my five year-old nephew Carter was there. Carter was the only child of my youngest brother Lyam and his wife Monica. He looked like a miniature Lyam, with his mother's mouth and nose. His little head was covered in a mop of deep chestnut curls that often got him mistaken for a girl, and his honey colored skin was glistening with a hint of sweat. He loved to color and draw; and, like his auntie, he was very meticulous when it came to his work. On that particular day, little Carter had separated himself from the other daycare children and had gone into the living room, where he was able to concentrate on coloring a page from his <u>Marvel Comics</u> coloring book. I sat on the couch and watched Carter as he deliberately colored each character, taking the time to match the colors perfectly from his over crowded box of broken, mixed, and matched crayons. He would use whatever piece of crayon he had until it rubbed down to the very tip of his tiny fingers; and then he would begin his archeological dig through the box to find an exact match, tear the paper off if he needed to, and continue working. Now I knew for a fact that Carter had several brand new boxes of crayons at his disposal, yet he insisted on struggling with this group of misfit crayons.

Finally I said to him, "Carter, why don't you throw away all those old crayons and use your new ones?" He stopped coloring, brushed the mop of curls out of his face, and looked at me with his sad brown eyes. The suggestion that he throw out his beloved crayons seemed to hurt him to his core. For a moment, I thought he might even cry. But then my beloved nephew uttered one of the most profound things I'd ever heard in my life, "But why Meme? They still work." And he went right back to his coloring, as if he had not proclaimed something life-shattering.

I sat back then and for the next hour I observed Carter as he worked diligently to finish his picture. If he required a green crayon, he worked for a green crayon, but not just any green. It had to be as close to an exact match as possible, regardless if it took ten seconds or ten minutes. Time was of no concern to Carter. The effort was worth it to obtain the results he wanted because, in the end, he would reap the benefits of his labor. Finally, his masterpiece was complete and he ran over to me with childlike pride in his eyes and presented it to me. "See Meme, this is for you." He smiled up at me.

"It's beautiful Carter, thank you." And it was. It was more beautiful than if it had been done with a brand new set of Crayola crayons with the built in sharpener. And, with my positive affirmation, Carter bounced off to his next activity, not knowing what he had just done for me. He and the Avengers had given me more than just a picture.

"But why Meme? They still work."

I pondered all those broken crayons, unsharpened and with paper torn off. Most people would have thrown them out. I would have thrown them out. But Carter didn't. Carter saw they still had value. The crayons had worth, a purpose beyond their brokenness.

As I watched Carter painstakingly go through those crayons looking for the perfect match, I felt like those broken crayons were a metaphor for how I lived most of my life. I don't ever recall a time in my life being in the brand new box of crayons. I don't ever recall being "showroom new." I was just a mismatched, half-used, broken, cast-aside, piece of nothing or something of nothing. Yet, I still worked. My life was like a Picasso. I knew from afar it could be a work of art; but up close, it was just a giant mess. Yet, somehow, it still managed to work.

I thank God for the Carters in my life who helped me believe I had a purpose because, if it were left up to me, I would have discarded myself long ago, just like I would've done with those crayons.

And, like Carter who saw that those crayons had so much value that he was willing to put the time and effort to dig through hundreds of pieces to find just the right shade of green to make the Incredible Hulk come alive, God, my husband, my children, my parents, my siblings, my church family and my close friends, doctors and therapist...they all believed I still had value. They believed I had a purpose. Like Carter, they were all willing to dig through all the broken bits to get to me, to keep me alive.

Yes, I was broken; but, by the grace of God and my human saviors, I still worked.

The Show Is Over, Say Goodbye

January, 2019

I can't say when the thoughts of ending my life became so obsessive; but one morning, with tears constantly stinging my eyes, that's all I could think of.

I was tired, tired of pretending, tired of donning the mask every single day for the sake of everyone else. My husband Jericho, our children, and my family needed me to be OK. On the outside, I did the right things and said the right things, just like I always did. All my life I majored in studying people, how to act, appropriate and inappropriate responses. Do this, not that. Laugh at this, cry at that. My responses to life were routinely not genuine. They were just how I learned to mimic the human condition. It was getting too burdensome to go on living like that. If I couldn't live authentically, what was the point of living at all? I was broken-down with the hurt I had been carrying all those years, all the painful, dirty little secrets I carried deep in my heart, secrets I dared not give voice to. Everything in my life was taking too much effort. Just getting a shower in the morning was an arduous task. I would go three or four days without seeing the inside of my tub. Personal wipes, witch hazel and alcohol swabs had become my best friends. My hair was a tangled mess. For the longest time, I was a mess; but no one noticed. My mask that broadcast to the world that I was OK was firmly in place.

No more. I could do it no more.

I thought about Jericho and our children and how they would urge me to continue to fight, but I was tired. I wanted to implore them, please, say goodbye to me tonight. Please just let me go. The children, Zander and Zeyonna, were young enough that they could go on with their lives. They could let me go before I caused them irreparable damage. This was the greatest gift I could give them. To my husband Jericho, my love, I thought, please, let me go. He deserved better. I didn't want him to one day look back on everything he had to sacrifice because of me and resent me for it. That would be worse than death. I wanted to say, please, set yourself free. Please just let me go... I'd lived in this world, but I had never belonged in this world. I didn't ever remember fitting in, not even amongst my siblings. I played the part well, but I've always known that there was something not quite right with Esmene. I think they knew it too. I had suffered way too long. My sin was being born. I'd paid the price for my sin. I wanted to tell the world, please, be kind and set me free...

I don't know what compelled me to reach out to Jericho and tell him my thoughts of suicide through a text message that morning, but I did. When I got home from work, he was waiting for me, having taken time off from work to take me to my psychiatrist, Dr. Diane. When I arrived, she asked "Are you finally ready to go to the hospital Esmene? They're waiting for you."

I looked at my phone, showing a picture of my children, Zander and Zeyonna, as a screensaver. I thought about the pain my death would cause them. I had to live for something. I had to live for them. I decided no one would say goodbye to me tonight. "Yes. Yes, I'll go." I looked at my husband who squeezed my hand tightly, silently letting me know he would be right by my side as I took a detour down a foreign road and embarked on a new journey. Just like always, he was supporting me along the way.

It was time to take the mask off.

Wet Dreams

In the fall of 1980, my parents, Bella and Barock, enrolled me in a Catholic preschool in East Camden at the ripe old age of three. They wanted to capitalize on my seemingly high intellect. The school was adjacent to the elementary school where Delilah, my older sister by four and a half years, was in the third grade. I was very young, so I have very few memories of my two years there; but one of the memories I have is branded in my brain for life.

Every day at dismissal time, my sister would walk over to the preschool to get me so we could walk the three blocks home together. And every single day that she came to pick me up, without fail, my napping cot would be outside drying because I had once again wet myself during naptime.

Every...Single...Day. I hated taking naps. I hated sleeping, period.

Angel, my uncle, would come to me when it was time to sleep, so sleeping was a time when I was most vulnerable. It was the time when bad things happened to me. Going to sleep caused me lots of anxiety. It's the reason why I suffer with such crippling insomnia to this day. No matter where I was, he would find me. And I knew, even with God and the nuns around me, he would find me there too. I would work myself into such a frenzy, I would release right onto my bed and relish the liquid warmth my urine would momentarily provide. Then the shame would come. It was the same shame I would feel whenever Uncle came to me.

At night, I would sing in bed to get my Mommy's attention, hoping she would come into my room and stay awhile, so Uncle would get scared and not come. But my singing was keeping Delilah up, so my Mommy told me that singing in bed would make the devil come get me. She didn't know how wrong she was. He'd get me when I was quiet. For he came for me more often than she knew. Only the devil wasn't red with horns and sharp teeth. The devil was an Angel. I never sang in bed again. Then nothing would deter the devil, for he was relentless. "Hush now. Don't cry. Don't make a sound," he would whisper hotly in my ear as his spider-like fingers would begin to travel over my non-existent busom. Don't cry. Don't scream. Don't tell. Don't fight. Don't sing. Don't pee. Don't sleep. Don't Don't Don't Don't Don't Don't Don't Don't Don't Don't...

And of course, being an older sibling, Delilah couldn't wait to run home and tell Mommy that once again I had failed to control my bladder in school. Mommy theorized something must be going on in school, because I never wet myself at home, which was true. I had only wet myself once (that they knew of) at home, and my father spanked me. I was going through enough at home and I didn't need Daddy spanking me too, so I learned to hide it if I did have an accident. Mommy asked me some questions and she thought maybe it was because the nuns were giving me a snack and then putting me down for a nap without letting me go to the bathroom. After all, I may have been on the same level with those kids intellectually, but by this time I had just turned four. Those kids were already five. Mommy wrote a note to the nuns telling them that if they gave me a snack, they should take me to the bathroom before putting me down for a nap. That seemed to solve the problem. What they didn't know was that I gave up trying to force myself to take a nap. While the other kids would drift off to a peaceful sleep, I would travel to another world that existed only in my mind. I would close my eyes and it would be like my mind would leave my body. I would be in a world all of my own. I can't tell you where I was, but I wasn't in preschool on that cot and I wasn't being assaulted in my bed. I was somewhere safe and happy. It was a place where "DON'T" didn't exist.

My aversion to napping has continued throughout my life. My children were never on a napping schedule when they were at home with me. If they told me they didn't want to take a nap...OK, no nap. If Jericho came home during the day and found me asleep, he immediately knew something was wrong. I slept during the day if I was sick or depressed. I could be absolutely exhausted at the end of the day; but as soon as my head hit the pillow, an inner alert would go off and I couldn't relax and fall asleep. I was at the time on five medications at night to help me sleep. I've been on many. This combo was working really well and I prayed it would continue.

But nothing would erase the memories of the nuns and that damn wet cot.

Grooming, on a Sunday Afternoon

My mother, Bella Simone, married my father, Barock Turner, shortly after she graduated high school in Philadelphia in 1971. They initially moved to Camden, NJ, but finally settled the family in Pennsauken NJ, where I currently live today. She was eighteen and my father was twenty-five. Mommy was a soft spoken girl who grew up in Philadelphia. She was the oldest girl of seven siblings, and my grandparents raised all their children together. Mommy was a short woman; in fact, none of us girls would reach past her diminutive height of five foot-two. Mommy had long, thick, dark brown hair that she had fashioned in a giant afro. Her slanted eyes paired well with her skin which was the color of coffee with just a tad extra cream in it, giving her an almost exotic look. I have to admit, Mommy had it going on. Daddy wasn't tall either. He stood about five foot-nine I would guess. He was born and raised in a small town in Virginia and lived with his mother, Kathleen. His younger sister, Marie, had been sent up north to New Jersey when she was a baby to be raised by other relatives because my grandmother was too young and couldn't care for both children. Daddy was a good looking man. His skin was smooth and rich like black silk. He had a normal build, not too muscular, not too thin. His most distinct feature was his high cheekbones, which is the primary thing my siblings and I inherited from him in the way of looks. Daddy loved to ride his motorcycle and he was even a member of a local motorcycle gang. Sometimes he would take me to the clubhouse but leave me outside in the van while he went inside to take care of "club business." But then I opened my big mouth about it and Mommy found out. No more trips to the club for me.

My sister, Delilah, was born within their first year of marriage in April, 1972. Daddy already had a daughter named Michaela who was five, from a previous relationship; but she lived with her mother, Ms. Leah, and her other siblings in Delaware. There was a second daughter born in April 1973; tragically the infant passed away shortly after birth. I was born in November of 1976. I was followed by my siblings Braxton in 1982, McKenna in 1983, and Lyam in 1984. Mommy was a stay at home mom. Her whole life was wrapped up into taking care of us kids. She never had a friend come over or had visitors. Daddy purchased one of those big conversion vans so she could travel with all of us when she needed to go somewhere. The people in the neighborhood dubbed us the Turner ducklings; we all filed out behind Mommy, each one of us a carbon copy of Mommy. Delilah and I were golden brown, while the three little ones were pale yellow. We all had slanted brown eyes as if we had some asian ancestry. Mommy didn't cut my brothers' hair until they started school, so we all had long, thick hair that mom kept braided. Daddy worked a lot at his job with the utility company in order to provide for all of us. We never really saw Daddy; we just knew a man lived in our house. He would be gone before we got up in the morning and he would still be gone when we went to bed at night. This routine continued up until his retirement. If we needed something from Daddy, we would leave a note by his dinner plate with our request. The next morning, we would know if our request was granted. Kids at school thought my siblings and I were lying that we had a dad. We would insist we did, but we had no proof. He didn't even come to our graduations. Surely, if you had a dad, he would be there, right? But Daddy had a choice to make and he made it. He sacrificed his relationships with his wife and children to provide for us, and we couldn't be upset about that. However, because Mommy was young, she had her hands full and needed help. Her immediate family lived in Philadelphia and Daddy's family was from Virginia, so other than Daddy's sister, Aunt Marie, and her two children, we didn't have many close relatives in New Jersey. Delilah was the oldest but she had attachment issues when it came to Mommy. If Mommy left Delilah to stay with anyone, Delilah would have major meltdowns and anxiety attacks. Leaving her with a sitter was not an option. Out of the blue, my younger siblings seemed to be plagued with medical issues and were constantly in the hospital or at a doctor's appointment. Then, when Delilah was twelve, she was diagnosed with diabetes, which started a series of hospitalizations and made her anxiety worse. It was too much for Mommy who was a very young parent. She needed help from someone. That's when Uncle Angel offered to step in to help. Since I never seemed to be sick or have any issues that needed attending, I was often left in Uncle's care.

Angel Christopher was not biologically my uncle. Biologically, he was my second cousin on my mother's side. My siblings and I started calling him Uncle because he was older than Mommy and we would play with his great nieces and nephews. They called him Uncle, so we followed suit. If I had to take a guess, he was probably in his early to mid thirties at the time when I was four. Uncle was a very charismatic man and quite handsome. He was about six foot three inches tall with a sturdy build. Due to his racial mix, African American and Italian, he was very fair complected, with long, dark, wavy hair that fell well below his shoulders. His eyes, depending on his temper, would be hazel or a shade of green. His lips were full and his teeth were pearly white. Uncle was smart, brilliant even. Well, at least he seemed brilliant to me. A lot of what I knew as a child I learned from him. I spent a lot of time with Uncle when I was a child. It wasn't because I wanted to. Our time spent together was born out of necessity. And in our time together, Uncle taught me many things, both good and bad.

I don't take baths as an adult. It's because of Uncle. Uncle would run a bath for me and let me play in the Mr. Bubble for about fifteen minutes. He would say "OK, Baby Girl, time for me to get you all clean." Mommy or my sister Delilah were the only ones who had bathed me previously; but Mommy told me to do what Uncle said, so I didn't put up a fuss.

Everything was fine until it was time to wash my private area. Something about his touch was different from Mommy's. He seemed to be sticking me, hurting me a little. I said "ouch" a few times. He said it hurt because we didn't have the same body parts and he was sorry if he was being a little rough. It was OK for me to tell him how I was feeling so he would know what to do to make me feel better.

Once I was done in the tub, Uncle would make me lie down on the bed and spread my legs. He said he needed to wipe inside my vagina with a rag to make sure he got all the soap out and to make sure I was all clean. I asked him what was a vagina and why he had to do that. Mommy didn't do that. He said vagina was the adult word for my private parts. Uncle said I was a big girl and didn't need to use baby words for my private areas. He said Mommy was still young and didn't always know the best way to do things. But Uncle said not to tell her because I would make her cry. I didn't want to make Mommy cry. He would make sure I was clean because if I smelled, the kids in school would make fun of me. Joshua was a little boy who had to sit in the back of the class. Everyone made fun of in school for smelling like poop and no one wanted to sit next to him. I didn't want to be another stinky kid in class. So even though it hurt a little and I would be sore, I was glad Uncle was thinking of what was best for me.

Thank you Uncle for taking care of me.

Uncle was very cunning. Uncle never wore a shirt when he gave me a bath. He didn't want it to get all wet, he said.

He always reminded me to make sure I didn't knock the plug out the drain, because I would go down the drain with the water. I believed it and it terrified me. Each time he bathed me, he would "accidentally" knock the plug out. I would scream and frantically throw my warm wet body onto his naked chest and wrap my little five year old body around him like a second skin. Uncle would hold me close, rub my back, caress my little bottom to sooth me, and then carry me to my bed.

"I'm sorry baby. Uncle has big hands and I guess my hands hit the plug again. But don't worry, I would never let my special girl go down the drain. I'll never let you go," Uncle would whisper into my neck. I would feel warm and safe in his arms as he would lay me back on my bed and perform his ritual of cleaning me to make sure I was fresh and clean.

Thank you Uncle for saving me.

Uncle always made sure to moisturize my skin. He would rub me down with baby oil or vaseline so I wouldn't be ashy. I remember the first time he asked me if it felt nice getting rubbed down after a bath. I said yes, it made me sleepy. He said he wished he had someone do that for him. I was eager to please Uncle after everything he had done for me. At this point, I was a little older, maybe seven. Surely, I could put Vaseline on my Uncle. He said he would appreciate such a gift. He took a quick shower and called me into the room he stayed in when he slept over. He had his robe on and had me start on his back. Then he had me move to the front and sit on his lap and start rubbing some on his chest. He made a sound like he was in pain. I jumped back. "Uncle, did I hurt you?"

He grabbed me by my waist and pulled me closer. "No baby, it feels real good. Keep going." I smiled, knowing I was doing it right, but Uncle had something on his lap poking me.

"Uncle, something's sticking me," I whined.

Uncle just smiled and asked if I wanted to see what it was. I nodded my consent. He scooted me back onto his knees and pulled his robe back. Protruding between his thighs was the ugliest thing I had ever seen. It was ramrod, straight with lines on it. It looked painful, like a monster. And it was a monster. I tried to back away, but Uncle held me by my waist. "Don't be afraid baby girl. It's called a penis. Women have vaginas. Men have a penis. And just like I make sure your vagina is clean, you need to make sure my penis is clean."

I remember shaking my head no so hard I gave myself a headache. "No. What do you mean no? As many times as I've cleaned your dirty behind? It's OK Baby Girl. I'll do it myself. I guess I love you more than you love me," he said with a sad look on his face.

Nooo ...that wasn't true. I loved Uncle. He saved me from the drain. He took care of me. So I held my little hand out for some Vaseline. Uncle smiled at me and kissed my cheek. "That's my baby."

I touched it. It jerked. My little hand could barely go half way around. Uncle told me to use both hands and rub the Vaseline up and down, especially around the top. It got really dry there and would hurt if I didn't do it right.

I didn't want Uncle to hurt. I started to rub it like he told me and Uncle started making the most God awful sounds I had ever heard him make. I believed I was hurting him but he kept telling me it felt good and to go faster. I did what Uncle told me to do but my little hands and wrists started to hurt. I told Uncle this and he told me just do it a little longer. His face looked like he was in agony. I didn't want to hurt Uncle so I slowed down. He grabbed my hands in a painful grip and pumped them up and down on his penis until suddenly a hot fluid erupted out of the top of his penis onto my little hands and his stomach. Uncle was moaning and groaning and his thighs were twitching.

Uncle laid back on the bed with me still sitting on his lap. I thought he had passed out but then he groaned again and his breathing was loud. I turned my hands over to examine the fluid that was now cooled on my fingers. It wasn't totally white but it wasn't clear either. I held it up to my nose to smell it. What the heck was it? "Uncle. Uncle?" I called out to him.

Uncle sat up and looked at me with sleepy eyes. "Thank you baby. Thank you. You're the best." Uncle took my face in his hands and kissed me right on the lips! He never did that before. I had only seen Mommy and Daddy do that.

"OK, Baby Girl, go wash your hands. Wash them good. And change your panties. I'm going to wash them. Then I'm going to take you to get your favorite ice cream for being such a good girl," he said and gave me a high five.

My favorite ice cream! Oh boy! "OK, Uncle," I said, still reeling from the events that just took place but excited about my reward for being good.

Uncle lifted me off of his lap and gave me a little slap on the buttocks to send me on my way. "Oh, and Esmene. Remember, this is our secret. What happens between us, stays between us. OK?"

"Yes Uncle," I said as I walked out, totally confused by the emotions tumbling around inside of me.

Unbeknownst to me, I had performed my first hand job. Yes, Uncle taught me many things.

Summer Solace

When I was a kid, summers were the best, but not because school was out. I was a nerd and I actually loved school until I got to high school. No, I loved summer because summer meant Michaela would be with me; and if Michaela was around, I would be safe. Michaela was my eldest sister, Dad's daughter from a previous relationship. She was ten years my senior. We didn't do halves in our family. Michaela was our sister; and when she was with us, she got treated just like the rest of us. During the school year, Michaela lived in Delaware with her mother, Ms. Leah, and her five other siblings. She wasn't the oldest of her other siblings but she was the oldest of us and she took her job very seriously.

I looked up to Michaela. She was everything I wasn't. She was popular, beautiful, tall, and thin. She had luxurious thick long hair that was down to her waist and made haters out of people. It looked beautiful against her chocolate skin. She reminded me of a Black Cherokee papoose. And talk about smart, this girl was brilliant. I wished I could be half as smart as she.

Delilah didn't like it too much when Michaela was in town because Michaela stole her thunder as the alpha sibling. I didn't care. I loved Michaela being there because while she was there, Uncle stayed away. She was very protective of her siblings and very outspoken. All I would have to do is say one word and she would have saved me.

So why didn't I ever say anything?

When Michaela was there, the world with Uncle in it did not exist. I didn't allow his presence to pollute the precious little time we had together. I was greedy, desperate for every minute I could get with her, not willing to give up a second of that attention over to him. I didn't think of what was going to happen once she left. That world didn't exist.

This world, where I was a child, a little sister being protected and loved by her big sister, that's the only world that mattered to me. But then the end of summer would come and reality would set in. Michaela's bags would make their dreaded appearance. And then so would Uncle. "Sis, don't be sad. I'll be back for Christmas this year," she said to reassure me. Christmas was a lifetime away for the hell I knew lay before me once she left. I would sit on the bed watching her pack and feel the heat of Uncle's gaze from the doorway watching us. I would pay dearly for my reprieve. "Don't cry Esme. You do this every time. What's wrong?" She sat on the bed and put her long arm around my shoulder. I nestled into the crook of her arm, knowing this was the last gentle touch I would feel for a while.

But I didn't take the chance to tell her anything. Uncle was watching.

Before I was ready, her bags were packed and she was in the back of the van, ready for Dad to take her back to Delaware. "Bye, everybody. See you at Christmas!" Michaela yelled and blew us a kiss. I ran over to the van, stepped up onto the runner, and pulled myself up with the door handle so I could see her one last time. She looked at me with worry in her eyes. "Esmene, what is it? What's wrong?" she asked as she reached out to grab my little hand.

Don't go, I thought to myself. I quickly glanced over at Uncle who was still watching. "I love you Michaela," I said and then hopped down and ran into the house. I couldn't bear to see her drive away. My fall was coming.

The Day Little Bobby Died

I will forever remember the day little Bobby died right before my eyes.

When I was nine, we had moved into a new home in Pennsauken, and our neighbors had a son who was about the same age as my little brother Braxton who at the time was four. The little boy was a handful for his mother and misbehaved often. One day, while looking out the window, I saw the young boy dressed in denim Osh Kosh overalls, a red shirt, and blue canvas sneakers along with his unmistakable platinum blond hair fluttering through our yard! I yelled out the window "Bobby! Bobby!"

He ran behind my father's work shed and had somehow managed to climb onto the roof. He was standing precariously on the edge looking down at the ground. "Mom, Bobby is on the roof of Dad's shed!" I called out to my mother. I could hear two sets of footsteps approaching the family room, one frantic and one even paced, as I turned my attention back to the scene outside.

"BOBBY GET BACK! YOU'RE GONNA FALL!!!" I yelled out the window.

And then it happened. In slow motion, little Bobby looked at me with that cherubic face and angelic smile. He held his arms out like eagles wings and jumped off the shed disappearing from my sight.

"NOOOO!!!" I screamed.

"What in the world is wrong with you?!" my mother demanded in her dulcet tone. Mom was a mild-mannered woman with the patience of a saint. Even when she yelled at us, it came off as sweet. I knew the even set of footsteps belonged to her. The other frantic, uneven footsteps belonged to Delilah who was now a teenager.

With tears streaming down my face, I told her, "Bobby's hurt. He just jumped off Dad's shed. He's got to be stuck behind it, hurt...or dead. Oh my God, he's probably dead!" I said in near hysterics.

My mother was looking out the window skeptically. "I don't see anything. Why would his mother let him be running through our yard like that? And how could he climb up on that shed? He's only four. What's gotten into you?" she asked, looking at me with concern all over her face. Delilah, who was now the same height as Mom, five foot-two, decided to chime in also. "There's nothing out there Es. Maybe you saw their cat run through the yard. She's white. Or maybe, I don't know, maybe you fell asleep and were dreaming? You should stop reading all that Stephen King crap and stuff like this wouldn't happen," she said, folding her arms like I imagine Dad would as she studied me.

By this time, Braxton, Mckenna, and Lyam had joined us in the family room. McKenna and Lyam were only two and one, so they weren't invested in what was going on; but Braxton had heard that his friend was outside, so he hopped up on the couch to look out the window too. "Where's Bobby Mommy? Can he come play?" Braxton turned to my mom and asked with a toothless smile. My mother in turn gave me an exasperated look because now she was going to have to deal with Braxton asking to play with Bobby and he couldn't because Bobby wasn't there. But I knew the truth. Braxton couldn't play with Bobby because Bobby was hurt...or worse.

At that I got angry and jumped off the couch. "I know what I saw!" I yelled before running outside and calling his name. But he didn't answer. Of course he didn't answer. He was probably unconscious...or worse, dead. I was too big to get behind the shed. My mother and sister were of no help, so I went to the one person I knew would help. I ran next door and rang the doorbell. Bobby's mother, a petite chestnut haired woman came to the door. I didn't even give her a chance to say anything.

"Bobby just jumped off the roof of my Dad's shed and he's... I think he's hurt!" I blurted out completely out of breath. I didn't want to tell her that her son was dead. An immediate look of horror came over her face, followed suddenly by disbelief. She let out a small laugh of relief. I was totally confused. "Honey, you must be mistaken. Bobby is upstairs taking his nap."

"No, he can't be. I saw him. He ran through the yard. He was on top of the shed. He looked right at me before he jumped!" I insisted, wondering why no one believed me. The sincerity in my voice caused doubt and something I couldn't define to seep into her eyes. She ushered me into the house and up the stairs, not only to calm me but I think to put herself at ease.

Slowly she pushed open Bobby's door. I prepared myself for screeching when she saw her little boy wasn't there... But on the bed, in an undershirt and Ninja Turtle Underwear, was Bobby peacefully sleeping. No Osh Kosh overalls. Not running through our yard. Not jumping off Dad's shed. Not dead.

"But...but I saw him," was all I could say. I could feel the burning of tears behind my eyes and nose.

"I know you did sweetie. Maybe you should get something to drink and go take a nap. It's really warm today," she said, giving me a sympathetic smile.

With a gentle hand on my shoulder she escorted me to the door. I turned to her, unable to meet her eyes. "I'm sorry."

"It's OK. I'm glad you were looking out for Bobby. Now go home and get some rest."

That incident was still the source of jokes with Mom, Delilah, and Braxton. At the time, none of us realized what was actually happening to me, the onset of psychosis.

.   Now I know, though I suspect I've known all along, something was seriously wrong with me. At the ripe old age of nine, I had experienced what was my first visual hallucination. It still amazes me how clearly I could envision Bobby on that day, more clearly than I can recall an experience that actually occurred yesterday.

Perhaps it actually did manifest, in a reality all of my own.

How to Save a Life

I remember my parents had taken the rare opportunity to go to the movies and do a bit of shopping at The Pennsauken Mart. The Mart, as it was known locally, was like an indoor flea market and the best place to spend your Friday nights and enjoy a hot, fresh soft pretzel from the Mart Pretzel Bakery. Uncle was watching us. I was ten and my younger brother Braxton was five. Delilah was at work. She had gotten a part-time job wrapping gifts at JCPenney in the Audubon Shopping Plaza. McKenna and Lyam had been dropped off with Dad's sister, Aunt Marie, because they could sometimes be too much for Uncle to handle without Delilah.

Braxton and I were in the living room watching <u>Fraggle Rock</u>. Uncle had been watching television in my parents' room. Halfway through the program, Uncle came out of the room and called for me. "Esme. Come here," he said in a heavy voice.

I wasn't even paying attention to the tone of his voice. I was upset that he was interrupting me at the climax of the show. His timing was the worst! "Hold on a second!" I yelled back, looking at Braxton and shaking my head.

"Come here now, Esmene!" he demanded. That voice got my attention. My heart started thumping in my chest.

My little brother looked up at me with a silent question in his eyes. Braxton was the quiet one of the group. Whatever question he had would go unasked. "Wait here B, I'll be right back," I told him. He just looked at me, nodded, and turned his attention back to the television.

I turned and slowly made my way back to my parents' bedroom. The door was left open a crack. I pushed the door open and Uncle was in there lying on the bed with his shirt off and his pants undone. "Come over here Esmene," he said.

I thought NO, not again. Not tonight. "No, I don't want to," I said quietly, unsure of myself. Uncle didn't like that. Uncle sat up on the bed and crossed his arms, looking at me. "Did you just tell me no?" I didn't dare look him in the face. I could feel the vomit starting to churn in my belly. "Yeah," I said. "Oh yeah?" he asked. I looked up at that, but did not respond. "OK, go on ahead, you can go," he said and then he waved me away with his hand.

Oh my gosh! I couldn't believe it! I stood up for myself and it worked! I walked back into the living room with a new sense of pride in myself. I sat down next to Braxton and...Uncle came from around the corner and picked Braxton up. "Hey Buddy, since your sister doesn't want to come watch TV with her favorite uncle, how about you?" Uncle looked at me pointedly as he tickled my brother's chin. He turned with my brother in his arms and I heard my parents' door close.

A cold panic swept through me like nothing I had ever felt before. What was he going to do to Braxton? How was I going to save him? I felt like my mind was short circuiting. Whatever I was going to do, I had to do it quickly. I couldn't let him do to Braxton what he had been doing to me.

Without much thought, I ran into the kitchen and grabbed a butter knife because I wasn't allowed to touch the sharp ones. I got to my parents' door and took a deep breath, trying to steady my hand so I could open it, praying it wasn't locked. I tried the knob and the door opened. When I went in the room, Uncle was laying on the bed with Braxton on his chest. I quickly hopped up on the bed to grab Braxton; and when Uncle tried to grab for me, I held the knife up to his face. "Whoa, whoa. What you think you about to do with that knife?" he asked with a sleazy smile.

By this time Braxton had climbed across the bed towards me and was on the floor safe. I backed off the bed towards Braxton and was still holding the butter knife in front of me to protect us. "I'll kill you! I swear to God I'll kill you! Stay away from him!" By this time I was crying hysterically. Braxton was looking between me and Uncle. His little hand grabbed mine.

Uncle chuckled and then held his hands up in surrender. "OK, OK tough girl. Go on, get out of here."

I started backing out of the room with Braxton, making sure Uncle wasn't moving towards us. I closed the door once we were out of the room so I could hear if he opened it. We quickly made our escape and I took Braxton up into the little crawlspace in my room. We climbed in there and hid behind some boxes. Braxton, being the quiet one, just looked at me with his silent question. I explained to him "We're going to play a game. Hide and seek. We have to hide from Uncle. If he doesn't find us, we win. Now we have to be quiet, OK?"

Braxton smiled up at me and nodded his head in understanding. I was so thankful this had not happened with McKenna or Lyam. There was no way they would have kept their mouths shut or would have been so trusting. There was a little light in the crawlspace and some old toys, so I turned the light on and we played. I would be able to hear if Uncle was coming up the steps.

After what seemed like an eternity, I heard my parents' car pull into the driveway. I let out a breath I didn't even know I was holding. Braxton heard it too and looked at me, his brown eyes wide with anticipation. I took the toys from his hands and turned his face to look at me. "OK, B," I said. "Mommy and Daddy are back so the game is over. We won! Uncle didn't find us!" I did a little high five celebration with him. "Since the game is over, we can leave our hiding space; but don't tell where our hiding space is so the next time we play, we can win the game again. OK?" Braxton nodded his head enthusiastically.

Gently, I opened the crawl space doors and let Braxton out. I slowly got out myself and made my way over to the steps to listen to the conversation downstairs. Uncle reported, "The kids were good. Didn't have a problem with them, right B?" I closed my door with shaky hands. I walked back over to the crawl space, found the butter knife, and then turned out the light. I placed the butter knife under my pillow where it would remain until it could be replaced by a sharp knife. And after securing my protection under my pillow, I succumbed to a thousand tears. I may not have ever saved myself, but on that night I saved my brother.

Sometimes, even now, my brother and I will share a look; and I often wonder if he remembers that night in the crawlspace all those years ago. For his sake, I hope that he doesn't. And if he does remember, I would want him to know I would do it all over again to protect him. I pray that, for his life, it's made all the difference.

Faustian Bargains

"Esmene..."

I heard the soft whisper of my name from across my darkened bedroom one night. I had just turned eleven years old and would at times share my room with my little sister Mckenna who was now four. We had just engaged in another battle over me keeping the light on in our room because I wanted to finish reading my current book. We made such a ruckus, Mom came up and made my sister sleep downstairs with my little brothers. I had to turn off my light. There would be no more reading for me that night.

"Eessmeeneee..."

She was such a brat. So now why was she back in the room bothering me? "Will you leave me alone? I'm trying to sleep!" I yelled at her.

Her voice was getting closer, but it sounded different; or maybe I was really getting pissed off. I reached beside my bed for the pile of books that lived there and threw one in the direction of her voice. "I said beat it or I'm telling Mom!" I huffed, punched my pillow a few times, and lay back down with my face towards the wall. I just assumed she left because I heard no footsteps. I never once stopped to think why would she be out of her bed. And that's when a new terror happened.

"ESMENE!"

The voice was a loud whisper in my ear, a voice that didn't belong to my sister. I jumped up and looked around in the dark for the source of the voice. I saw nothing in the shadows. I was too terrified to reach for the light, terrified to see what was in my room; but I turned on the light anyway.

Nothing! There was nothing and no one. Whoever or whatever it was must have hidden in my closet...or worse, under my bed. Whatever I was going to do, I was going to have to do swiftly before IT got me. I gathered all the courage I could muster, scampered like a bunny rabbit into the next room, and slammed the door. It was the first time I willingly went into a room with Uncle. "What the hell's wrong with you?" he murmured.

"There's something in my room Uncle. Something's calling my name," I told him, my voice shaking with fear.

He buried his face further in his pillow. "Girl you just had a bad dream. Go on back to bed and stop with your nonsense. You're too smart to be imagining stuff."

I was near hysterics. I jumped on the bed and grabbed his shoulders, the first time I willingly grabbed his unclothed body. "I wasn't dreaming!" I yelled with tears streaming down my little face. "There's something in my room. You have to go look. Please Uncle, I'm scared!"

He rolled over and looked at me then. This time he REALLY looked at me. "OK baby girl. If you that scared, you can sleep in here with me," he said with a wicked sneer.

I felt like someone had punched me in the chest. I didn't want to sleep in the room with Uncle. I knew what that might lead to but I didn't want to be in the room with IT either. What was I to do? So I said "OK, come with me to get my pillow and blanket. I'll sleep on the floor."

Uncle smiled at me and pulled back the covers. He was clad only in his underwear and I could see that he was already aroused. My fear had excited him. "Now you know I won't let my Baby Girl sleep on the floor. You either get in this bed with me or go back to your room. And hurry up and choose. It's cold in here."

I looked back at his closed door, tempted to run back, open the door, and go wake up Mom. But then I remembered the Bobby incident, how she didn't believe me, and how the incident had become a family joke at my expense. No, I thought, I couldn't go to Mom. But maybe Delilah? No, Delilah slept like the dead. Something would kill me before she woke up. In my eleven year old mind, I only had two choices: dance with the devil I knew or face the new one I didn't know.

So I chose to sell my soul to the devil I knew for the protection he would give. Uncle would hurt me, but I was accustomed to his brand of hurt. And I knew Uncle would never allow me to be hurt by anyone else because I was his, his alone. I was terrified because I didn't know what this new devil had in store for me.

But as I lay there that night, being soiled by this Uncle who claimed to love me, I vowed to align myself with the new devil. Whatever it was, I realized, nothing could be worse than the crushing hell I was experiencing with Uncle at that moment.

So began our Tango down the Caramingo, my auditory hallucinations and I. It has been a love-hate relationship between us, one I've both despised and held onto tighter than my true love.

Yes, I sold my soul to two devils that night. It cost me more than I bargained for.

<u>Share My World</u>

Mom and Dad had gone out to Seafood Shanty in Cherry Hill one evening to celebrate their anniversary. All of us kids were home and, of course, Uncle was there to keep an eye on us. Delilah was now fifteen and I was a few months shy of turning twelve, so we were old enough to watch ourselves and the little ones; but my parents weren't comfortable leaving us at night. So, as usual, Uncle was more than willing to accommodate them.

Delilah, Braxton, McKenna, and Lyam were all downstairs watching a movie; and I was up in my room trying to put all my books in some kind of order. Dad had come up into my room, saw my books lying all over the room, and told Mom not to buy me any more until I got my mess under control. So, I was in my room putting them into neat little stacks in the corner. When he got home, I was going to ask him if he could buy me a bookcase.

I heard the doorbell and it made me jump. I had been doing that a lot lately, I realized. I was startled so easily. Uncle came out of his room. He asked as he flashed his pearly white smile, "Whatcha doin' Baby Girl?"

"Dad said I had to clean up my books or I couldn't get any new ones," I explained. Then I turned back to my work.

"OK, well I got my buddy coming up, but we just gonna be in my room talkin' 'bout some business," he said. Then he went down the steps to answer the door.

I didn't like that. A strange man was coming in the house? I was immediately on alert. I could feel the anxiety creeping into my chest. I looked at the mountain of books surrounding me and wondered if I could get away with shoving them in my closet. But I knew Dad and his room inspections. Dad's job forced him to take a one week vacation every year because he never took a day off from work. During that week, each one of our rooms received a thorough inspection. The closets and under the beds were his target spots. You couldn't get away with hiding stuff there. I began to work quicker. Instead of keeping the books together by genre, I just started stacking them. I did, however, still keep them grouped by author. My undetected OCD wasn't going to take the chaos that far.

I heard two sets of heavy footsteps jog up the steps. "Baby Girl, this my homeboy, Jon-Jon," Uncle said, making the introduction.

Jon-Jon smiled at me with his gold tooth and asked "How you doin' Sweetheart?" He was shorter than Uncle and was very thin with a dark complexion. He had on a green track suit with a matching Kangol hat.

I didn't greet him back. I just turned back to my books, my little hands moving faster. I couldn't tell you how much time had elapsed. My copy of Charlotte's Web had fallen open; and, after a quick glance at the page, I was quickly immersed into the world of Charlotte and Wilbur. All thoughts of book organization and Uncle and Jon-Jon were a world away. The opening of Uncle's door served to bring me back to the present. Jon-Jon asked "You still messin' around with those books girl?"

I just sat there looking at them, but no words would come out of my mouth. Jon-Jon was smiling at me. He slowly walked into my room and made his way over to where I was sitting on the floor. I was paralyzed under his gaze. He bent down in front of me and picked up the book I was reading. "Have you read all these books, little girl?" he asked. I didn't say anything. He turned to look at Uncle and then back at me. "You awfully quiet. You don't want to rap?" he asked as he threw my book down.

I looked at him quizzically. What did music have to do with this? Not knowing what he meant by rap, I began shaking my head. "No, no I don't like rap music," I said, which was true. I mean, I liked a song here and there; but for the most part, I didn't care for it. I must have said something awfully funny, because Uncle and Jon-Jon started laughing and snorting. I didn't like that. I didn't like them laughing at me.

Jon-Jon glanced at Uncle. "She's cute. I like the quiet ones." And before I knew it I was on my back looking up at the ceiling. Jon-Jon may have had a small stature, but he was strong. I was robbed of the use of my legs and my arms were trapped between our bodies. His lips were on mine. I felt dizzy and nauseous. I wasn't breathing. I heard a voice. Someone was angry, yelling. It was Uncle. What was he saying? That's when I acted with the only weapon I had. I opened my mouth and bit down as hard as I could. I felt his upper body lift off of mine and I took in a deep, desperate inhale of air. His hand was on his mouth and he was mumbling "Ouch, you little bitch. That hurt!" He looked at me with murder in his eyes. "I'm gonna teach you to bite me!"

He swung his arm back as if to hit me. I flinched and brought my arms up to protect my face. Then Uncle threatened him. "YO! Lay a hand on her and see what I do to you. Nigga, get up and get out 'fore I kick yo ass." Jon-Jon lifted up on his knees. I rolled out from under him and made my escape. I ran past Uncle, down the steps.

"Esmene! Esmene!" I heard Uncle calling me. But I didn't stop. I ran through the living room, into the kitchen, through the family room where my siblings were watching The Neverending Story, and out the back door.

I took in big gulps of cool autumn air. It was burning my lungs to the point where it brought tears to my eyes, but I didn't care. My need was great. I stood there in my backyard with my hands on my knees, in a state of disbelief over what had just transpired. Why me? I wondered. What was wrong with me? What was I doing wrong? "God," I asked, "please tell me."

"Es?" I heard a little voice calling to me from the doorway. The door opened and out came little McKenna in her pigtails and clutching a doll. She came down the steps and walked over to stand next to me. "Es, we're not supposed to be outside when Mommy and Daddy aren't home," she reminded gently.

I looked at her, barely able to make out her baby face in the dark. "I know Kenni, but I felt sick. I didn't want to get sick in the house and make a mess so I ran outside."

"Do you have a tummy ache?"

No, it's a heartache, I thought to myself. "Yeah, Kenni. I have a tummy ache."

"Well you want to come lay in my bed with my doll? That's what I do when my tummy hurts," she offered me.

And her offer was so innocent and so kind, the only kindness being offered to me in a world of distress. I could feel the tears slide down my face. "Does it help Kenni? Does it help your ache?" I asked.

McKenna nodded her head vigorously and her barrettes clicked together. "Yup, cause I'm not sick alone," she said with a big smile.

I didn't want to be sick alone anymore. "OK, Kenni. I'll go lay down with your doll. Thanks for sharing with me."

"Well, you walk me home from school every day so I want to help you feel better."

And as I allowed myself to be led to the bed of this child, I couldn't recall a time in my short life when I felt safer or more loved.

Mr. Potato Head

It was a beautiful summer day in 1990. I was thirteen years old and would be starting high school in the fall. It wasn't too hot and I had an old fan with metal blades that let out the best air. I was sitting on my bed doing something I rarely did, playing with toys. More specifically, I was playing with Mr. Potato Head. Mr. Potato Head had always been one of my most favorite toys. You could put his mouth where his eyes belonged or his mustache where his nose belonged. His arms could be substituted for his ears. He was still the cool toy or maybe a really popular toy. No matter what form he was in, Mr. Potato Head was always accepted.

I envied Mr. Potato Head. I, too, felt all mixed up. I didn't feel accepted. I spent a lot of time watching other people, studying how to fit in. I had already learned being myself was not going to be acceptable. No one was going to think it was cute that my lips were where my eyes should be. So, playing with Mr. Potato Head let me express my feelings and he would understand.

The house was quiet, except for the noises of nature. Mom had gone to take the younger ones to their doctors' appointments and Delilah went with her to help. I was left at home...with Uncle. I heard the door to his bedroom open. I pretended like I didn't hear it, like I didn't know he was standing there in my doorway. I could feel his eyes boring into my soul. "Esmene," he called to me. His voice was hoarse, as if he had just woken up.

"Yeah," I answered casually, trying not to show the anxiety gripping my body.

"Esmene, put those toys down and come in here."

That's when I turned to look at him. Uncle had a white tank top on and some black shorts, no socks or shoes. His long hair hung loose around his shoulders. I knew better than to defy Uncle. If I said no to him, he would hurt me. He had left bruises on me before that Mom had never seen. I didn't want to get hurt again, so I bid goodbye to Mr. Potato head and went to him.

When I walked through the door, I stood just inside the room. I heard him close the door and turn the lock. I swallowed hard. I felt the heat from his body up against my back. I had on an orange halter top with white shorts with orange stripes that day. My hair hung past my shoulders in two tangled ponytails which were brushed to the sides. I could feel his hands beginning to massage my naked shoulders. I cursed myself: stupid, stupid! Why hadn't I changed?

A gentle kiss was dropped on my shoulder blade. My breath caught in my throat. My eyes were tightly shut and my little hands were balled into tight fists. Uncle didn't make me open my eyes, but I felt myself being moved over to the bed and he pushed me down on it.

My heart was thumping so loudly I swore he could hear it. I heard nothing but the sound of my heart for a few minutes. I didn't open my eyes to see what Uncle was doing, but I was curious. Did he leave and I just didn't hear him over my beating heart? I prayed for such mercy; but then I felt a dip in the bed, and suddenly his body was covering mine. He was naked. Well, I sensed he was naked. I don't know how I knew, but I knew.

He kissed me then. He kissed me like I had seen Victor Newman kiss Nikki on <u>The Young and The Restless</u>. It was an adult kiss. I kept my mouth shut tight but his tongue was insisting on entrance. Yuck. He pulled back. "Open your mouth Esmene," he demanded. My eyes were still closed. I shook my head in defiance.

Suddenly a sharp pain shot through my scalp where he viciously pulled my hair and I cried out in pain. His tongue wasted no time invading my mouth. I couldn't breath. I wanted to vomit. I wanted to sink my teeth into his slimy tongue.

I felt his greedy fingers grab at my halter top. No, no, no, I thought. But what was I going to do to stop him? Tears started running down the sides of my face as I realized I was powerless to stop him. The only thing that would save me was if one of my parents came home or if God was merciful enough to take me before he could.

I'm not sure how or when Uncle got all my clothes off, but he did. His body was intimately pressed up against mine. His fingers were exploring me in a foreign place. I became even more nauseous because it actually felt a little nice. I got a warm feeling in my belly and I had to fight to keep my body from responding to him. Somehow, he knew that. "See Baby Girl, I knew you liked it," he said as he sucked on my barely developed breast.

My eyes were still screwed tight and I felt light headed because I was only taking a breath once every two minutes. God, I wondered, what was he going to do to me? I quickly got my answer.

Without any preamble, he inserted the tip of his penis (not sure how I knew it was the tip, I just knew) at my virginal opening, grabbed my right thigh and brought it up over his hip. He kissed me again, his tongue once again invading my mouth right before the most god awful pain I had ever known in my life ripped through my body.

I was screaming. I was crying. I was scratching at him, biting him. The taste of copper filled my mouth as I bit down on his tongue (or was it mine?) or maybe it was my lips (or was it his?) I didn't know. I was begging and pleading with him to stop. I felt like I was being ripped in two. I thought I was dying. I even prayed for it. Surely death would be more merciful than what I was enduring. He stayed still, but only for a moment, before his body began to rhythmically thrust into mine.

Suddenly, I was back in my room, sitting on my bed. I had Mr. Potato head in my hands with his pieces: his eyes and ears and hats and noses. So we sat there, Mr. Potato Head and I; and I asked him how he wanted to look that day. He said he wanted to be whole. He wanted to be complete. He told me what eyes he wanted, the ears, mouth and so on. I put him together just the way he wanted to be. Perfect, unadulterated. I took him from a shattered place and made him whole again. Whole again, like I would never be.

After I had put Mr. Potato Head together, every piece in its exact place, I sat back to admire such perfection. Suddenly, Mr. Potato Head's lips that once held a smile, turned into a frown and seemed to melt off his face. The arms, ears, hat and nose also fell. Blood began to flow from his orifices. Mr. Potato Head had been ruined.

I felt a sting on my face. "Esme. Esme!" Uncle was calling my name slapping my face. I opened my eyes. Uncle was hovering over me. I was back in his room. His body was no longer violating mine. Uncle stood up, grabbed his shorts off the floor, and pulled them on. He seemed in a hurry. "Go get your robe and come downstairs. You need to get cleaned up before your Mom gets home. Hurry up! I'll let you take a bath if you hurry."

I heard his hurried footsteps disappear down the stairs and into the bathroom. I had yet to move. I wasn't even sure what had happened. But my body knew. I began to move and I was sore all over, like the way it feels now after weight lifting at the gym. I gingerly moved over to the edge of the bed and that's when I saw my virginal blood spilled all over his sheets. I don't know why I did it, but I stuck my fingers in it. I played with it between my fingers. I then gathered up a little bit more. I got up to look in the full-length mirror. I felt the cooling mixture of blood and semen running down the inside of my thigh. I smeared what little bit there was on my face like tribal war paint. My body had been through a battle, a battle I didn't win. Blood had been spilled and it was mine.

So, I had to wear my shame.

"Esmene get down here!" Uncle yelled up to me.

I gingerly made my way into my room, put on my robe and grabbed my towel and washcloth. Uncle was standing outside the bathroom. "Girl, what the hell is that on your face? You done lost your mind or something?" I thought, you just raped me, Uncle; but you're asking me if I lost my mind? Have I lost my mind? Maybe I had. How could I possibly still be sane after you just raped me? Uncle continued, "Never mind that. I put some Mr. Bubble in there for you. Make sure you wash good and get that shit off your face. Don't take too long."

"Yes sir," I whispered and continued into the bathroom. I heard him run up the stairs, probably to change his sheets.

I took off my robe and eased my tender, battered body into the welcoming water. It was hotter than I could usually tolerate; but I got in and sat down, enduring the punishment for my sin. I sat there in the tub, sweating from the combined heat of the water and the heat of the day. Strangely, I did not cry. I did not weep. I simply sat and watched the snow white bubbles I had once loved become defiled and turn a bubble gum pink, resembling the bottle from which they came.

I hate Mr. Bubble.

Why You So Obsessed with Me?

No, my number one love wasn't some grade school friend that I used to invite over for sleepovers where we would hide under blanket forts and giggle about the cutest boys in school. In fact, I never had a sleepover with any friend. I barely had any friends.

No, it wasn't my favorite stuffed animal or Cabbage Patch Doll that was all the rage at that time, with names like Emily Sue or Leo Carl. No, that would be too normal for me.

No, it wasn't a favorite blankie that I carried around, old, tattered, and dirty, that I refused to let go of because it brought me so much comfort. There were no such conventions in my life.

It wasn't even the books I read so voraciously that could take this number one spot.

That devotion belonged to my one true love, food. I can't tell you when my relationship with food began to morph into something abnormal; but when it did, it was like an avalanche, silent and deadly. Once I was caught up in it, I was powerless to do anything to fight it. I found a comfort in food I had not found in anything else, even my precious books. My favorite thing to do was to stop at the papi store on the corner, get a bag full of goodies, hide them in my bookbag, and go straight to my room. I would quickly do any homework I had and then the party would begin. I would grab a book and my bag of goodies and then wander off into a mystical land where there was no hurt, no pain. This was a world where I was safe. I was loved. I was beautiful. I was special. I was protected. No one was hurting me. No one was bullying me. I was perfect. My world was perfect. Food gave me a reality that I couldn't manufacture for myself.

In one summer, between sixth and seventh grade, I gained fifty pounds.

When I didn't have money to go to the store, I relied on the same tricks that a junkie would employ on the street. No, I didn't sell my body; but I did become an accomplished thief. I would get up in the middle of the night and sneak food out of the freezer or pantry. My parents soon realized someone was stealing food. Delilah and I had both put on weight, so we were both suspects. "Which one of you is sitting up at night eating up all the food in this house?" Dad demanded to know in a strongly worded note he left for us on the kitchen table one morning. His question was reiterated by Mom. "I know one or both of you've been sneaking food and it's going to STOP TODAY!" The next morning when we went down for breakfast, there was a lock on the chest freezer and pantry. But I wouldn't be deterred. I learned how to pick both locks; and when my parents were gone, I would quickly go in and take what I needed to satisfy the intense hunger clawing inside of me demanding to be satisfied. On days when I would come home from school and no one would be home, I would cook whole packs of bacon; and while I was waiting for that to cook, I would eat cakes and cookies to sooth the anxious excitement I was feeling while waiting for the bacon to cook.

When I started eighth grade at twelve years old, I was at my max height of five foot two inches and weighed one hundred and seventy-five pounds.

I'm embarrassed and ashamed to admit that I didn't stop at stealing food from my house. Dad didn't believe in giving us an allowance, so I stole money too. I'd take dollars out of Dad's work pants that he hung in the closet to be washed after he came home from work. I even stole money from my classmates at school. In eighth grade, I was attending the local parochial school and we had a little store at lunch time where we sold candy to raise money for our trip to New York. I would steal money from the store, a quarter here, fifty cents there. I worked my way up to taking dollars. Once I took a whole ten dollar bill. I didn't care that I was taking away from my classmates' hard work. I needed my food fix to feel even remotely normal and nothing was going to stand in the way of the one thing in my life that made me happy.

To my eighth grade class and teacher, I want to say I'm sorry. I continued to spiral out of control; and, by the time I graduated from Pennsauken High School at seventeen, I weighed two hundred and thirty pounds.

I took my binge eating to college with me. It was a little harder to hide my food relationship but I managed to make it work. I went to LaSalle University, a predominantly white college, so I didn't feel like I fit in with the fraternity/sorority scene on campus anyway. Besides, I wasn't a drinker at all. I was an eater. So while my doormmates spent the weekend partying, my food and I had our own party. We were free to enjoy each other's company, uninterrupted. I would order a large pizza, fries, mozzarella sticks, stromboli...whatever I wanted. It was especially easy because by then I had a credit card. I would take my food back to my room and my bestie and I would have a wonderful night in, just the two of us. And the next day when my friends would regale me with stories of their dates and whom they hooked up with, I would smile to myself and think, I had a really good hookup too. Despite my clandestine rendezvous, my weight had stabilized while in college. I gained and lost as the years went by. By the time I left college at twenty-one, I still weighed two hundred and twenty-five pounds.

Looking back now, I wonder if the reason why I turned to food had an underlying catalyst that I never realized when I was younger. Being overweight unfortunately has often been equated with being unattractive. Maybe I thought that by putting on all those extra pounds, I'd become unappealing to Uncle. Or perhaps in my childish mind, I thought size equated to strength; and if I became bigger, I'd then be stronger and be able to protect myself against Uncle. Maybe I was inspired by the thought of both. Maybe I didn't think about either of those things and just wanted to forget the pain I was in and continued to eat. But it never mattered how much I weighed. My bestie was always there, never judging, with arms opened wide, always ready to welcome me home.

You'll Always Be on the Outside

I hated high school. It started out bad on day one and just went downhill from there. After what had happened with Uncle, I felt like I was marked like Cane after he killed his brother Abel and everyone could see it. The fact that no matter what I did, I just never fit in only confirmed that for me. In order to blend in, I began to watch the "cool" kids and tried to emulate what they did. Needless to say, I couldn't pull it off; and it only caused me to become the target of more ridicule.

I'd put on a lot of weight over the last couple of years, and anyone who was overweight in high school knows the hell of being bullied. I remember one day my sophomore year, I had to go up to do an oral presentation in Spanish class. When I got up to speak, a boy named Elliot sat up. He looked right at me and said "God, you're ugly". Gym started causing me so much anxiety that my blood pressure would go sky high and I would get sick. During my last two years of high school, I had a medical exemption from gym.

Although my family was nowhere near poor, my dad didn't believe in spending a lot of money on expensive clothes and shoes which meant I never had the latest or greatest. I was always neat and clean in my Kmart or Bradlees gear. Kids laughed at my Bobos that squeaked on the floor as I walked down the hall and my knock off FUBU shirts. I was just a hot mess, a walking disaster from head to toe.

I did manage to have a few friends though. They were Tisha, Nakita, and Luna, whom I am still in contact with today. Also, I was friendly with Lauren, Wayne, and my first boyfriend William. But even they weren't as low on the popularity scale as I was. If there was a list of where everyone was ranked, I know I was probably on the bottom.

The only thing that I ever had going for me was that I was smart, but I wasn't even one of the smartest. I was just smart enough to be in advanced placement classes. Most days after school, I would go home, sit in my closet, and cry. I was tired of being treated like trash. This is what led to my first suicide attempt during my senior year.

One day while I was in the school library, someone came up behind me and grabbed my breast. I jumped and turned around to see it was a guy named Lance, one of the guys who was always making fun of me. Why would he be touching my breast? Before I could ask him, he smiled at me and said, "I was checking to see if they were real. I knew you wouldn't mind someone finally touching you." He laughed and walked away.

That day after school, I stopped at the RiteAid and shoplifted a giant bottle of aspirin.   That night I lay up in my bed crying, knowing that I was going to die alone after having been violated by Uncle and bullied by my classmates for being different. I prayed for God to take my soul to keep as I began to swallow as many pills as I could, just about the whole bottle. I don't remember how many were in there but it was a lot. Then I lay down and just waited to die. As I drifted off to sleep, I remember thinking I would now be in peace and I was actually happy.

Hours later, my heavy lids opened allowing my eyes to take in the same scene it looked upon every morning. To my dismay, I was still alive. Not only was I alive, but I was sick. I was throwing up all day. Mom thought I had some kind of virus. Every time I moved, I threw up. I seriously considered grabbing the replacement sharp knife from underneath my pillow and stabbing myself. All I kept thinking about as I made white and green speckled chunky offerings the porcelain throne was how much this episode solidified me as a loser. I mean, I couldn't even kill myself correctly.

Finally, I confessed to Mom why I was so sick. She didn't do or say anything. Back then, I took it as though she didn't really know how to deal with something like that. Now that I am older, I think maybe she was shocked and didn't know what to do. I know a lot more now at forty than I did at seventeen. I didn't realize how young and naive Mom was. She didn't seek medical care for me and just watched me for the rest of the day as I continued to throw up. Three months later at my high school graduation, I could still feel the effects of my amateur suicide attempt. I was certainly glad to be getting my diploma and to be leaving my high school experience behind. It was over. I would be leaving for college in a couple of months, where no one would know me and I could start a new life.

I was certain this would never happen to me again. I would never try to end my life by my own hands. I was wrong.

The Lion and the Honey

It was November 24, 1994, Thanksgiving evening. It was the usual gathering for our Thanksgiving dinner. Both of my parents were in attendance that year, all of my siblings, Uncle, Aunt Marie, and her two kids. Aunt Marie was Dad's little sister, three or four years his junior. She was raised in New Jersey by their maternal aunt because Grandmom had had both kids as a very young teenager and couldn't care for both of them. Dad and Aunt Marie visited with each other while they were growing up; and then when Dad turned eighteen, he made his way to New Jersey to be with his sister. Aunt Marie was a medium built woman, about five foot five, with cocoa colored skin and short brown hair. She was the single mother of two kids Veronica, eleven, and Kenneth, ten. That's it. They were all sitting around, bellies full, chatting about those things which adults chat about; and the younger kids were playing Mall Madness in the back room. Delilah had taken the opportunity to escape to the sanctuary of her bedroom.

What was I doing? I was one hundred percent immersed in the most riveting movie I'd ever seen in my life. It was Silence of the Lambs, starring Jodie Foster as the no nonsense FBI training academy student, Clarice Starling, and the brilliant, psychopathic and somehow sexy cannibal, Hannibal Lector, played by the intense Anthony Hopkins.

How had I not seen this before? I was mesmerized the first time I heard Hannibal say "Hello Clarice." The dialogue between the naive yet ambitious Clarice and the charming yet dangerous Hannibal was ingenious. My seventeen year old self could feel the chemistry between the two ignite right there on the screen. And what was this? Clarice and Dr. Lecter (for I would never disrespect the good doctor and call him Hannibal) introduced me to something that would develop into an obsession of mine for over the next twenty-five years: the serial killer. I'd never heard the term before. I didn't know what it was, but after seeing the movie I was able to get a glimpse into the macabre world of the psychopathic killer.

Mom admonished me, calling out "Esme, what's that you're watching? And stop sitting so close to the TV. You'll hurt your eyes." I didn't even acknowledge her question with an answer. I didn't want to miss a second of Clarice's mission as, with the help of Dr. Lecter, she desperately tried to find the elusive serial killer of big girls, Buffalo Bill.

After seeing the movie, I dove head first into finding out every little thing I could about these serial killers such as Ted Bundy, John Wayne Gacy, Jeffrey Dahmer, and even Ed Gein, whom Buffalo Bill was loosely based on. This was, of course, when the world wide web was in its infancy, so most of my research was done in the Pennsauken Public Library, which was fine by me. It just so happened at that time, Time Life Books came out with a True Crime Series on Serial Killers and Mass Murderers (another term foreign to me at the time), and I begged Mom to get them for me. It helped that she had a little bit of interest herself. Those books then became my most prized possessions. In fact, I still have them to this day. I read them cover to cover, devouring every little detail of these deranged individuals who killed people like they were no more than pesky ants.

What was wrong with these people? What was going on in the minds of these predominantly male villains that would cause them to have such an appetite for murder and mayhem? I wanted to know. In my mind, the only way I could find out was if I followed in the footsteps of Ms. Clarice Starling. Maybe I wouldn't be going all the way to the FBI, but I knew my future lay within the field of psychology.

Something had gone wrong with these people. Was it congenital or was it something nurtured by their environment? Also, something was wrong with me. Albeit, I certainly didn't have the desire to kill people and bury them under my house or to eat them; but something wasn't right with me. Was I born this way or had Uncle made me this way? If I could figure out what was wrong with them, surely I could discover what was wrong with me. Maybe I could even cure myself so, for once in my life, I could be like everyone else. My mind was made up. I was going to become a psychologist with a focus on serial killers.

Over the years, I had amassed quite a collection. I had serial killer books, magazines, and trading cards. I watched serial killer documentaries all day if no one was home; and much to my future husband Jericho's chagrin, I slept with the books next to the bed. I found out a lot about what drove these people to commit the perverse acts on humanity that they did.

As for my self-discovery, I found out I wasn't a psychopath or a sociopath. I wasn't a narcissist, a pedophile, a necrophile, or a cannibal. But what I still didn't know then was what **WAS** wrong with me. My issues were not wrapped up in a neat little package and written up in any book I'd come across. I was, however, still convinced that psychology would be my only way to find out. I believed that if Dr. Lector could silence Clarice's lambs, I could silence my demons as well.

Dear Mama

Aunt Marie was Dad's only sibling and the only one of our aunts who lived in New Jersey, so we were very close to her. Her two children, Veronica and Kenneth, were complete opposites of each other. Veronica, the oldest, was a tall sturdy girl who looked just like her father. She was a quiet, studious girl and a bit of a loner. She often acted like a second mother in the home. Kenneth was not as tall as Veronica but he was just as sturdy. He looked more like Aunt Marie but he didn't act like her. He was a menace. He caused trouble everywhere he went. We couldn't believe that our sweet Aunt Marie had raised such a little terror. Sometimes we would ask Mom to lie and say we weren't home so she wouldn't come over and bring the kids with her. But Aunt Marie was the BEST. She had a rough time in life, but that didn't change her from being one of the kindest people I had ever known. Aunt Marie was on public assistance while trying to get her life back together, so she didn't have much; but what she did have she would willingly share with anyone. Her door was always open to us, and some of our fondest moments were spent with her.

At this time, I was eighteen and had just finished my freshman year in college. It was Friday, May 8th, 1995, when I called my beloved Aunt to tell her I just got my first job at the local Food Town grocery store in Cherry Hill. Yes, Food Town. Imagine me wanting to work around food. Aunt Marie was always so proud of me. Her genius niece is what she always called me. The details of that call are fuzzy to me today, overshadowed by the events that followed not long after.

Just a few hours after my call to Aunt Marie, Mom received a phone call from Aunt Marie's best friend, Dana, saying she was at her house knocking on the door but my aunt wasn't answering. Mom was on her way over anyway, so she told Dana to wait for her. Mom left with

Delilah and I stayed behind with my younger siblings. We all thought she was probably just sleeping. Unfortunately we were all wrong. About forty-five minutes later the phone rang. "Hello," I yelled into the phone trying to be heard over the noise my siblings and their friends were making playing basketball in the backyard.

"Esme..." at least that's what I think I heard, and it sounded like Mom, but something was wrong.

"Hello?" I said again, not yelling this time because I wasn't so sure I wanted a response.

I heard Mom say again, her voice hoarse with tears, "Esmene...Esmene, call your father. Tell him to get to Aunt Marie's house. She's dead." Mom finished before she was consumed by gut wrenching sobs.

I drifted away briefly. Aunt Marie's dead? That just can't be? I just spoke to her a few hours ago. She sounded fine. What happened? "Esmene....ESMENE!!" My mom was yelling my name through the phone. I don't know how much time had elapsed, but I was holding the phone and sobbing uncontrollably. "Esme baby. The ambulance is here. Do you think you can call your Dad and tell him?"

I wiped my eyes and nose with my hand. "Yes," I told her.

"OK, I also need you to call her pastor. Pastor Huntsman. The number is in my book. Can you do that too?"

I thought no. No, I can't call a stranger and tell him that my aunt is dead. No. But I said "Yeah. I can do it."

"Good girl. Just keep everything calm until we get there." The line went dead.

OH GOD, OH GOD, OH GOD....How was I going to call my Dad and tell him this? I could barely talk? I was literally choking on my tears. But Mom was depending on me, so I did what I had to do. This was a time when cell phones were in their infancy, so people still memorized phone numbers. I quickly dialed Dad's number, silently hoping he would not pick up.

But his gruff voice came through the phone. "Hello?"

I didn't even have a chance to think about what I was going to say, so I just blurted it out. "Dad, you need to get to Aunt Marie's house. She's dead."

After a moment of silence he asked "What did you say?"

I started crying again in earnest at the pitiful sound of his voice. "Mom called. She's at Aunt Marie's house. She said for you to go there. She's dead." I prayed he understood so I would not be forced to say it again.

"Ah shit!" was all Dad said before he hung up on me. I was fine with that.

The call with her Pastor went about the same, sans the four letter expletive. Hours later, my parents came home with my cousins in tow. We were told they would be living with us now, as their father had left them years ago. Once my siblings were informed, sleeping arrangements were made, the kids got settled, and I finally got the full story.

By the time Mom and Delilah got to my Aunt's house, my cousin Veronica had come home from school. She had a key, so she unlocked the door. She and Dana went into the house. When they walked in, they found my aunt laying in the middle of the living room floor, arms spread wide, with the Mother's Day cards we had sent her spread around her like she was reading them when she fell. Mom got there not too long after that and started CPR but she knew it was too late. Aunt Marie's lips were blue and her body was already cold. My father declined to get an autopsy done, so we don't know what caused her death; but she had recently been in the hospital for heart problems. Everyone assumed it was related to that.

Something happened to me when Aunt Marie died but I never realized it until years later. It was as if a circuit had been tripped. When Aunt Marie died, I had just finished my freshman year in college; and I had done well. But once sophomore year started, something had changed. I was struggling in ways I had never struggled before. My head was filled with a lot of noise. I was becoming reckless and neglecting my responsibilities, doing anything I could to escape the constant chatter in my head. The more I tried to gain control, the more my life spun out of control. I tried to fix it, but I had no idea what I was dealing with.

I was on a runaway train, about to embark on a journey beyond my imagination.

Grubin and Lovin

I met Marcus my sophomore year at LaSalle University. My dormmates and I were pulling another all-nighter. We all either had papers due or tests the next day; and since we all wanted to do well, we waited like idiots until the night before for a good old cram session. It was a food run to a diner that brought me to Marcus.

"Evie," I whined at my friend and roommate that night at around nine-thirty pm. She was sitting at her desk as usual, twirling a lock of her curly fiery red hair around her finger with her other hand punching in numbers on a calculator. Eve was an accounting major, perfect for her personality.

Eve finally looked over to where I was lounging on a bean bag chair. "What is it Meme?" she asked, peering at me over her glasses. Even though Eve was my roommate, she was a senior. Her sister, Tai, a sophomore, was also our roommate. Unlike Eve, Tai's head was covered with dark curls that hung past her shoulders and she was sweet and soft spoken. Eve and Tai were as different as night and day but I loved them both dearly.

I whined "I can't focus. I think I need a snack. Writing about serial killers makes me hungry."

"Es," Tai said from where she sat perched on the top bunk, her curly dark brown hair in a messy bun, "if you buckle down and focus, you can get done with that paper and you won't have to be up all night."

Alexis, our neighbor across the hall, was sitting on my bed and had ceased her furious typing. She said "Es, a snack doesn't sound like a bad idea. I'm starting to get sleepy. Maybe if I eat something, I'll get a second wind." She yawned, raising her long, slender arms over her head and stretching her back so that her long, straight hair brushed her trim waist.

Just then there was a knock at the door and the phone rang at the same time. Evie threw her hands in the air in frustration and yelled, "Come in!"

"Hello," I answered the phone, just as Luna and Bliss from down the hall walked into the room. "Hey Chris. Yeah, she's here. Alexis, Chris is on the phone for you."

Alexis ran to get the phone. "Hello. Oh, I didn't know you were coming. OK, be right down." she hung up. "Chris is here," she told us. Chris was her boyfriend. "I'm going to go down and sign him in. Then we'll see what we can do about your killer appetite," she joked.

"Hurry back!" I yelled as the door closed behind her. I knew with Chris being here we'd be up all night. He was a student at Drexel but he spent most of his time here with us. He was nineteen also. Chris was African American, so he gave the campus a little more ethnicity. We needed it. At the time LaSalle literally had about eight black students in Neumann Hall where we lived. Chris was about the same height as Alexis with a sturdy muscular build. He kept his hair and facial hair cut low and had adorable dimples on both cheeks. Chris was a good guy and he loved Alexis. They looked good together.

"You guys going to get something to eat?" Luna asked. Luna and I had gone to high school together. She'd graduated the year after me. She was a Hispanic girl who stood about five foot seven with a head full of hazelnut brown wild curls that reached all the way down her back.

"I said I want a snack or something to pick me up. You know, get the creative juices flowing." I told her.

Bliss asked as she picked up some of my notes, "What are you working on?" Bliss was an African American girl who was a political science major. She was my height with a very petite build. Bliss had what would be considered very long hair for a black girl. It was a little longer than mine, past the shoulders but on the thinner side. It looked jet black and she wore it straight with a part down the middle. She would never be accused of being a social butterfly but she managed to find her place in our group and we liked her.

"A research paper about serial killers. It's making me hungry." I replied.

Bliss made a face. "Eww, how can writing about slaughter make you hungry? You're so weird with this stuff. Eve, Tai, I don't know how you feel safe sharing a room with her. She's creepy. You've somehow got me interested in this stuff now."

Eve turned to look at Bliss and said "It's not too bad until she brings out the trading cards and tries to get a game going. Then it gets really weird."

Luna laughed at that. "Meme you're crazy with this stuff."

In no time at all I heard the combination being entered into the keypad on the door and in came the dynamic duo, Chris and his ever present duffle bag. We never saw what he actually had in that thing. I hoped it wasn't a body. "Ladies!" came his enthusiastic greeting.

We all greeted him in return.

Chris dropped his duffle bag on the floor, plopped down on my bed with Alexis, grabbed her around the waist, and dragged her onto his lap. They were so cute. "So," he asked, "what are my ladies up to tonight?"

Alexis leaned her temple against his forehead and sighed. "Well, I have a paper due tomorrow in Psych, Es has a paper due tomorrow in English Lit, Tai and Evie both have tests, and I'm not sure about Bliss and Luna, so we decided to work together to keep each other motivated and awake."

"I finished my paper two days ago," Bliss said while looking around in our mini fridge. Alexis and I mimicked her and made faces.

Luna kicked back on Eve's bed. "You guys got me scared. I don't have any tests or papers due. At least I don't think I do. Now I have to double check," she said with a frown on her face.

Chris gave a laugh at that and asked "So anyway, how's it been going?" Chris knew Alexis and me well enough to know nothing had gotten accomplished thus far.

Alexis smacked his arm and said "We've been working, or at least I'VE been working. Esmene is whining that she's hungry and needs something to eat. The student union and dining hall are closed. Intermissions isn't open tonight. We could order pizza?"

I made a face. "I'm tired of pizza. We just had broccoli tomato pie last night which is basically pizza."

"Well what do you want? We're wasting time," Alexis implored.

"How about the Explorer's Den? Their steaks are the bomb," Luna said. Everyone nodded their heads in agreement. Explorer's Den had the best steaks in the area.

Chris suggested. "Ladies, ladies. I know where we can get some food that's not pizza or steaks. How about we go to a diner?"

Alexis rolled her eyes. "Oh God Chris, not IHOP."

"I love IHOP," Bliss said with a pout.

Chris explained, saying "No baby, not IHOP. It's a diner I've been hearing the kids on campus talk about. They go there all the time during late night study sessions and after campus parties. It's over on Rising Sun Avenue. The food is supposedly really good."

"How are we going to get there?" I asked. "We don't have a car, unless we get Eve to drive us." Eve just looked at us, rolled her eyes, and went back to studying. "And I'm not standing on Broad Street waiting for a bus at this time of night. I'm hungry, not desperate."

Chris laughed. "We'll catch the shuttle up to Broad Street and then catch a hack cab to the diner. We can get a hack back or catch the bus back," he said, checking his watch to see what time it was.

I wasn't from Philly, so a hack cab sounded dangerous to me. "I don't know Chris. Is that safe?"

He gave me a double dimpled smile. "Don't worry kid. You'll be safe with me."

And that's how I found myself seated in Nelly's diner. It really did look like a classic diner with the little jukeboxes at every table to play music. I had to hand it to Chris. The place was nostalgic, the food was good, and there was this cute guy who kept coming from out of the kitchen making eyes at me.

"Esme, did you hear me?" Alexis said.

"Huh?" I replied.

"What are you looking at?" Alexis and Chris both turned to look behind them. Thank God Marcus wasn't there.

"Don't look!" I said through clenched teeth. "This man keeps coming out of the kitchen, standing there smiling at me. He's kind of cute."

Alexis was all teeth. "Where is he now? I want to see!" She was being obvious in her search for my admirer.

I grabbed her arm. "Will you control yourself? We're adults, not children. Besides, I'll let you know when he's coming again. Just act natural." I was telling her to act naturally, but I had butterflies in my stomach. I'd never had a man look at me like that before. And he was a man. I didn't know how old he was but he was long past his high school years.

Luna kicked me under the table. "Here he comes, here he comes. Be subtle Lex."

This time he came right up to the table. "Hello, how are y'all doing tonight?" he asked while looking at me. He wasn't tall, about five foot seven with the build of a guy who worked and drank beer. There was nothing extraordinary about him, but there was definitely something attracting me to this man like a moth to a flame.

Alexis answered for all of us. "We're doing well. Thanks for asking. How about you?" She smiled up at him. He looked over at her and smiled. "I'm good, thanks. I hope you enjoyed the food this evening. I prepared it for you." What was it I ordered, I wondered to myself. God it was delicious. "It was delicious," I finally squeaked out. He turned those brown eyes back on me. "I'm Marcus by the way." He shook hands with Alexis, Luna, Bliss and Chris. Then he took my hand. "Would it be OK if I spoke to you in the back for a few minutes?" he asked. I thought hell yeah it would. Control yourself Esmene. Deep breath. "Yes, that'd be fine," I said, hoping my voice was as calm as I was trying to appear. He gave me a charming smile and gestured for me to follow him. I looked to Alexis and I could see she was ready to burst but she was totally keeping it casual. Chris was sipping his soda, rolling his eyes.

When we got outside he asked. "Are you from Philly?"

"No. No, I'm from New Jersey.

"Oh a Jersey girl. Where in Jersey?"

"Pennsauken," Here we go, I thought.

"Pennsauken? Never heard of that. Where is it?"

"It's between Camden and Cherry Hill," I explained. He shook his head. No recognition. "You ever heard of the Mart?" I asked him.

"Oh yeah, yeah. Now I know what you're talking about. Pennsauken, OK," he acknowledged. Since living in Philly, I realized no one ever knew where Pennsauken was until you mentioned the Mart.

An awkward silence settled between us. I began to play with my fingers. "Well...?" he asked.

Well what?"

"Aren't you going to ask anything about me?" he teased with a smirk on his lips.

I wanted to smack myself on the forehead. Idiot. Of course, ask questions about him. Show him you're interested. I was blowing it. "So, how long have you worked here?"

"Ten years."

Ten years? That seemed like a long time. So I asked "How old are you?"

"I'm thirty-two. I'll be thirty-three in November. Is that a problem?" he asked, taking a step back from me.

To me, no, it wasn't a problem. Thanks to Uncle, I found myself attracted to men much older than myself. One would think older men disgusted me, but in actuality the opposite was true. "What a coincidence, my birthday is in November too. Umm, you're not married are you?" I asked.

He smiled again. He was cute in that subtle sort of way. "No. No wife, no girlfriend either. I do have a twelve year old son though. I hope that's OK."

OK for what, I thought? What are we doing? There was only one way to find out. "Marcus, you ask if that's a problem or is that OK. OK for what? What are you expecting? What do you want?" I asked shyly.

Marcus took both my hands in his and rubbed my knuckles and said "I think you're beautiful. And now that I've spoken to you, I think you're a very nice young lady. I'd like the chance to get to know you better. Would you like to get to know me better? Talk on the phone, see each other outside of here?"

YES, YES, YES my inner voice said. "That would be nice," I told him. "Yes, I would like that."

"Good. Now I have to get back to work, but I'm really glad you came in tonight. Now I have a couple more questions for you."

"Really? What?"

"Can I ask how old you are?"

"Eighteen," I said.

"Eighteen?" he repeated with a hint of disbelief in his voice. I was often mistaken for being younger than my age.

'Yes, Eighteen. Is that a problem?" I asked, a little annoyed.

He offered up an adorable smile. "Nope, no problem at all," he said. "And what's your name?" he asked while drying his hands on his apron.

My mouth was dry and I stuttered a little bit. "Es...Esmene."

"Esmene," he repeated with a smirk. "I never heard that name before. It's pretty. I've never seen you in here before. You live around here now or are you still in Jersey?"

"Well, I'm a student at LaSalle. I live on campus," I said with butterflies in my stomach. I noticed he took a step back at that.

"LaSalle huh? Good school. OK, one final question. Can I kiss you?"

Oh My God I was going to faint! "I umm..." I hesitated.

"Hey, listen, if I'm moving too fast, just tell me. I'm not trying to pressure you..."

"No, it's OK. A kiss would be OK," I assured him.

Still holding my hands, soothing my nerves, he leaned into me and gently caressed my lips with his own. It was a whisper of a kiss, with a promise of more when I was ready. He stepped back and kissed both my hands.

"Tonight turned out better than I thought it would," he said with a genuine smile. "Come on." We exited the back and he took me right up to the front where the register was. He got a piece of paper and wrote his number on it and had me do likewise. He then told the cashier not to worry about the check for our table, that he'd take care of it. She just chuckled and shook her head.

"Sweet dreams Esmene." he said.

"Goodnight Marcus." I replied.

Natural Woman

I was nervous. It was eleven-thirty, pm, on a Saturday. Marcus and I were sitting on the couch in the living room of my campus apartment that I shared with Alexis. I was nineteen now and he was thirty-three. It was the first time we'd been alone together since we met four months ago. He'd avoided all attempts from me to get him alone, but then I pulled a childish stunt of showing up to his job escorted by another guy. So now, here we were. I got what I wanted but now I didn't know what to do with him.

What will I do, I thought. Marcus was sitting casually with his arm draped along the back of the couch, drinking his beer and watching the news. I didn't want to interrupt his beer or his focus on the news. This was quickly looking like a bad idea. The news went off and Marcus got up to throw his empty beer can in the trash. He came back and plopped down on the sofa closer to me. "So, Ms. Esmene, what'd you have in mind for this evening?" He gave me one of his dimpled smiles. Usually that would make me smile too, but not tonight.

My stomach was in knots. "I..I don't know," I stuttered, looking down at my lap.

He lifted my chin with his finger. "You don't know? You went through an awful lot of trouble with that stunt you pulled to get me here. You must've had a good reason."

He was gently caressing my chin, with an impish grin on his face. He was teasing me because of my childish antics to get a rise out of him; but it worked, so I didn't care. Since I'd gone through so much trouble to get him to this place, he wasn't going to make it easy for me. I was going to have to ask for what I wanted. The feeling of his hand gently caressing my face had calmed my nerves and my eyes had closed just to enjoy the feeling. I then felt his other hand sliding up and down my left thigh. "Esmene," he said my name, like a prayer. I opened my eyes to meet his chocolate brown orbs.

Suddenly, I knew it was inevitable. As Marcus hovered over me, I had to keep opening and closing my eyes, as he kept morphing between himself and Uncle. Every time he became Uncle, I would squeeze my eyes shut and then open them and he would be Marcus again.

"You alright?" he asked.

I attempted to smile at him. "Right as rain."

For some reason, I didn't think there'd be blood or pain involved thanks to Uncle's unsolicited initiation years before; but there was both. At his initial thrust, I was transported back to that day in Uncle's room and panic set in. My eyes shot open. The room was spinning around me as if I'd drunk a fifth of vodka. My chest felt compressed underneath his weight. My hands had balled up into fists and were against his chest. He grabbed my wrists and held both my arms above my head. I couldn't get away.

Hot. I was hot. I felt like I was going to be sick. He was everywhere. On me, in me, around me. I couldn't get away. Then that dreaded jingle started playing in my head. "Mr. Potato Head. With eyes and ears and hats and noses. And hands you can bend in so many poses..."

And then it was over. Marcus's body lay still on top of mine. I opened my eyes to see Marcus, not Uncle. I easily moved his body off of me. I jumped up and locked myself in the bathroom. My head hurt. My chest hurt. I couldn't get enough air in my lungs. I looked down between my thighs. The blood! Oh God, the blood was there. Not again, I thought. I turned to the toilet and threw up the limited contents of my stomach.

"Esmene. Are you alright?" Marcus's concerned voice came through the door.

"I'm OK...I just...I need to clean myself up. Just give me a few minutes, OK?"

"Esmene, why didn't you tell me you were a virgin. I could've hurt you. You should've told me," he said with tenderness in his voice. I heard him move away from the door.

I started up the shower, hopped in and quickly began to clean up the evidence of our coupling. Though I was using a warm vanilla scented body wash, the overwhelming sickening sweet smell of bubble gum was invading my olfactory senses. When I was done in the shower, I saw Marcus had made his way back into the living room and was drinking another beer. I went in my room, dried off, dressed in some university sweats, and joined him on the couch. "Marcus, I'm sorry, I said. "I didn't think it was a big deal."

He turned towards me. "Not a big deal? It's a very big deal. It was your first time. I could've been a lot gentler. I thought you had experience, that you knew what you wanted and what you were doing. I didn't even wrap it up," he said shaking his head and taking another sip of his beer.

I didn't care about any condom. I cared about him. In fact, I was pretty sure I was in love with him. Using a condom never even entered my mind. "Marcus, listen, I'm OK. A little panicked, but OK. Now that I know what to expect, the next time will be better."

He looked at me and smiled. "You want to do it again?"

Did I want to do it again? But you love him, my mind whispered. My heart countered that I had loved Uncle too and my love for him only brought me pain. But I ignored my heart and said "Yes."

April, 1996

"I just can't believe he broke up with me," I cried to Alexis, Luna, Bliss and anyone else who would listen for the thousandth time. Eve had graduated and Tai lived in another apartment, so they were both saved from my melodrama

Luna rubbed my back. "I know Mama, but maybe he's right. He's too old for you. You should probably find someone closer to your own age. It'd be better for you."

"Well shouldn't he have told me that BEFORE he had sex with me!" I said through gritted teeth. "He had a couple of months of fun. Then when he realized how much I was in love with him he gave me this BS about how he's too old for me, all he's going to do is ruin my life, and I deserve someone better. I don't want someone better. I WANT HIM!"

"I'm sorry sweetheart, but you can't force him to be with you. If it's over, it's over," Alexis said.

Bliss added, "I don't know what you see in him anyway. I mean he's nice and all, but you're going to college to have a better life. He's a cook in a diner with a kid and no car." Luna punched her on the leg. "Ouch! What was that for?" Bliss then said to Luna and Alexis, "Come on you two. You both know I'm telling the truth. She doesn't need to spend money on a college education to get a guy like him. She could land someone like him if she had a GED and save herself a lot of money."

"BLISS!" Luna and Alexis exclaimed in unison.

"I can't take it," I moaned. "I can literally feel my heart breaking inside my chest. What did I do wrong? Why am I not good enough for him? I'd do anything for him. How can he not see that?"

Luna said "Es, you're more than good enough for him. This is his loss, not yours! Now come on, stop beating yourself up. You've been crying for two weeks now."

"What time is it?" I asked suddenly.

They all looked at each other confused. "Ten forty-five. Why?" Alexis asked.

I sat up and reached for my box of tissues. One left. "Come on, let's go," I started blowing my nose as I shoved my feet into my sneakers.

"Go?" Luna asked. "Go where?"

"To the diner. He'll be getting off soon and he should be waiting on the bus stop right out front, unless he has some new woman who's picking him up and taking him home."

Bliss' eyes almost fell out of their sockets. "Es, you're NOT serious! You're going to stalk him?"

"Nooo, I don't stalk him. I just want to see him. I miss him sooo much. Now are you guys coming 'cause, if not, I'm going by myself." I got up, grabbed my keys, and headed for the door.

The sounds of grumbling soon followed me out the door.

August, 1996

I was on the phone with Justine who said "Es, I'm worried about you. All you do is carry that phone around with you all day, hoping Marcus calls and then you cry when he doesn't. This isn't healthy." Justine was one of my besties. She was a year and a half younger than I was. We had gone to high school together. She could be very caring and also a little dramatic as demonstrated by this phone call.

"Well, what else am I supposed to do?" I told her. "I'm not worthy of love so I might as well just stay in this house and die. There's no purpose in doing anything anymore. I might as well just do whatever the heck I want. What does it matter in the end anyway?"

"Esmene, you're not even making sense right now. You know what? I'm getting you out of the house today. Go get showered because I know you haven't showered in a couple of days. Put on clean clothes and I'll be there to pick you up in thirty minutes."

"But what if he calls and I'm not here to answer the phone?" I asked pathetically.

"Sweetie, it's been months. He's not going to call."

"But according to Murphy's Law, he would call today because I'm going out. No, I'm not going."

"Thirty minutes Es or I'm telling your Mom." The line went dead.

I showered and dressed in clean clothes as demanded. I left my hair in its natural curly state out of indifference. About forty minutes later there was a knock at the door. I opened the door to Justine who was looking rather nice in her multi-colored top and denim skirt with a split up the side. Justine was about five foot seven with long legs. She was a sturdy girl, so she did the skirt some justice. Her hair was all done up real cute and I think I saw a hint of lip gloss.

I looked down at myself. I looked like a street urchin. I had on an oversized football jersey and jeans that were too long so the bottoms were tattered. My sneakers could have used a good cleaning and my hair was in a curly afro. I didn't care. I was secretly hoping she would be embarrassed to be seen with someone who looked like her little brother. Maybe she would tell me to stay home. I didn't care about going anywhere. I didn't care about my clothes or hair. I didn't care about anything anymore because no matter what I did, the people I loved either hurt me or died. And where the heck were we going anyway? Was she taking me to the diner? Of course I wouldn't get so lucky. "Where are we going?" I inquired.

"South Street," she said.

I groaned. "Oh no. Not South Street. Mom always said nothing good happens on South Street."

"Well I'm claiming today to be your lucky day." She gave me a sly smile.

We actually found parking without too much trouble and began our stroll down South Street. There was plenty to see, so Justine started to grab my hand to duck in and out of every little bizarre shop we passed. I knew her mission was to get my mind off of Marcus, and I appreciated the effort; but he was all I could think about. My heart was crushed and I felt like a little more of me was dying every single second. I was no doctor but I was pretty sure I was dying from a broken heart.

"Come on. This place looks cool. Let's go in here," Justine said, grabbing my hand once again. I looked up at the sign and read SoHo. Inside was a cramped store of assorted odds and ends. They had graphic tees, sunglasses, novelty items, shot glasses, and some sex toys A little bit of this, a little bit of that. There were four guys already in the store making it seem smaller because the store was crammed with so much stuff. One of the guys made a beeline for Justine.

Oh brother. Before I knew what was happening, Justine had gotten a severe case of the giggles over what this guy was saying to her. I couldn't have cared less, so I busied myself looking at the sunglasses until Romeo finished. I found a pair that looked interesting, so I turned to the mirror and tried them on. As I was admiring my reflection, a tower of a person stepped right in front of me to look at himself in the mirror.

Real ignorant, I thought. I waited for a second to see if Mr. Ignorant was going to move; but he didn't, so I tapped him on the back. Mr. Ignorant turned around; and failing to look down he didn't see anyone, so he turned back to the mirror. I huffed and puffed, slapped my arms against my sides and tapped Mr. Ignorant again. This time he turned around and he did look down. He looked me right in my eyes and said in a deep voice that matched his stature, "Oh, I'm sorry. I didn't see you there." Then he moved away from in front of the mirror.

He smiled at me with this goofy smile and I impolitely rolled my eyes at him. I didn't know if he was being serious or if he was trying to be funny. As tall as he was, he probably really didn't see me. He was one of the tallest people I'd ever seen in real life, except for maybe the basketball players on campus. He was massive! It didn't take much to be taller than I was, but I felt like a spec of humanity next to him. He was tall and thin and about two shades darker than I was, but I could tell the darker shade was from the sun. He had a thin mustache and a goatee and was sporting those waves all the guys had in the nineties. He was dressed in the standard Philly dress code: white tee, khaki cargo pants and Timbs. Other than the fact that he was tall, I took no other notice of him and I was just ready to move along.

I wasn't one bit sorry that I was going to have to break up Justine's love connection. "Justine, I'm ready to go," I said exasperated.

She gave me a look and said "Really?"

I responded with my own look. "Yes, really. Come on, let's go," I said and headed towards the door.

"Which way you ladies walking?" I heard her new friend ask.

Justine giggled. I rolled my eyes for the tenth time that day. Pretty soon my eyes would be rolling down South Street on their own. I decided at that moment that I was going to stop answering the phone when I saw Justine's number come up on the caller ID. Hadn't I suffered enough? "We're just walking up and down the street," she told her new friend. "We're not going anywhere specific," she added and did a little flirty thing with her fingers.

"OK, so are we. Maybe we'll run into you again," he said.

I thought, with the luck I'm having today, we probably will run into you again. I opened the door, a signal that I was ready to go with or without her. Justine said her goodbyes then shoved me out the door. "Really Esme? We were having a great conversation. He's really nice. You couldn't just let us finish talking?" Justine whined.

"We're supposed to be here for me, not for you. Remember? Get Mr. Wonderful's number and chat with him on your own time," I said unsympathetically.

"His name is Dominic," she said pouting.

"Sorry. Dominic," I replied.

"Esmene..." Justine started to whine and drag her feet.

"Justine don't start with me. You brought me here. I didn't ask to come. If you wanted to come here to meet men, you could've come here alone. Now if that's what you want to do, that's fine. I'll catch the bus home. But just know, don't you even think about trying to get me out of my house again. Are we clear?" I asked through gritted teeth.

Justine let out a sigh. "No, that's not what I want. You're right. This was for you, not for me. If I run into him again, I'll just get his number. I'm sorry Es. Forgive me?" she asked with a poked out lip.

I smiled for the first time that day. "I shouldn't, you giant baby, but I do. Come on, let's see what other weird stuff we find out here."

Of course we found Dominic and his crew again inside of a Chinese restaurant. It was like they were following us. So we were sitting in a generic Chinese restaurant on South Street, with Justine and Dominic playing getting to know you. The only things I wanted to know were what was in my shrimp fried rice and why was Mr. Ignorant sitting in the corner staring holes into me.

I found out Mr. Ignorant's name was Jericho. Jericho and Dominic were brothers, the youngest two out of eleven siblings. Dominic was twenty-two and Jericho was twenty-six. The two other guys who were with them, Ricky and John, both teenagers, were their nephews.

Dominic was the talker, hence, the one I didn't trust. I think it might've had something to do with his assertion that the famous Philly R&B group, Boyz II Men, was originally supposed to have five members, not four. He was the supposed fifth member. We sat in that restaurant for quite some time listening to Dominic shovel the bull; and, to be honest, he turned out to be quite entertaining. He had us all laughing and managed to take my mind off of Marcus for a few minutes.

But Jericho caught my attention. He never said a word, still sitting there with that deep penetrating gaze focused right on me. What was this guy, I wondered, some kind of psycho?

It was getting late and I was ready to go. We all left the restaurant together, Dominic and Justine having exchanged phone numbers. When we were almost to our car, I heard a foreign, deep voice call out ,"Hey, hey, what did you say your name was again?"

Justine and I both turned to look but I immediately knew that voice belonged to Jericho. He was smiling at me. I had no time for his nonsense. I rolled my eyes at him. "My name's not hey," I said, then turned around and kept walking.

"Es, I think he likes you," Justine said, playfully bumping my shoulder.

"Justine, I've got books about guys like him." We laughed and we both got in the car.

September, 1996

Justine and Dominic had started seeing each other, but Justine was not comfortable driving in Philly. That meant that I'd become her chauffeur when she wanted to see him. And, of course, every time she wanted to see him, Jericho would tag along, so it would be hours of them making out in the backseat, with Jericho and me sitting in awkward silence in the front. The only thing we seemed to bond over was the death of Tupac and his song I Ain't Mad at Cha, which is now officially "our" song. How romantic, I always think.

It was Justine who told me Jericho was really interested in me. "Justine," I asked when we were alone, "how can he possibly be in love with me? He's barely said two words to me both times he's seen me."

"Esmene, he's really shy; but Dominic said every time we leave he says that he's in love with you," Justine insisted.

"This from Dominic, the fifth member of Boyz II Men?"

We both laughed. "Come on Es, give him a chance," she said.

"A chance to do what?" I asked. "I've nothing to give him. My heart belonged to Marcus and he broke it. I'm still waiting for him to call me and tell me he loves me and that he'll take me back. I don't care about anything else. Nothing has any meaning anymore without Marcus in my life. I have a thousand things in my head and I can't grab hold of what's relevant in the moment. I don't know what's wrong with me. He's ruined me. I'll never be good for anything." Then I started to cry.

Justine laughed and asked "Are you done, Cicely Tyson? You're so freakin dramatic. Don't get me wrong, Marcus was nice and cute; but he was this little, old, short order cook with no car. Are you really going to let the loss of him ruin your life? You're crazy!"

I jumped up off my bed ready to defend my man. "How dare you? That may be all he was to you but to me he was my everything! He still is. Can't you see I'm broken? Can't you understand my heartbreak? Even in my sleep his demon minions come and torment me in my dreams. There's no escaping him."

"Have you been drinking again?" she asked.

"You're such a bitch, you know that?"

"You never used to drink and now all of sudden you're drinking Zima. I mean, that's not the hard stuff, but for you it is. You can't handle your liquor. Is that what you're going to do for the rest of your life? Sit in your room, get drunk, smoke Black & Milds, and be a drama queen? What's gotten into you? What's wrong with you?"

"You know what?" I spit out angrily, "I don't know what's wrong with me and I don't even care. I don't care about anything anymore."

October, 1996

After about four weeks of sitting next to Jericho in the front seat of my car in Fairmount Park listening to Justin and Dominic make out in the backseat, Jericho asked if we could talk, just the two of us. I agreed. It had gotten too cold to sit in the car, so we went back to his place. "So this is your room?" I asked Jericho as we entered the dark room and he closed the door behind us.

"Yeah. I share it with Dom."

I saw there were two single beds, one on each side of the room. I thought how the heck did he fit on that bed?

"Have a seat," Jericho said. I could hear he was nervous.

"This is the first time I've ever been in a guy's room," I said truthfully. I had never been in Marcus's room, though I had been in his house.

"Really?" Jericho asked. "Am I making you uncomfortable? Do you want to go back downstairs?" he asked politely.

I had to admit that for a man his size, all six feet seven inches of him, he was a gentle giant. "No, I'm OK. It's just my ex usually came over to my place." I saw Jericho look down at the floor. "Oh, I'm sorry. I shouldn't have brought him up. That was inappropriate."

"No, no. It's OK. If you need to talk about him, it's OK. I'll listen. It's no problem,"
Jericho said while holding my hand.

And that's exactly what I did for the next hour. I cried my heart out over the man I loved; and Jericho sat there, holding my hand, listening to every word, and getting me tissues to wipe my face. When I'd finally exhausted myself of tears, he looked at me. "Are you OK now?" he asked, sounding genuinely concerned

I sniffed. "Yeah, I'm OK. Thank you. I don't know many guys who would've been as patient as you were."

He looked down shyly. "I just want you to be OK." His caramel eyes met mine again. "Would it be OK if I kissed you?"

I felt a slight stab of betrayal hit me. How could I kiss this man when my heart belonged to Marcus? But he sat here and listened to me pour my heart out. Certainly he deserved a kiss. Anyway, Marcus made it clear he didn't want me, so I wasn't betraying anyone. "Yeah, you can kiss me."

And it was there, in his bedroom, that we shared our first kiss. The kiss quickly progressed into something more and pretty soon we were about to engage in the horizontal lambada. "Wait Esmene, I don't have a condom." Jericho's voice was strained from holding back.

"Who the heck cares? I don't, do you?"

And that was the end of that conversation.

January, 1997

"Jericho, we need to talk," I said when he answered the phone.

"Right now? I was just leaving to..."

"I'm pregnant."

"You're pregnant?"

"Yeah, that's what I said."

"Are you sure?"

"Yes, I'm sure. The doctor confirmed it yesterday."

"I mean, you're sure it's mine?" he asked after a deep resounding sigh. I didn't even bother to answer. He should have known I'd been with no one else.

"OK, what do we do?"

"Well, first you need to come and meet my dad."

"Your dad? Why?" his voice squeaked.

"I think my dad would want to meet the man who knocked up his daughter," I said, exasperated.

"I don't know what to say to your dad."

"Well you better think of something. Oh, and one more thing."

"What?"

"What's your last name?"

Drinking the Kool-Aid

March, 1995

Aunt Marie was a sweetheart, despite having some rough times in life. However, despite her struggles, Aunt Marie began to turn her life around. She managed to get a place for herself and the kids, procured stable employment, and started going to church.

Now, like most people who started going to church, once they started attending, they wanted to bring everyone they know along with them. When Aunt Marie made this transition, I was an incoming freshman in college, so I was mostly hearing about it from Mom. Any time there was some ladies' function, Aunt Marie was inviting Mom and Mom would politely decline. I was glad I wasn't there because I had my own opinions about church. I loved God. God and I were cool. It was the people in church I didn't trust. I'd seen too many people who quoted scripture on Sunday morning and did the devil's work Monday through Saturday. Uncle was one of those hypocritical, upstanding Christians.

Anyway, during one of my school breaks, Aunt Marie was hosting a ladies' luncheon for the women of The Living Word Fellowship Church at her home and she asked Mom and me to come. I did NOT want to go and told Mom but she said Aunt Marie really wanted us there. I loved my Aunt Marie, so I did it for her.

When Mom and I got there, I was already on high alert. The ladies from Living Word were already there and they greeted us with the biggest smiles I'd ever seen.

Strike one: I didn't trust people who smiled a lot. Strike two: They were being so nice and friendly to me. No one is that nice unless he or she wants something. Strike three: My Aunt Marie had actually cooked! Aunt Marie never cooked. Suddenly, it all became clear. Poor Aunt Marie had drunk the Kool-Aid!

I rudely rolled my eyes at those charlatans and followed my aunt into the kitchen. "Aunt Marie, how did you get mixed up with these people anyway. They're weird," I said to her as she tossed salads and loaded plates.

"Baby they're not weird, they're Godly women and I wish you'd get to know them. I told them all about my brilliant niece and they wanted to meet you. Now be nice Esme," Aunt Marie pleaded with me.

I generally didn't "do nice" but for her sake I was going to perpetrate the fraud. But if she was serving any punch, I was out of there. I walked back out into the dining room with Aunt Marie, with a fake smile pasted on my lips, to be introduced to these mighty women of God.

There was the Pastor's wife, Doreen Huntsman. She seemed OK, a petite lady about Mom's age. She reminded me of Patty Labelle. There was her older sister, Darla Weldon, also about Mom's age and equally attractive but taller than her younger sister. I had my eye on that one. She smiled at me but I saw an eyebrow go up. She might have been on to me. There was The Mother of the church, who was also their mother, Mom-Mom Dottie. Now she was a cutie, a woman in her late seventies who looked really good for her age. She had a beautiful smile. It was almost beautiful enough to fool me. Lastly, there was Darla's daughter, Amelia. She was grinning from ear to ear too and she had big bright eyes that said "hey, let's be friends." I was hoping mine said "no thanks." I didn't know how old she was, but she looked to be about my age. All I could think was you poor baby, they got you too. Take my hand and run away with me. I'll save you. I gave that child a sympathetic look and she responded with that same smile. What have you all done to this poor, clueless baby, I wondered.

I'm not going to act like I remember one thing that happened at that women's meeting that day, because I don't; and I never thought I'd see those women again, so it didn't matter. But God doesn't do anything without a reason.

When Aunt Marie died, Mom was determined to keep her kids, Veronica and Kenneth, in the church. Because the church was about a half hour away in Marlton, she ended up staying for the services herself and she began taking my brothers and little sister along as well. The next thing I knew, not only had my mother drunk the Kool-Aid; but she had given it to my younger siblings. Now they were all members of this cult. I still had Delilah and Dad with me as free agents.

However, it wasn't too much longer before Delilah drank the forbidden juice too. They REALLY got Delilah! Delilah must have had super sized serving, because when they got her, they got her good. She became a sanctimonious, Bible toting, scripture quoting, pointing out my every sin, Christian that I could not stand. Every time I came home from school for a visit, she was beating me down about how I needed to get saved from my sin, how I needed to go to church, and how I needed to get a relationship with God and accept Jesus as my personal Savior. She would follow me into the bathroom holding her Bible in her hand. I remember thinking that must have been some powerful Kool-Aid she drank. It must have been grape.

So one day more than a year after Aunt Marie had passed away, I was home for a weekend in October; and Delilah was following me around the house with that darn Bible again, giving me an earful because I didn't go to church with the rest of the family that day. I'd had it. I opened my bedroom door and turned back to face her. "You know what Delilah? You know when I'll go to church? When I have kids because I want them to be raised up in a good church right from the beginning, and not try to force it

on them when they're my age. Now leave...me...alone!"
And with that I stomped into my room and slammed the
door in her face.

That would shut her up for a while. I had no plans to
have any kids.

January, 1997

No one had ever told me God had a sense of humor.
My plan not to have children anytime soon was quickly
derailed. A cold winter day found me and Delilah playing a
game of iSpy. Delilah whined "It's freezing. Can we close
the window now?"

"No, the natural light is better to read them," I said. "Stop
being such a punk. Here, look at them now."

Delilah looked at the two white plastic sticks as she held
them out the window into the sunlight. She shook her head.
"Esme, I don't care what kind of light you put on these.
They both show two lines, which means they're positive.
You're pregnant!"

My heart was in my throat. I held the tests out the
window and looked for myself. The pink lines were faint,
but they were there. I put the storm window back down.
"Maybe it's a false positive," I tried to reason.

"Two false positives on two different tests? I don't think
so Sis. You're pregnant. Wait until Dad finds out."

"Oh shut up!" I said. "You're supposed to be my big
sister. Help me. What do I do?"

She sighed heavily and took the tests from my hand.
"Call and make an appointment with Dr. Borero. He'll order
blood tests to find out for sure. Then he'll tell you what to
do."

A Week Later

I was sitting in the family room pretending to be
watching television, but I could feel Mom's eyes on me as

she finished her dinner at the table. I wondered why Mom kept staring at me. She knew. She had to know.

I had my appointment with Dr. Borero five days earlier. Dr. Borero wasn't actually certain that I was pregnant based on the dates of my last menstrual cycle and exam, but I got the call that afternoon. Yes, I was indeed pregnant. I needed to make an appointment with an OB/GYN. I needed to tell my parents. Mom was looking at me, looking at my stomach. Mom was very calm by nature and had an eternal poker face, but she couldn't fool me this time. My Mom knew.

Well guess what? I wasn't going to let her get one up on me. I was a woman now and I was going to confront her before she confronted me. About ten minutes later, Mom cleared her plate off the table and made her way back into her room. With my heart thumping in my chest, I followed her. When I got to her door, I took a deep breath and then knocked. "Come in," she said.

I knew it; she was waiting for me. Mom was bent over looking for something in her closet. I took the coward's way out. "Mom, I just found out that I'm pregnant. I'm keeping the baby and there's nothing you can do about it." I opened the door and left. I went to my room and didn't see Mom for the rest of the night.

It wasn't until the next day that my Mom called me into her room. "Esme, were you telling me the truth yesterday when you said you're pregnant?"

"Yes, ma'am," I whispered.

"And how do you know for sure?"

"I took two home pregnancy tests that came up positive, so then I went to Dr. Borero and got a blood test to confirm it." I put my head down in shame. "I'm sorry."

Mom inhaled deeply and sat with her back straight but didn't say a word. Finally, I looked up and met her eyes. They were full of doubt. I didn't blame her. "I...I have an OB/GYN appointment this Friday at eleven. Do you think you could take me?" I asked her. If she went to the appointment with me, she would know that what I was telling her was true.

Mom let out another sigh but still remained calm. "OK, Esme. I'll take you to see what's going on." I knew by her tone that I was being dismissed so I got up and left the room. Mom and I didn't discuss it again, not even on our way to my appointment.

It wasn't until after I came out from my exam with all my pamphlets, samples, scripts for vitamins and she heard the receptionist telling me how to make an appointment for my first ultrasound, that reality finally sunk in for Mom. I was really pregnant and she was going to be a grandmother. But, what a shock! She was ecstatic. Mom loved babies. Mom babbled on about this and that and all the things I needed to do to get ready but still there was only one thing I could think about. How was I going to tell Dad? However, before I told Dad there was another thing I needed to do.

On Sunday morning I got up, got myself ready, and went to church with my family. It was an uncomfortable experience for me. I never expected to be sitting in church, pregnant out of wedlock, feeling like I had let my parents down. I certainly didn't want anyone in the church to know I was pregnant for fear they would ridicule me. At that time, I just needed to get what I could get from the Lord before everyone else ran me away. Ironically, one of the things the Pastor spoke about was being careful about the words that came out of your mouth. Whatever you spoke into the atmosphere would come into existence. Great, I thought, now you tell me.

After the message, there was an altar call for which I was chosen to go up. Mom came up to support me. I was an emotional mess. I kept telling Mom I was sorry and she told me it was OK and she wasn't mad at me. Right there, I accepted Jesus as my Lord and Savior. Unfortunately, in the middle of accepting Jesus Christ, my stomach was rejecting my breakfast. I had to run to the bathroom.

As I was finishing up in the stall, I heard someone come in the bathroom. I came out and saw a woman standing there with kind eyes that I had not yet been introduced to. I learned later her name was Lillian. "Are you alright?" she asked me with a gentle voice.

"Yes, I'm OK," I said hoping I didn't have regurgitated scrambled egg on my mouth.

"How far along are you?" she asked.

My mouth hung open. "How'd you…?"

She smiled sweetly at me. "He told me when He prompted me to come check on you."

"He who?" I wanted to know who was snitching on me.

"God, our Father," she said. "He speaks to us. Don't worry. You'll learn to discern His voice too. Now finish up. The Pastor wants to finish praying over you."

"Please don't tell anyone," I pleaded with her.

"Girl, it's not for me to tell. Now let's go."

So back out I went up to the altar, where Pastor Langston Huntsman and his wife Doreen prayed the prayer of salvation with me, and I also became an official member of the church. After service I was welcomed by all the members and given materials to start my new members classes. It was just a flurry of activity but it was OK. For the first time since this all started, I felt like I was going to be alright. I didn't feel alone.

Refreshments were quickly given out before everything was packed up and we were ready to leave. It wasn't until we were all in the car and I looked at my siblings enjoying their Capri Suns in the back seat that I started laughing out loud. "What's so funny?" Mom asked.

"I drank the Kool-Aid."

<u>The Proposal</u>

<u>Over three years later...</u>
At three am, I sat straight up in bed and turned the bedside lamp on. "Jericho," I reached over to shake his shoulder to wake him up, "Rico," I said again.

"What? What happened?" he asked groggily without moving or opening his eyes.

I slapped my hands against the comforter in frustration "Rico, I can't do this anymore."

"Huh?" he questioned, still not moving.

"I said I can't do this anymore," I repeated with frustration in my voice.

"Can't do what anymore? Sleep?" he asked, turning further into his pillow.

"No Rico. I can't do this! Us! This living together in sin! I can't do it anymore!" Jericho and I had been living together since Zander, our son, turned a year old. He'd just celebrated his third birthday.

Jericho quickly flipped over and fixed me with a glare, before he reached over to grab the alarm cock to see what time it was. "It's three o'clock in the morning and you decided now was a good time to talk about us living in sin. I swear, I'd love to know what the hell goes on in your head sometimes," he said. Then he thought about it, "On second thought, maybe I don't want to know."

Jericho may have thought it was odd, but it had been playing in my head like a tape stuck on repeat since I had gone to bed. I couldn't get it to stop. Maybe now it would stop. "I'm being serious Rico. It doesn't bother you that we're Christians, yet we continue to live in sin?" I asked, trying to reason with him.

Jericho flipped over onto his back and put his forearm across his eyes. "Esmene, I don't really think about it. It's not like we set out to live together. Living together was born out of necessity. You and the baby had nowhere to go. I wasn't going to leave you on the street, so you moved in here. Case closed. I'm not going to feel guilty for providing for my son and his mother."

Jericho had a point, but I wasn't ready to concede. "Yes but that was almost two years ago and we're still doing it."

Jericho sat up. "Esmene, I'm not holding you hostage here. If you're trying to tell me you want to leave, just come out and tell me; but don't think you're taking my son with you to go be with some other dude. That ain't happening. If you think there's some man out there better for you than me, you're more than welcome to go be with him; but my son stays with me," he declared angrily.

"Your son stays with you? I'm his mother!"

"And I'm his father! Mothers always think they get to pull rank because they're mom. You wouldn't let me run off with Zander and go live with some woman trying to act like his mommy, would you? Why should you get to run off to be with some man trying to act like his daddy? Come on now…" he finished, throwing back the comforter and swinging his legs over the side of the bed.

I grabbed his arm. This was going all wrong. "Wait, wait! No, you misunderstood. I don't want to leave to be with some other man. That's not what I was saying. Please, come back," I pleaded with him as I pulled him back to the bed.

Jericho shook his head and ran his hand down his face, "Well, Es, what are you saying, 'cause you about to drive me nuts here?"

I looked down at the comforter while I got my thoughts together and then wondered why I never noticed the design pattern looked like little demon faces. "What I'm saying is, if I don't plan on going anywhere and if you don't plan on going anywhere, why are we wasting our time playing house? I mean, if we're not going to go our separate ways, we should probably just get married."

Jericho's head whipped around to me so fast I heard his neck crack. "Did you just say married? We should get married?" his voice squeaked. "Well think about it. We'd all have the same last name. I could finally legally change Zander's last name to Munroe since he uses it in school anyway. I could finally put you on my medical benefits. I'd like to have another baby and I would prefer to be married when I do. And it'd be nice if they had the same father. Oh and then there's the tax break..." I rattled those facts off nervously in my girly moment.

Jericho smiled at me, enjoying watching me squirm as I lay down my argument as to why it would be beneficial for us to get married. I'd finally come to the end of my assertion as to all the reasons why we should get married. Jericho reclined with his back against the headboard with his eyes closed, not saying anything.

After a few minutes had passed I had to say something. "Well, what do you think? Don't leave me hanging here," I said anxiously.

His soft brown eyes opened to meet mine. I put my head down. He was going to say no. He moved over towards me, took my chin in his long fingers, and lifted my head up so my eyes would once again meet his. A gentle smile graced his full lips. "Well Es, I'm not a stupid man and I'd have to be some kind of idiot to turn down that tax break." We both laughed. "So yeah, I think we should just go ahead and get married too." He dropped a gentle kiss on my lips.

"OK," I said.

Then, suddenly, Jericho turned out the light and pushed me down on my pillow. "Now what was that thing you said about another baby?" he asked as he laughed.

"That's for AFTER we're married goofball," I said giggling at his antics.

"Oh," he said with a grin. "I guess I missed that part."

Just a Little on the Wrist

Pregnancy never did agree with me.
I was twenty-four and working at Cendant Mortgage
when I was pregnant with Zeyonna. Jericho and I had been
married just two months before I found out I was pregnant.
This pregnancy was a little better than Zander's. I hadn't
passed out anywhere but I was still sick all day. I had to
wear these motion sickness bands on my wrist and take
medication to help combat the morning sickness that
plagued me all day.

At the time, Jericho was working a low wage job in
Philadelphia, so I was supporting the family. Don't get me
wrong, he did what he could; but my salary paid the
majority of the bills. However, we started to run into
financial trouble due to the pregnancy because I was sick
so much. I'd used all my personal and sick time, so I was
at the point that I had to take unpaid days off. We quickly
found ourselves short on money to meet our monthly
obligations.

But I didn't worry. We were good and faithful Christians.
We prayed every day and often quoted Romans 13:8 "Owe
no man anything, but to love one another, for that loveth
hath fulfilled the law." I even wrote it on the checks I was
able to send out. I had the faith of a mustard seed that my
God would see us through.

On the day after Christmas, 2000, at about four pm, I'd
been babysitting my nephew Nathan who was the same
age as Zander. Nathan was the son Justine had with
Jericho's brother Dominic before they broke up. I grabbed
my keys and bundled the boys up so I could take my
nephew to his grandmother's house. We got downstairs;
and when I opened the door, I saw that my car was gone. I
was shocked: who the hell stole my car? My car was a
little unusual. It was a Chevy Metro, like the color of gold. I
called her Goldie. I ran upstairs and called the police. While

I waited for them to arrive, I called my nephew's mom to come get him when she got out of work. The police came and made a report. They advised me to call my insurance and finance companies to report the theft.

I called the insurance company first to report the car stolen. Then I called the finance company. Ms. Obnoxious spoke to me, saying "Mrs. Munroe, your car wasn't stolen. Your car was repossessed for non-payment."

"Non-payment? I'm only a month behind. I'll be sending in a payment when I get paid next week. Please, I need my car!" I pleaded.

Her reply was "By then it'll be sixty days past due. You have thirty days to come up with the remaining balance of the loan or the car will be sold at auction."

"The remaining balance of the car loan? That's ridiculous! Why can't I just bring it up to date?" I asked with a great deal of anger.

Ms. Obnoxious replied again: "It's too late for that. You had your chance. Now we want the full balance of the car. And with your past history with us, good luck finding a new finance company to give you that kind of loan."

Ms. Obnoxious was a bitch. I refused to cry, even though the tears were burning the inside of my nose and behind my eyes. I wouldn't give Ms. Obnoxious the satisfaction. I took a deep breath and asked "Where's my car?" very slowly to keep my composure.

"OUR car is in a lot in Bordentown," she sneered. She then rattled off an address and told me I could pick up my personal belongings if I wanted to. "It'll be there for thirty days and then it goes to auction." Ms. Obnoxious told me in a sing-song voice. She was loving this.

I slammed down the phone, not even saying good-bye, and fell into hysterics. I was so thankful Zander and my nephew were in the bedroom playing. Repossessed? How the heck did this happen? I was so upset and embarrassed. What should I say? How could I tell people?

What was I going to tell Jericho? It was the only car we had.

Everything was falling apart. Our car was gone. Our rent was past due. Zander's school tuition was past due. We were drowning and I could see no way out. My carefully erected house of cards was falling down around me and it was all my fault. In the midst of my silent meltdown, Justine came to pick up my nephew. She brought me a gift and asked me where hers was. I quickly and thoroughly cursed her out at that point and threw her gift back at her, momentarily forgetting all my Christian values. Then I slammed the door in her face.

"Mommy?" Zander asked in his little voice laced with concern. "What's wrong?" I leaned down and took his sweet little face in my hands. I thought of how he deserved so much better than this. He deserved better than to be living under the threat of being put out of school. He deserved better than to be living under the threat of eviction. He deserved better than living with the embarrassment of his parents' car being repossessed. He deserved better than a failure like me.

"Nothing baby. Mommy's going to make everything right. Now go to your room and play." I kissed him on both his little cheeks and silently said a goodbye that was so much more serious than he knew.

After I heard his footsteps disappear into his room, I went into the kitchen and grabbed a large serrated knife. I started to cry in earnest now. I loved my son. I would miss watching him grow up but he'd be better off without me. And the baby that I was carrying now? Hopefully Jericho would make it home in time to get me to a hospital so they could save her. He should be home soon. If not, she'd be with me and then I wouldn't be alone. Jericho would have Zander and I'd have her. Jericho would come to understand I was doing what was best for everyone. My life insurance payout would be more than enough for him to start over again and get out of this mess I made for him. I loved him too much to continue to cause him this much pain and embarrassment. I was nothing but a burden. It was time for me to go.

I rubbed my six and a half month belly and whispered, "I'm sorry baby." I had the knife in my right hand and held it to my left wrist. I began to pray Psalm 23 "The Lord is my shepherd, I shall not want..." Then I pressed down as I began to slide the knife across my delicate wrist. I could see the first signs of blood...

"MOMMY!" I instantly dropped the knife into the sink, held my wrist down, and turned towards Zander.

"What is it?" I said through gritted teeth from the pain. My heart was thumping in my ears. Blood was trickling down my hand into the sink.

"Mommy, Toy Story is over. Can I watch Monsters Inc again?"

I looked into his slanted bright eyes and thought what the hell are you doing? I looked down at my arm. There was blood slowly dripping out of the one slice I made, traveling down my hand, onto my finger to land in the sink. "Mommy?" Zander questioned again, wanting to know what land his Mommy had disappeared to so suddenly.

"Sure Baby. Go back in the room. Mommy will be there in a minute," I said softly to him to ease his anxieties. I turned on the cold water and ran it over my wrist to rinse the evidence down the drain. I didn't know if cold water would hurt or help my wound but it felt good. I turned the water off and examined the cut. It wasn't too deep, but it was deep enough for it to bleed as if I had cut myself while cooking. I grabbed some paper towels, enough that I could wrap around my wrist until I could tend to it better later. I splashed some cold water on my face and dried it off. I said a quick prayer asking God to forgive me.

"Mommyyy come on," Zander cried. And Mommy, still alive, went off to tend to her son.

Wait, Watch Her

Several years had passed after my second failed suicide attempt. I was still working at the mortgage company now known as PHH. Jericho had embarked on a new career as a CDL driver. Zander was in school. Zeyonna would be starting kindergarten soon. And I was still struggling with my weight. When I visited my primary physician, Dr. Larry, he said pointedly. "I think it's time for you to look into attending a meeting at Overeaters Anonymous. I think you have some serious eating issues, young lady."

Wait, I thought, did this man just tell me that I have an eating issue? No kidding. Guess who's late to the party? I'd been big since I'd been his patient. Granted I wasn't this big, but seriously? Overeaters Anonymous? "Dr. Larry, don't you think you're overreacting?" I asked, trying to keep my voice calm.

Dr. Larry took his glasses off and turned his whole body towards me. "Young lady, no, I don't. You're twenty-eight years old and two hundred sixty-three pounds. That's the highest weight you've ever been. Your blood pressure is outrageous and your sugar levels are rising. Now I need you to get your eating under control. You have two young children; and at the rate you're going, you won't be around to raise them."

Ouch. I didn't want to hear that, but was he right? Two-hundred and sixty three pounds was a lot of weight on a five foot two inch frame. But Overeaters Anonymous? Surely there was an alternative? "Dr. Larry," I told him, "my job has just partnered with Weight Watchers. A representative comes every week and does the weigh-ins and has the classes right at work. Could I do that instead?"

Dr. Larry seemed to consider the idea for a moment. "Weight Watchers is an excellent program if you apply yourself. OK, let's see how much progress you make in six weeks. If you do well, we won't have to revisit this topic. Sound good?"

"Sounds like a plan. Thank you Dr." I said.

"My pleasure. I'll see you back in six weeks. Good luck to you sweetheart." He bid me goodbye.

Soon after I got back to the office, I talked my supervisor Ms. Nadine and my cubby buddy Ms. Doris into signing up with me. Ms. Nadine was a sixty-two year old African American woman with a husband and twin daughters. Ms. Doris was a Caucasion and about the same age. She lived with her husband, daughter, and mother. Regardless of our ages or race, we all had one thing in common: we needed to shed some pounds.

So we went to a meeting, signed up, did our initial weigh-in (embarrassing), and got our materials. It was a pretty straight-forward plan. The way the program worked was most foods were assigned a point value. Each individual was allowed a certain amount of points per day based on his or her weight. The goal was to stay within your point values each day and you would lose weight. Plus, you had cheat points to use throughout the week.

It was simple. Well, the first two weeks went great for Ms. Nadine and Ms. Doris. They had each lost six pounds. However, I gained a total of five. At the end of the meeting in the second week, the facilitator pulled me aside and said if I came back the next week and gained again, we'd have to talk to see what I was doing wrong. It was like a punch in the gut. I wondered why I couldn't get this right. Was Dr. Larry right? Did I need Overeaters Anonymous? No, I did NOT need Overeaters Anonymous. I was going to do better.

That happened on a Friday. On Wednesday of the following week, I caught some kind of twenty four hour bug. Everything I ate I brought it back up. I couldn't keep anything down. Friday was the Weight Watcher weigh in, the moment of truth. I held my breath as I stood on the scale.....Hallelujah! I was down five pounds in one shot! I got a gold star in my book! I was so excited. Ms. Doris and Ms. Nadine were so happy for me. They asked me how I did it. I said it must have been because of the stomach bug I had. I couldn't keep anything down for the last couple of days.

"Well it worked kiddo," said Ms. Doris, giving me an affectionate pat on the back.

It certainly did work. It really did. I then considered what it was that worked? I couldn't keep anything down. But I was sick. If I'm not sick now, what if I gain the weight back next week? I could always make myself sick the day before weigh in, just as an extra precaution against weight gain. I'd still work the program, of course.

So getting sick had gotten me over the hump. It gave me a little push. I wouldn't need it all the time, only when I stalled and needed a little help along my journey. Intentionally getting sick was my new secret weapon to help me along the way when the scale maybe wasn't moving in the direction I would like it to move. This was great. It was times like this that I loved being smart. So I told myself to wait until I see Dr. Larry in three weeks. He is going to be so proud of my success. Better health, here I come.

Woman's Work

I loved my job at PHH. It was my first real job out of college; and although it was not in my field of study, it was a steady career with a decent salary and good benefits, both of which were needed in order to support my children. I moved up quickly in the company and held several different positions over the years. It was the company from which I expected to retire one day. And I did, just not in the way I thought I would.

The first signs of trouble came not too long after I returned to work, having given birth to Zeyonna. I just couldn't seem to get myself together. I was run down and tired all the time. I was easily irritated and argumentative. And all I really wanted to do was sleep or eat. Jericho reasoned it was the combination of the addition of the new baby and our still precarious financial situation that was causing me stress. His reasoning was plausible, so I went with it.

But then one day, the tears started. I would cry uncontrollably throughout the day. At work. In my car. In the shower. In bed. It didn't matter where I was. I was crying. "Esmene?" asked my buddy Emily as she turned around to look at me one afternoon. "Honey, are you OK?"

"Yeah," I told her. I was in the midst of wiping my face, so I nodded an affirmative, which was totally in contrast with how I looked at the moment. I threw my wet tissues in the trash and looked up at Emily's concerned face.

I adored Emily. She was a sweet petite girl with brown hair that fell in beautiful ringlets down her back. She was two years younger than I was with a very slender build. If your feelings got hurt easily, it was probably in your best interest to steer clear of Emily. She wasn't mean but she just didn't bite her tongue. On the other hand, if you wanted honesty, which I appreciated, Emily was the person to go to. A lot of people didn't appreciate my girl's candor, but

Emily was one of the most compassionate people I'd ever met. "You don't look OK to me," she said. "In fact, you look like hell. You're not OK are you?"

That caused more tears. "No, no I'm not OK, but I don't know what's wrong either. I just can't seem to stop crying. I just started crying one day and now I can't stop. It's so frustrating!" I angrily grabbed more tissues.

Emily got up out of her chair and came around to hug my shoulders from behind. "Sweetie, maybe you need to see your doctor, get checked out, and make sure everything's alright."

"You want me to go to the doctor because I can't stop crying?"

"You just had a baby. This could be hormonal. Healthy people don't just cry all day," Emily suggested.

"Thanks Mama. I didn't think of that. I'll call my doctor during our lunch break." I gave her hand an affectionate pat.

"You're welcome, Honey."

I was able to get the last appointment that evening. When Dr. Larry walked in the examination room, he said "Esmene, tell me what's going on?"

"I'm not sure, doctor. It started out with me being tired and irritated. Then I started crying for no apparent reason. I'll be at my desk at work and suddenly I just burst into tears. I just want to lay in bed and cry all day but I have to force myself to get up to go to work. Jericho has started on his new career and we're almost back on our feet financially after the hit we took during the pregnancy. I don't have time for this."

"And *this* would be...?" he asked.

"I don't know," I said exasperated. "Why do you think I'm here? I want YOU to tell me what *this* is."

Dr. Larry took his glasses off and perched them on top of his head. Then he reclined a little and placed his hands behind his head, his thinking pose. "When did this start?"

"About two weeks ago."

"Has this ever happened to you before?"

"Once, when I was pregnant. It was after I attempted suicide."

"You attempted suicide while pregnant? My God Esmene," he said in disbelief as he sat up in his chair and studied my eyes. Then he collapsed back into his chair and ran his hand down his face to rest on his mouth before shaking his head. "I certainly don't have that in my file," he said sitting up and grabbing my file.

"No, you don't. I was seeing my OB/GYN exclusively at the time. My sister McKenna took me to see Dr. Angeles."

"OK, OK," he said nodding his head, resuming his former pose. "So what happened? What did he do?"

"Umm, he prescribed me anti-depressants. He said I was depressed. He gave the samples to my sister and explained to her how I was supposed to take them. He told her not to give them all to me because I was a suicide risk. She gave them to Jericho," I explained.

"Did they help you?"

"No. I didn't take them. I was afraid they would hurt my baby."

That explanation earned me an incredulous look. "Let me get this straight. You attempted suicide while pregnant; but when given medication to help you so you wouldn't do it again, you didn't take the said medication because you didn't want to harm your baby. Do I have that right?" he asked incredulously.

"Exactly."

Dr. Larry shook his head, put his glasses back on, and opened up my file. "Esmene, I agree with Dr. Angeles. I believe you're dealing with depression. I'm going to prescribe you an antidepressant to see if that helps with some or all of your symptoms. Now you may have some side effects, so it would probably be a good idea to take a few days off."

Then I shook my head. "I can't. I took all my paid time off while I was pregnant. If I take any days off now, they'll be unpaid. We can't afford it." Tears started running down my face.

Dr. Larry handed me a tissue. "What if you take a short-term medical leave. That would be paid, right?"

I nodded my head. "Yes, I believe so."

"OK just get the paperwork over to the office and I'll get it completed for you. In the meantime, here's your script for the medication. Esmene, please take the medication this time. It can't help you if you don't take it."

"I will doctor. I promise."

That appointment led to the first time a doctor took me out of work for a medical leave. Also, I was prescribed antidepressants again. Just like the first time, I didn't take them. After about a week at home, I woke up one morning feeling like my old self, like nothing had happened, no crying, no tears. I waited a few more days to see if the spell was truly over and it was. I went back to work and all was well with the world. And I did it without antidepressants.

That same scenario played out several times over my years at PHH, with each episode lasting a little bit longer than the previous one. Each time I was taken out for a medical leave, I was prescribed an antidepressant that I never took. It always amazed me how there was no follow up by my doctor to find out if I was even taking the drugs. Someone had to notice that I never needed refills.

Then, in 2006, when I was twenty-nine, I started crying one day, and I just couldn't stop. At that time I was in account management and my work had begun to suffer. My supervisor at the time was doing all she could to cover for me but she could only do so much. I said to my supervisor after another trip to the bathroom "Ms. Nadine, I think I'm going to leave early. I'm not feeling well." It was obvious I'd been crying again.

She sighed. "What are you going to do when you get home?" she asked, voice full of concern. I shrugged my shoulders. "Is Jericho home?"

"No," I answered.

Ms. Nadine shook her head. "I'm sorry Esmene, I can't let you leave. I don't care if you sit at that desk and do nothing but cry all day. But I can't let you leave. I'm worried about you. Something's wrong and I'd never forgive myself if something happened to you," she said sympathetically.

"I can't just sit here and do nothing. I can't think. All of my spreadsheets need to be reconciled and e-mailed to the director by three. I can tell you right now, it's not going to happen because of the way I'm feeling." So I pleaded with her, "At least if I'm out sick, there'll be a reason why it didn't get done."

"Don't worry, I'll get it done. You just go sit down and get yourself together. When you're feeling a little better, you can come over and help me," she said gently and dismissed me.

"But Ms. Nadine..." I started to protest.

"No buts. Now go have a seat. Get some coffee. Go take a walk. Just don't leave the premises."

I felt like the biggest loser that day and I knew I couldn't let this farce go on much longer. Ms. Nadine was putting her job on the line for me and that wasn't fair. By the grace of God, a blessing showed up in my email about a month later. The company was going through a restructuring. They were offering to buy selected employees out of their employment contracts. The employees who accepted would get settled upon benefits for taking the buyout; and because they were not actually quitting, they'd be allowed to collect unemployment.

The day after receiving that email I gave my notice. "Ms. Nadine, I'm taking the package."

"I don't want you to go. You can get through this," Ms. Nadine said.

I shook my head. "Ms. Nadine, I can't stay. Something's wrong with me. I've changed and it's not fair for you to keep covering for me. Someone's going to find out and I don't want you getting into trouble because of me. This way, I can walk out on my own terms, with money in my pocket and not be put out with nothing," I reasoned.

Ms. Nadine nodded her head in understanding. "I guess that makes sense but I'll miss you Esme. Please promise me you'll get the help that you need. I want you to find the real Esmene in there." She gave me a motherly hug.

I didn't have the heart to tell her I was already lost.

Blurred Lines

Nancy was the therapist I had started seeing in the summer of 2006. I found her very easy to talk to and very knowledgeable but just talking wasn't making my symptoms any better. I was still crying a lot and my energy level was in the toilet. Even my hygiene was beginning to suffer. That's why it was decided that it was time for me to see a psychiatrist to get a concrete diagnosis and start medication. This was my first appointment with Nancy since seeing the psychiatrist.

When I arrived, Nancy motioned for me to follow her to her office. "So, Esmene, how was your appointment with the psychiatrist?" Nancy asked.

"It was OK. She's very nice. I like her. A lot of questions. It seemed like she was asking the same question three or four times, just changing the wording."

Nancy smiled and nodded her head in agreement knowing what I was referring to. "So after all the questions, what did the doctor conclude? By the way, what's her name again?"

"Dr. Diane. She initially diagnosed me with Major Depressive Disorder. She prescribed me Lexapro." Nancy turned and made a note in my file.

"Now Esmene, have you started taking the Lexapro? And what do you mean by initially?"

"Yes. Yes, I actually started taking it the next day. She started me on ten mg a day. I didn't feel any difference though. Well, I didn't notice any difference at first," I said with much disappointment.

"Well, you won't, not right away. These medications usually take about two to six weeks before you start feeling any effects from them. But it sounds like you had some kind of side effect from it?

"You could say that."

"Really? Tell me about it," Nancy encouraged as she settled back into her leather chair.

"Some of the details are fuzzy, but I remember being antsy all morning and I just needed something to do. Zander and Zeyonna, who are now ten and six were also bored so..."

While talking to Nancy, I relayed the events that had transpired...

November 17th, 2007

"Zander, come over here and wash the tires!" I yelled.

"OK, I need some water."

"I'll give you some water." I laughed and I squirted him all over with the water hose. He screamed and squealed, ran away from the cold water, and hid behind the minivan. Zeyonna was standing on the sidewalk laughing, holding a sponge, so I got her next.

"Mommy, Mommy, stop! It's cold," she yelled, laughing as she ran through the backyard.

"Esmene, what the hell are you doing!" Jericho yelled as he threw open the front door.

I stopped chasing the kids with the hose and looked over at him. "The kids are helping me wash the cars," I said as I turned the hose towards Zander to squirt him again.

"Esmene don't! What's wrong with you? Are you crazy?" He stormed out the house towards Zander.

I stood there confused. I couldn't understand why he was angry. "What's wrong? We're just having fun?"

"Having fun!" his eyes were full of rage as he dragged Zander with him towards the backyard to get Zeyonna. He took in her wet appearance and looked at me with disgust in his eyes. "Esmene, it's thirty degrees outside and you have the kids out here squirting them with cold water! Look at the baby. She's soaked!" He picked up Zeyonna, grabbed Zander, and took them in the house.

I stood there, alone in the middle of the street, trying to get a grasp of what just happened. Was it really that cold outside? I'd never purposely hurt my children. I thought washing the cars would be fun. But Jericho was so upset with me. What had I done that was so wrong?

I walked inside the house and closed the door. The living room was empty, so I moved through the house towards the bedrooms. I could hear water running in the bathroom. When I got to the door, I saw the baby standing there with a towel on, shaking. I walked up behind her. "Are you OK Baby?" I asked her softly.

"I'm cold Mommy," she said, her little teeth chattering.

I felt tears prick at the corners of my eyes. "Mommy's sorry Baby. I didn't mean to hurt you," I said.

"You didn't hurt me, Mommy. I had lots of fun!" she said with a toothless grin. Just then Jericho came out the bedroom, pushed past me, grabbed Zeyonna, and disappeared into the bathroom. I wanted to go in there and tell him I'd bathe her. I was more comfortable bathing the kids, but I thought better of it and just went back in the living room to take my coat and shoes off.

"Zander, you OK Buddy?" I asked my son when I walked in his room.

"I'm fine Mom, but Dad's really mad at me," he said.

"He's not mad at you, Babe. He's mad at me. You didn't do anything wrong. Are you cold?"

He nodded in the affirmative. "Just a little. Dad said I have to get a shower even though I already took one today. Can we have hot chocolate with marshmallows when I get done?"

"Sure," I said.

"And some Oreos too?" he asked with a smile.

I knew I was letting myself be manipulated by a ten year old, but what the heck. "Yes, and Oreos. Now get ready for your shower."

Both kids were bathed and warm in fresh pajamas. They had their hot chocolate with marshmallows and were watching their favorite programs on the Disney Channel when Jericho came into the living room. "Esme, I need to talk to you." His voice was devoid of emotion as he turned to walk towards the bedroom.

I gave the kids a reassuring smile and made my way to the bedroom. As soon as I passed through the doorway, Jericho closed the door. "Do you want to tell me what the hell is going on with you?" he asked under his breath.

"I don't know what you mean. So OK, I didn't realize how cold it was today and I shouldn't have been squirting the kids with water. It was poor judgement. I'm sorry. I don't know what else you want me to say."

"What do I want you to say? Esme, I just came from the laundry room. Why are you going to Sam's Club every day buying giant packs of paper towels and toilet paper? The whole laundry room is full of toilet paper and paper towels and you still keep going every day to buy more. Just last month, we kept running out of toilet paper. Now we have enough to give to Zander when he graduates college. Why are you doing this?"

"Like you said, we kept running out. I'm just trying to make sure that doesn't happen again. I thought you would be happy about not having to run out to buy a roll of toilet paper," I said, confused by his anger.

"Es, one pack of that toilet paper from Sam's has thirty-six rolls. We have five packs of them. I think we're good now. And the paper towels? Each pack has sixteen rolls. There are six packs of those in the laundry room. We could open up a store. Something's not right with your judgment, Es. Listen, do you think it could be the medication?"

"I don't know. I don't think so, but I really don't know," I said sitting down on the bed with my head down.

Jericho sat down next to me. "Look, I'm sorry I yelled at you but I was afraid of the kids getting sick. I want you to call that doctor first thing Monday morning. Tell her what's been going on and see if it could possibly be the medication. Will you do that?"

"Yeah. Yeah, I'll do that." I turned to look at him and said "I'm sorry."

Jericho put his long arm around my shoulders and placed a kiss on my temple. "I know you are Baby. The kids are OK. Let's just make sure you're OK too."

The Next Monday Afternoon

Thankfully, when I called my psychiatrist's office and explained my situation to Dr. Diane's receptionist, she was able to give me an appointment for that afternoon. I was hoping Dr. Diane would be able to give me some insight on my odd behavior over the weekend.

"And when was the incident with your children?" Dr. Diane asked.

"It was this past weekend. Doctor, my husband's really concerned and now so am I. I thought it was the medication doing its job. I was more alert. I had energy. I was getting stuff done. I was going out. I was cooking and my house was clean. But then these other things have us concerned. Something's not quite right."

Dr. Diane was looking at me nodding her head. Then she pulled out my file and began looking it over. "Esmene, have you ever heard of Bipolar Disorder?" she asked.

"Yeah, it used to be Manic Depressive Disorder."

"Exactly right. The depressive symptoms of Bipolar Disorder mimic Major Depressive Disorder. How I usually find out a patient is bipolar is when I prescribe him or her an antidepressant and it throws him or her into a manic phase. What you've been describing to me are signs of mania. Based on what you've told me, I'm changing your diagnosis to Bipolar I Disorder. The PTSD is still the same."

I was stunned. I never expected to hear that diagnosis. What was I supposed to do with that? "How did I get it?" I asked, as if I had an STD.

"Well, bipolar is largely hereditary, but it can be triggered by traumatic events, even drugs and alcohol. Do you know if anyone in your family has a history of Bipolar Disorder or any mental health issues?"

"I don't know."

"It's OK. What's important right now is that we manage your symptoms. Now, along with your antidepressant, I'm going to have to prescribe you a mood stabilizer. I doubt if you'll have too many manic episodes, but mania can be dangerous. The point is to keep you in the middle."

"Is this the reason why I binge and purge?" I asked.

"Your binging and purging is an unhealthy coping mechanism that you use to deal with your bipolar and PTSD symptoms and it needs to be addressed. There are some antidepressants that help curb that behavior but cognitive behavioral therapy is best. Have you given the Crenshaw Center a call?"

"Yeah, I called them. My husband is taking me next Friday." The Crenshaw Center was an Eating Disorder Center.

"Good. Alright. Let me get your script ready for you and you can be on your way. Same instructions as last time. If you have any problems, just give the office a call."

Can You Help Me

"Are you nervous?" Jericho asked me as he expertly maneuvered our Toyota Sienna around the curves and up the hills of Manayunk. I was on my way to my appointment at the Crenshaw Center and I had no idea what to expect.

"Yeah, I am. I've never known anyone who had an eating disorder. I've only seen it on TV or read about it. And the people never looked like me. They were always young white girls. In fact, you know what Bliss said to me on the phone last night when I finally told her why I had to leave my job and revealed everything that I was going through? She said, 'Esme, what do you mean you have an eating disorder. You're not white.' I was so pissed I hung up on her but then I couldn't sleep because I kept thinking about it. And she's right." Jericho reached over to grab my hand and squeezed it. "I don't know if going to this place is such a good idea," I told him.

Jericho quickly glanced over at me, giving me a reassuring smile before turning his attention back to the road. "You'll go there and see what they have to offer you in the form of treatment. If they can help you, great. If they can't, oh well, thanks anyway. No harm done going there to at least check the place out. You may go there and find lots of women like you. You can't believe everything you see on TV," he said. He was right, I wouldn't know until I got there.

We arrived at the center a half hour early as suggested in order to fill out the evaluation forms. We were greeted by a very perky secretary. I couldn't help but notice she was young and white. "Mrs. Munroe, we're glad to have you come visit our facility today. Now these are the evaluation forms that need to be completed before you can see one of our counselors. You can have a seat right here in the waiting area and fill those out. When you're done, you can bring them back up to me; and then a counselor will be with you shortly thereafter," she explained with a giant Vanna White smile.

"Great, thank you," I said with much less enthusiasm. We turned and headed for two seats in the corner of the waiting room. As usual, I took the seat that would allow me to have my back to the wall. I didn't like to have my back exposed so someone could walk up behind me when I was unaware. I wanted to be able to see everyone's comings and goings.

In between filling out the pile of evaluation forms, I glanced around the office looking for clues about what the client base probably looked like. There was a poster on the wall that showed three young white girls sitting on a lawn, having a small picnic lunch. I looked above where Jericho was sitting and there was a poster with a picture of all the counselors at the center. Each one of them was white. I was starting to feel uneasy.

I continued filling out the paperwork, still determined to give the place a chance. I really couldn't make a judgement based on whom they decided to use in their advertisements or the fact that their staff was entirely white. That didn't mean that they didn't have the tools to help me. As I got to the last few pages of the evaluation, I started to see some of the clients coming and going from the facility. Maybe I just came on the wrong day, but every girl I saw was no older than twenty, white, and thin as a pencil. They were nothing like me.

"Mrs. Munroe, are you almost finished with your paperwork?" the secretary asked.

I stood up, gathering up the papers and said, "Actually, I've changed my mind about the appointment. I don't think this is the right place for me, but thank you for your time." I turned to Jericho to find him staring at me, "Come on Babe, let's go." I motioned my head towards the door. Jericho looked totally confused, but put down his magazine and followed me to the door.

"Wait. Mrs. Munroe, wait!" I turned back around with my hand still on the door. "Is something wrong?" the secretary asked. "Why don't you wait for one of the counselors to discuss any concerns you might have. I'm sure we can address them here."

Just then, I felt a tugging on the door. Someone was trying to come in. I let go and there were more clients looking like genetic clones of all the other clients I had seen. I looked at them and then looked down at myself. I turned back to the secretary.

"No, you can't help me. Goodbye," I said as I opened the door.

Once in the car, Jericho asked, "Es, what was that all about?"

I sighed deeply, rested my head on the headrest, and turned to watch the scenery out the window. "It's like Bliss said. I'm not white."

It wasn't long before my next appointment with Nancy. I knew I would have to explain my actions to her when I saw her. Nancy probably wouldn't understand why I left either. I wanted to be able to get help from someone who was at least familiar with the community and culture that I identify with. We do things differently. We have different values, different beliefs. How could someone help me when he or she didn't even know where I'm coming from? People like that can't identify with me. No, it was never going to work there. "Esmene," Nancy asked soon after my next appointment started, "did you even give them a chance to tell you if they had any African American clientele?"

"No. I know they didn't. Every girl who walked through there looked like she worked at Abercrombie and Fitch. They were kids, not much older than my son. All day those white counselors deal with young, thin white girls. And there's nothing wrong with that. Except I'm a black, thirty year old mother of two, who is far from thin. My BMI would classify me as obese. I still don't understand why you and

Dr. Larry insist on saying I'm bulimic in the first place. I've never even heard of a black person having an eating disorder."

"Oh come on Esmene, stop being ridiculous. People of all races have eating disorders, just like people of all races have mental problems," she said.

"Well if they do have them, they certainly don't talk about them. Now that I think about it, I don't even know of another black person who goes to therapy or sees a psychiatrist!"

"Where is all of this coming from? Why are you trying to make mental health into a race issue? You're here aren't you?" Nancy pointed out.

"Yes, I'm here, but I'm the exception, not the rule. How many other black clients do you have?" I asked her.

"Well at the moment you're the only one," she admitted.

I challenged her by asking "When was the last time you had one?" Nancy had no answer. "There are four other therapists in this office. How many black people have you seen in the waiting room? I've never seen one besides myself."

"OK Esmene, you've made your point. But just because black people are not a general part of their clientele doesn't mean they can't help you," she tried to reason.

"They wouldn't be able to help me, Nancy. There would always be a disconnect between us. They would try to treat me like they treat their other patients and that wouldn't work. I'm not like their other patients. We don't come from the same backgrounds. We don't have the same home life. We don't have the same responsibilities or expectations. No, they couldn't help me."

Nancy nodded her head. "I understand Esmene. I'll help you the best way I can. I just want you to know, though, just because it's not talked about in the black community, that doesn't mean it's not happening. I think you would be shocked to know just how prevalent these disorders are amongst the African American population."

"I just feel so alone, like no one can understand. I'm embarrassed and ashamed. If I really am a bulimic, I'm a really bad one because I'm fat; and I'm an embarrassment to my community because I'm black. Then there's the whole Christian factor. If I was such a great Christian, I wouldn't need to take medication. I would already be healed from these disorders. So, on top of being a bulimic and an embarrassment to the black community, I'm also a failed Christian. Nancy, why do I even continue to breathe?" I asked seriously.

"Stop it. You stop it right now. You're not a failure and you're not an embarrassment. You're someone who has some challenges and you're doing the right thing by seeking help for them. That's not failing. You're going to come out winning because you'll have the tools you need to get you through when things get a little rough for you. You'll learn positive coping skills instead of the negative ones you've been using your whole life. You're not alone. I'm going to help you get there. Also, you have something that a lot of my clients don't have, a supportive spouse. Let me tell you, that makes a HUGE difference. We don't have to rush this. Slow and steady wins the race. We're going to do this together, OK?"

I looked at Nancy and the look in her eyes was so sincere that I had no choice but to believe her. "OK, Nancy," I said, surrendering to her will. "We'll do this together."

My journey was headed down a new path.

Justify Me

"Mom, can I go to Laylah's skating party Friday night?" Zeyonna asked me one afternoon when she was in the fifth grade.

"Sure. Is it going to be in Cherry Hill as usual?" I asked as I continued to wash dishes.

"Yeah. If you want, I can ask Taliyah if I can ride with her Alisha and Ayannah so you won't have to drop me off. I think her mom is staying to skate too."

"Well as long as it's OK with her mom, it's fine with me. Saves me two trips," I said happily.

Peaceful silence hung in the air between us as I finished the dishes and tended to dinner on the stove. Peaceful silence never lasted too long in my house. "Mommy?" Zeyonna asked.

"Yes, Baby?"

"Why do you hate skating so much?"

I immediately tensed up and went on the defensive. "I don't hate skating, I just don't like skating. I never actually learned how to skate," I said hoping she would leave it at that.

But of course she didn't because she's my daughter and that response was less than satisfactory. "Mom, you absolutely hate skating. Just opening the door to go inside to the rink makes you look like you're about to barf. You've never let me or Zander have a skating party, no matter how much we beg you."

I weakly tried to deflect, saying "I just think it's dangerous. I don't want you to get hurt."

"But I don't understand why? Your brothers and sisters skate and most of our cousins skate, so what's the deal with you?"

And then as I drifted back into the past I thought Mommy got a raw deal. That's the deal with me and I pray she'll never understand. I was nine years old when the seeds of hatred for skating were planted deep within my soul.

My older sister Delilah impatiently yelled at me, "Come on Esme, stop being such a big baby. I'm missing my friends while I'm messing around with you!" We were in our basement and Delilah was supposed to be teaching me how to skate. Delilah, who was then fourteen, had the patience of a tic and had no time for her little sister who couldn't jump double-dutch and apparently couldn't learn to skate. For all her tutelage, all I learned how to do was land on my butt instead of my knees. It hurt less.

She was once again pulling me off my butt by my arms. "Ouch Dee, stop being so rough. It hurts!" I cried.

"Well it wouldn't hurt if you would stay off the ground Dummy," Delilah said, sticking out her tongue.

"Stop calling me names. I'm telling Mommy," I whined, rubbing my sore bottom.

"That's what babies do, cry and tattletale. If you could skate as good as you whined, we'd be outside instead of this hot stinky basement!"

"Oh shut up Delilah!"

"No, you shut up!"

"Whoa. whoa, whoa. What's going on down here?" A deep voice rang out.

We both knew who it was. Standing there at the bottom of the steps, wearing a red and white Adidas jogging suit with matching Adidas sneakers, his long dark hair in a ponytail against his pale brown skin, was Uncle. Delilah's eyes lit up. "Hey Uncle." She ran to give him a hug. Everyone loved Uncle, including me despite all that he had done to me. The thought made me sick.

He dropped a quick kiss to the top of her head. "Hey there Dee. Now what's all the fussin' I hear goin' on down here?" He flashed his smile at her before finally resting his eyes on me. A shiver ran through my body.

As usual, Delilah noticed nothing strange. "I'm trying to teach Esme how to skate, but she is the worst student EVER! I'm never going to get to play with my friends if I have to stay down here with her all day," she whined.

Uncle's smile got even wider. Oh no, I thought. He bent down to look at Dee. "Well Dee, guess what? Uncle may be able to help you."

"You can?" She asked with childlike enthusiasm. I thought, please, Delilah, don't leave me.

"Yeah, I can." He turned his head towards me and eyed me cooly. "I'm Uncle. I can do anything."

"Whatcha gonna do Uncle?" Delilah asked with excitement.

"Well, believe it or not, Uncle was a pretty good skater back in the day. I think I still know enough to be able to teach Esme to stay off her butt so you can go play with your friends."

Delilah threw her short arms around his waist. "Thank you Uncle!" Then she turned to me. "See Esme, now you have an even better teacher. The bestest! You'll be out there skating with us in no time!"

I was shaking now. For the love of God! My mind was screaming at her back as she turned to retreat. Then she was gone. She left me. I couldn't believe she'd left me. What was I going to do? Maybe I could feign sickness, disease. Explosive diarrhea? "OK Baby Girl, let's get started," he said.

We had been down there for about an hour and I had to admit the lessons were going well. Uncle really was a better teacher than Delilah. But just when I let my guard down and started to feel safe, I somehow landed on my back behind some boxes with Uncle on top of me.

My heart was thumping. I began sweating. My arms were trapped between our bodies. I didn't know much about height advantage back then, but Uncle was a lot taller than I was. I felt overwhelmed by him. I began to squirm in my panic but that only seemed to excite him more. "You're such a little tease," he whispered in my ear with his hot breath.

I stopped moving. I wanted to scream. Mommy was right upstairs but I was scared that he would hurt me. The cold look in his eyes told me he would. From my body language, he knew when I had given in. He raised up on his knees and pulled my pants and underwear down. I focused on the fact that it was Saturday and I had Wednesday's underwear on. Maybe he would think I had not bathed since Wednesday and he would leave me alone. No such blessing would come my way that day.

After he pulled down my pants, he pulled down his sweatpants and underwear. He laid on me so that our private parts would be lined up. He then proceeded to rock himself back and forth between my chubby thighs, groaning, licking my neck, and murmuring things I didn't understand. Blood rushed to my face, hot with humiliation.

I looked up at Uncle, this man I loved and admired so much and searched the secret places of my mind in an attempt to recall the offense I had committed that caused me to deserve such cruelty. As I lay underneath his rocking body, I thought about my short life and the kind of person I perceived myself to be. I had always considered myself a good girl. I rarely got reprimanded by Mommy or Daddy and not once had I ever been reprimanded in school. I didn't fight or say the naughty words that I heard some of the other kids say. So I didn't deserve this.

I suddenly got a heavy feeling in my chest. A deep sadness had come over me and I felt my eyes begin to water. Uncle was supposed to be a good man and I loved him. He wouldn't do this to me for no reason. I may have hated what he was doing but this must have been my punishment for something I had done wrong. I had to make up for my sin. In a most pitiful voice I said his name, "Uncle," as tears ran down both sides of my face. His eyes shot open and he looked at me with a look in his eyes that I can now describe as possible regret. He reached between our bodies and fished out one of my little hands and placed a gentle kiss on my palm and held it to his chest.

After what seemed like forever, his breathing became erratic and his thrusting was harder. Suddenly, he groaned and I felt the liquid heat seep between my thighs and between my butt cheeks. I looked up at Uncle. His eyes were closed and his mouth was shut tight. I couldn't tell if he was in pain or what. I didn't care, I just wanted him off of me. I felt dirty, especially with his sticky wet stuff on me now. But my punishment had been paid.

Uncle let out a little chuckle. "Good God Girl, you gonna be something else when you get grown." Then he dropped a kiss on my cheek and told me not to move. He took the white towel that he had tucked in the back of his pants to wipe off sweat and wiped off the evidence of our rendezvous. He jumped up like a spring chicken and pulled his pants back up. I, on the other hand, got up like an old man. My whole body hurt like I had been in a fight. He bent down, took my skates off, helped me up, and pulled my pants up. He told me to go to the bathroom and clean up. Then we would go to the store to get some goodies.

Those skates have remained in that same spot. I never picked them up again. Experience really was the best teacher. My Baby was right. I hated skating.

Is This the End

    Thanksgiving, 2009, was a very special Thanksgiving. It was my first time preparing Thanksgiving dinner all on my own and I was hosting it at my home. Most of my relatives didn't come, though. Only Lyam and Braxton were in attendance. The rest of the family decided to have dinner at Mckenna's new house that she and her husband Cedric had recently purchased. I'm not going to lie, I felt slighted; but, nevertheless, I was thankful for the time I was going to have to spend with those who would be attending in my home, making memories that would last a lifetime. I had made the decision about a month beforehand. This would be my last Thanksgiving.

    I was tired; and if I was tired, I knew those around me had to be tired too. It had gotten to the point where I couldn't even be bothered with getting up in the morning to make sure the kids got to the bus stop safely, even though it was just around the corner. Some days, they barely made it to school because I would wake them up late. Ms. Lilly from church would come by the house just about every day to get Zeyonna and take her outside to play after school and keep her entertained so I could rest. No one would ever comprehend how that made me feel. I would go for days without showering, brushing my teeth or combing my hair.

    Who had I become? I was a sick, sorry, sad, pathetic shell of a person. I was tired of being tired. I was tired of being sick. I was tired of being sad. I was tired of being pathetic. I was tired of this life. It was like playing the longest game of Monopoly in the history of Monopoly and I didn't want to play anymore. I wanted to turn over all of my money and property and forfeit the game. I was done.

    Since I knew I was going to take my life, I wanted to make the aftermath easier for Jericho and the kids, so I had Jericho, who was now a CDL driver for a moving company, bring home packing boxes a few weeks ahead of time under the pretense that I wanted to clean out my closet. The whole week leading up to Thanksgiving, I boxed up most of my clothes and hid the boxes in the basement. This way, when I was gone, he wouldn't have to worry about packing up all of my belongings. Most of it would be done for him.

That's the least I could do for him, since he'd always been so supportive of me through this whole battle. It wasn't even a battle, just a slaughter really. Bipolar and PTSD had just come in and took what they wanted from me. They took my job, my finances, my sanity, my will to fight, and my will to live. I didn't deserve to live and surely my children deserved a better mother than I'd been, a mother who would fight for them in times of trouble. No, they didn't need me. They would be better if I were gone.

So, the day before, I had withdrawn all the money from my personal accounts and put the money in an envelope in my top drawer where Jericho would easily find it. I'd not decided on whether to leave a note. I figured I would know when the time came. I came home and actually felt good about myself. I felt I was finally being selfless and doing what was best for my family. I was actually smiling and singing while I made the final preparations for dinner.

"Well this is new," Jericho said as he placed a gentle kiss on my cheek.

I smiled up at him. "I feel new. I feel good today, at peace. Everything is going to be as it should be."

Jericho came over and put his hands on my shoulders and looked me in the eyes, "Everything OK Esme?" he asked with a worried brow.

I stood on tiptoe to kiss his chin. "Everything is just fine, Babe."

Dinner was phenomenal. I impressed myself with it being my first time cooking a turkey and all the fixings. Everyone walked away from the dinner table content. I was glad. This was exactly how I wanted that night to be. This was the lasting memory I wanted to leave my husband and children. I knew they would be hurting the next morning and knew they wouldn't understand at first that I was doing this for them, but they would eventually realize the gift of freedom I had given them and they would think back on Thanksgiving and have wonderful memories of me.

Dinner was over and the guests had bid goodnight. All the leftovers had been packed away and the dishes had been cleaned. With overstuffed bellies, Jericho and the kids crawled into bed. "Babe, you're not coming to bed yet?" Jericho asked.

"I just want to finish up some stuff in the living room. I won't be long," I answered. I knew he was tired from all the food he stuffed himself with and I wouldn't get an argument back.

I walked out into the darkened living room, dug around under the couch, and found my stash: sixty, two-mg Ativan tablets. I was prescribed Ativan on a regular basis but rarely took it because I was scared to become addicted to it. Well, now I had a use for it. I would throw in some of my other medications like Geodon, Zoloft and Sonata just to make sure this worked. I was going to take them all. No aspirin this time.

I went into the kitchen to get the other pills when I heard my phone ringing. I had left it in the bedroom. I quickly ran in there to get it because I didn't want Jericho to wake up. My heart was thumping. Please don't wake up, I prayed.

I read missed call: Sister Lilly. I took the phone, closed the bedroom door, and headed back to the kitchen for the rest of my pills. The phone started ringing again. I groaned, my eyes rolling up to the ceiling. I thought, you're kidding me, right?

It was Sister Lilly again. I knew if I didn't answer she would just keep calling so I answered. "Hello," I said, trying not to sound like a woman on the verge of swallowing almost one hundred pills.

"What's up Bud? How was dinner?" Sister Lilly asked in her chipper as usual voice.

"Dinner was good. Real good. Everything went fine."

She must have detected something odd in my voice. "Are you alright?" she asked me, not so chipper anymore.

She knows something is up, I thought. I never should have answered the phone. "Why yes, I'm fine. It's just been a long day so I'd like to go to bed now," I said hoping to get her off the phone.

And of course it didn't work. A moment of silence hung between us. "So where's everyone else?"

"They're already asleep," I answered.

"They're all asleep and you're still up? What are you up doing?" Sister Lilly and God are best friends. They talk all day, every day. There was no way that I was going to lie to this woman and get away with it but I was going to try to be slick.

"I was just tying up some loose ends," I said. I thought I was being clever. Good one Esmene I said to myself. I was being honest. I WAS tying up loose ends.

There was a stretch of silence that started to make me squirm, even though we were not face to face. Finally she spoke. "Uh huh. OK, well did you finish up those loose ends?" she asked.

"Um, not quite, I was just about..."

"OK, well you can finish them up while we're on the phone," she said cheerfully, "So, tell me about dinner. I know you were nervous because it was your first time making a turkey. How did it turn out?"

And that conversation stretched on until three in the morning. We laughed, we cried, we reminisced, we prayed. We did it all. It was one of the best conversations I'd ever had. I would have missed it if I'd tied up those loose ends.

"Well Bud, you should probably go get some rest. How do you feel?" She had me reconsidering my suicide. Am I going to dump the pills, unpack the boxes and stay here with everyone?

"I feel good. I'm OK now," I hoped she could hear my answer. I knew in my heart that God sent her to call me and save me from myself. And maybe I wanted to save myself too. Maybe my tone had let her know I was really troubled. I thanked God for loving me more than I loved myself, and I said a prayer of thanks for Sister Lilly being in my life.

"He loves you Esmene, you know that, don't you?"

"Yes ma'am," I said, my voice heavy with emotion.

"And I love you too. We all do, but none of us love you like He does," she said with a fierceness in her voice. "He will never leave you, never forsake you. God is your refuge and your strength, a very present help in times of trouble. Remember that Esmene. You're never alone. He's a friend who sticks closer than a brother. You hear me Esmene?"

"Yes," I whispered. I heard her.

"Now you're going to hang up this phone and go lay down with your husband and go to sleep right?"

"Yes ma'am."

"And if you need me, you call me. I'll be right here. I love you Esmene, I truly do," she said in a gentle voice.

I knew she did. I could hear it in her voice. I could feel it over the phone, "I love you too. Thank you. What can I ever do to repay you?"

"You can stand Esmene. And having done all you can, just stand."

More Money, More Problems

My favorite board game is Monopoly. However, most people won't play it with me because they say I get too serious. They're not lying; I'll play for hours. The only one who would go toe to toe with me was my cousin Kenny; but he was away in the army, so I began collecting various versions of the game in the hopes that once my children became old enough, I could teach them the joys of playing Monopoly.

We finally emerged from our financial troubles and were able to purchase our very first home in 2011. We were so proud. We didn't think it would ever happen, especially with me being out of work; but God is good and faithful to His word. We prayed and believed for a new home and we received it. It was a fully renovated three bedroom, with one and a half baths and a finished basement, just enough room for the four of us. We were finally living the American dream.

About a year later, Jericho noticed something peculiar was happening. Packages began to appear on our doorstep, almost daily. "Babe, did you order something else?" Jericho asked me, while bringing in one, sometimes two packages off the front step.

"Oh yeah, just a little something I found on Ebay. It was a great deal. Just put it in the corner," I would say while mindlessly scrolling through Ebay for that next great deal.

It wasn't long before I had a pile of unopened boxes in my dining room, with more packages arriving daily. Now there were packages from other places like Modells. "Oh, they had North Face hoodies on sale, I told Jericho. "I couldn't pass that up. You know how expensive they are. And Macy's. They had a twenty-five percent off customer appreciation sale. Zander needed new basketball shorts. I got some really good deals.

Jericho yelled after yet another package was delivered, "Petsmart? Es, we don't have any pets."

"Oh, I know. My friend volunteers at a shelter and she said they needed food donations. This was a great buy. Twenty-four cans of cat food for $9.99? What a steal!"

I was making a lot of strategic and wise purchases and Jericho was lucky to have me overseeing the finances and being so responsible. But Jericho stormed into the bedroom one evening while I was sitting on the bed scrolling through Ebay. "Esmene, what's this?"

I looked up at him and saw him holding a letter of some kind in his hand. "What's what?" I said innocently, because I didn't have a clue.

"It's a notice. A notice from the mortgage company that our payment bounced! What the hell's going on Es?" Jericho asked furiously. Jericho didn't write checks for a reason. He had check-writing anxiety since I'd known him. As soon as he sent a check to anyone, he would constantly check the account to see if it was cashed. He couldn't rest until it was. And he hated bounced checks. Finally, it got to the point that if he had to pay a bill, he made out a money order or paid in cash.

I smiled up at him sweetly. "Rico, it's probably some error. Calm down. Banks make mistakes too. Come here. Let's check the accounts."

Jericho was not computer savvy. We did a lot of banking online which meant I was the one in charge of the finances. He left it up to me to pay the bills and he rarely knew what was in the accounts. He sat next to me on the bed as I pulled up our bank accounts, confident that there would be no issue. My confidence instantly faded as I saw there was indeed an issue: a major issue. Our checking account had nothing in it, and our overdraft account only had $350.00 left in it. Where had all of our money gone I wondered before Jericho echoed my thought as he jumped up off the bed. "Esmene, where did all our money go? We have nothing here!"

I was dumbfounded. How had this happened? "Rico, we must have been hacked. We're victims of identity fraud. Someone got access to our accounts and stole our money," I reasoned to him.

"You think?" he asked.

"I think so. Let's check the transactions."

Jericho sat back down and I clicked on the transaction details, expecting to see someone bought plane tickets to Jamaica. Instead, this is what we saw:

Paypal: $19.99
Paypal: $29.99
Paypal: $15.99
Paypal: $9.99
Macy's: $57.98
Paypal: $19.99
Modells: $62.78

And the list went on and on. There were no plane tickets to an exotic place, no extravagant shopping sprees in a foreign land, just a housewife with a computer who had embarked on a thirty day manic buying binge. What the heck did I buy, I wondered.

"Esmene, what the hell? Is that what's in all those boxes downstairs? You haven't even opened them! We just pile them against the wall and let them sit there! You spent over $1,600 on bullshit?" He paced up and down the bedroom like a caged animal, his hands on top of his head, dropping the f-bomb like nobody's business. He stopped pacing and fixed me with a cold stare. "Downstairs Es. NOW!" he demanded.

He headed downstairs and I didn't hesitate to follow behind him. By the time my little legs caught up with his, he was standing in the living room surveying the mountain of boxes. He turned to me. "We're going to open each and every one of these boxes and see what the hell you spent

$1,600 dollars on, Esmene. Do you understand me?" he asked through gritted teeth.

I couldn't even speak. I just nodded and went into the kitchen to grab a pair of scissors so I could cut open the boxes. I sat down on the floor signaling I was ready. Jericho grabbed five or six off the top and sat them down in front of me. As I gently started to cut them open, Jericho started ripping boxes open with his bare hands like a mad man. Cardboard was flying everywhere!

With each Monopoly game he unboxed, he became more incensed. There were all different versions of Monopoly: Christmas Story, UPS, 70th Anniversary, Pearl, Onyx, Pink Boutique, Zappos, Sun Maid, Monopoly 2000, FAO Schwarz…You name it, I had it. And to make matters even worse, I had purchased some duplicates.

Jericho's rage was finally spent with the last box ripped open. He looked at the mountain of games, clothes, and pet food lying at his feet. Then turned his cold gaze towards me. "Just answer me one question Esmene, why? Why would you do this?"

I looked around at the evidence of what I'd done and the tears were clogging up my throat. I was in disbelief, but the evidence was right in front of me. Hot, silent tears made their way down my face and warm salty snot was leaking past my lips. I just sat there, looking and dripping. I looked up at Jericho just then, him standing over me with his arms spread wide, gesticulating at the mess I had made. He resembled a kaleidoscope through my tears. "I don't know," I whispered.

"You don't know!" he yelled back.

"I DON'T KNOW!...I DON"T KNOW!...I DON'T KNOW!... I DON'T KNOW!…" I was screaming now, throwing boxes at him from my place on the floor. He was easily knocking them away from his person, looking at me with shocked wide eyes that I dare to throw boxes at him. "I DON'T KNOW!...I DON"T KNOW!...I DON'T KNOW!... I

DON'T KNOW!..." my mantra continued. I now had my hands clasped behind my head, my head nestled between my forearms, and my knees curled up to my chest. I was rocking myself back and forth.

I'm not certain how long I sat there like that, yelling and rocking and crying; but after a while, I felt Jericho's strong hands peeling my arms away from my head, and then he nestled my head against the hardness of his chest. His heart was beating loud and fast.

It soothed me. He took over rocking me back and forth, the way a parent would soothe a small child. He was gently rubbing my back, whispering words he didn't understand and I couldn't consciously hear, but somehow they managed to do the job they were intended to do. "It's OK, Baby. It's OK," he breathed into my ear.

"No, no it's not OK. I'm sorry. I'm sorry. I don't know why I did this. We're going to be homeless because of me," I cried.

"No, we're not. We're going to be OK," he assured me.

"Why did I do this? What the hell is wrong with me?!" I screamed into his chest.

He breathed a kiss into my temple. "I don't know Babe. I don't know, but we'll figure it out."

Nights Like This

On a fall night when I was thirty-five, my head was consumed with static. It was static like the static on the radio when you're not getting a good signal. It started out low, in the recesses of my brain. There was a lot going on in my house that night and I couldn't get any peace. Jericho and Zeyonna had been arguing about something for at least an hour. I didn't want to get in the middle of their argument because, of course, according to Jericho, that meant I was siding with Zeyonna. All I wanted to do was change into my pajamas and go to bed because the static was getting exponentially louder. And so were they.

I couldn't tell what they were arguing about. Perhaps it was one of the things a father and his preteen daughter argue about, I suppose. I was in my room taking off my pants and I heard Zander's door open. I guess he didn't want to miss out on the action. I remember yelling "Will you two please shut up?" Or did I? Maybe I said it in my head. I don't know, I couldn't think straight and the static was louder now. I had started sweating on that cool evening. My body was vibrating with tension and I just kept thinking dear God, please just shut up!

They were still going at it, getting louder and louder. Jericho had gotten in the bed so he was yelling loud enough for Zeyonna to hear him in her room. She, in order to not be outdone, was of course yelling back. Zander had quickly lost interest in their verbal jousting and went back into his room. I looked at my bed with longing but it just swam in front of my eyes. My head hurt and I couldn't focus. I was hot. I couldn't hear or think.

I quickly put my shirt and pants back on, sans bra, which, being full-figured, was risky. I grabbed my phone and a jacket, ran downstairs, and went out the front door to take in a deep breath of precious cool air. I then went on a short walk to clear my head and regain control. At least that's what I think happened. That's all I remember.

I awoke to the sound of some guy asking "Ma'am. Can you hear me? Have you been drinking this evening?" I lifted my head up wondering why my pillow felt like stone and why Jericho was flashing a flashlight in my face. I put my arm up to block my eyes from the light and asked him what he was doing.

"What am I doing? What are you doing laying out here in the street like this? You could've gotten yourself killed!" the male voice exclaimed.

Lying in the street? What the...oh no no no. I put my arm down to brace myself and that's when I realized I was indeed lying on cold, black asphalt right next to the curb painted yellow. There was a stop sign maybe ten feet away. To my right, I saw that I was directly in front of the church I went to when I attended St. Cecilia's Elementary School back when I was somewhat sane. If ever there was a time I needed prayer and protection, this was it. Thank you God I said to myself.

"Ma'am..." the male voice called to me again.

I looked back towards the source of the voice. The bright flashlight was still pointed towards my face. I forced myself to look past the light and into the eyes of the police officer. "No officer. No, I haven't been drinking or taking any drugs," I said, my voice hoarse with impending tears.

He turned off the flashlight and he and his partner, Officer Important and Officer Skeptical, moved to stand in front of me, waiting for an answer. Officer Skeptical took out a note pad just as an ambulance showed up. "OK. So why are you laying out here in the street?" Officer Important wanted to know.

I started to cry. "I don't know. I just don't know. I was in my house. I was tired. I wanted to go to bed. I don't know how I got here," I explained between sobs.

The officers looked at each other quizzically, then turned back to me. Officer Skeptical asked, "What's your name Miss?"

I had to think for a minute. "Esmene. Esmene Munroe," I said, unsure of myself.

"OK Ms. Munroe. What's your date of birth?" he asked slowly.

"November 20, 1976," I quickly replied.

"Good. Your address?"

"Oh it's...my address?" I started to wonder, what the heck was my address? I should know this. Where was I living now? I had moved a few times. Was I in the apartment? The rented house? I know we were in the process of buying a home. Did we go to the closing? Were we living there? Where did I live?

Officer Important: "Ma'am, you can't remember where you live?" I began to panic. Oh my gosh, I thought, had I been assaulted, hit on the head with something and now had amnesia? That just couldn't be. I remembered everything else. Where did I leave from? I remembered getting dressed. What room was I in...

Skeptical then asked "Who do you live with?"

In an unlady like gesture I wiped my snot on my sleeve before answering. "I live with my husband and two kids. I just don't remember where."

"What's your husband's name and phone number?"

Why are they asking me all these difficult questions, I thought. I didn't know his number. "I DON'T KNOW!! His name is Jericho. I don't know his number. I don't know anything! There's something wrong with my memory." I felt around for a tissue and found my phone. I had my phone. I quickly scrolled through the names until I got to the labeled savior: Mom.

I handed it over to Officer Important because I didn't even know what to say when she answered the phone. I don't recall the conversation that Officer Important had with my Mom, but within five minutes, I saw a Midnight Blue mini van speeding down the street towards us and screeching to a stop. Five people hurriedly jumped out. Zander and Zeyonna rushed over to hug me. My poor Zeyonna was in tears. Mom was crying too, hugging Officers Important and Skeptical for finding her daughter. Jericho just stood by looking shocked, helpless and lost.

Officer Important asked me if I was OK, if I thought I needed to go to the hospital to get checked out. I told him I just wanted to go home. I apologized for all the trouble I had caused. Officer Skeptical said it was no trouble. They were just glad I didn't get hurt. Officer Important didn't look like he agreed with the no trouble assessment but he didn't say anything.

After they bid us a goodnight, we drove home in awkward silence, none of us knowing what to say to each other. When we got home, I was glad to see we pulled up to our new home. Yes, I remembered then. We lived across the street from my parents. I gave my Mom a hug and a kiss. I told her I was sorry and I wouldn't do that again. We all went in the house and Jericho locked everything up tight. We went up to bed, everyone thankful that I was back home and safe. I was thankful that everyone had held off asking me the one question I knew they wanted an answer to: what happened? What caused you to walk a mile away from your home and decide it was a good idea to lie down in the middle of the street?

How could they understand? I didn't tell them. I had stopped taking all my medications and seeing my doctors and Nancy almost a year before. I felt good at the time, so I decided I didn't need them anymore. I fell into the bipolar trap of thinking the problem's gone and it almost cost me my life.

And the Rivers Run Red

Some months later, I was up at two o'clock on another sleepless night. Jericho, Zander and Zeyonna were all sleeping soundly in bed and I was left to roam the house like an ancient spirit. I didn't read, nor did I watch TV. I didn't listen to any music. I didn't turn on the computer. I didn't eat, nor did I drink.

I sat on my living room couch, staring through the television, trying to channel something, anything. I felt so empty, so lost. I wasn't dead but I didn't feel like I was alive either. Even the usual painful emotions that I despised weren't present. I felt nothing at all. I was like a black hole where things came in and got lost forever. I felt so cold, not the cold you felt from the weather. This was a cold from the inside, from the emptiness of my soul. Nothing was stirring. I held my breath. Could I hear the beating of my cold heart? I began to question my very existence.

I got up and went into the bathroom. I looked in the medicine cabinet, found what I needed, and then went back to my place on the sofa. I took a deep breath. Did I feel my heart beating? I held out my left arm. In the dim light I admired its paleness, the greenish-blue veins that formed a road map of the highways of warm blood traveling through my body that was keeping me alive. I could see a deep vein running from my hand up my wrist. I ran my fingers over the delicate area. It was so soft, so smooth.

I opened my right hand to study the shiny, new straight razor. It too was smooth. I hesitantly held it against the delicate skin of my left wrist. I'll cut just a little bit, not too deep I thought. I ran the razor lightly across my delicate skin. Nothing. I must be dead, I thought; but then I thought I can't be dead, so I did it again, but this time with more conviction. I held the razor closer to my wrist and cut. This time my blood trickled forth. AHH! What glorious relief.

Again the blade went across my wrist and my blood continued to flow. The warm, sticky blood was trickling down my arm to my elbow. Yes! I felt it, the pain. What beautiful pain! Once more I sliced into my yielding flesh.

I looked down at the narrow stream of blood running down my left arm. It was my life's blood, a deep, passionate red. I sat the razor down on the coffee table and then I took the fingers of my right hand to touch the cuts I had made. The blood was starting to cool, the cuts pulsing with pain. I could feel my heart beating. I was alive. Uncle was right. There was beauty in pain.

I wiped the blood away to see what kind of damage I had done, only to have more blood seep out and replace it. It didn't really matter to me. What mattered was that, before, I was cold and unfeeling. Now I was warm and alive. I took the blood on my fingers and smeared it on my face like war paint. I had fought another battle. But this one was different.

Something made me stop. Death wasn't going to take me yet. And with that thought, I reclined back on my couch as I wrapped a wet towel around the wounds so my life source would continue to flow within me.

Crash and Burn

In the summer of 2016, I experienced a severe mood shift. I had been in my bed for three days and I awoke totally disoriented. My eyes were attempting to open. They were so heavy. Did I just have surgery or something? I was trying to think. Where was I? Was I in a hospital? Was I at home? Nothing was coming to me. I was lost in the fog of my mind.

"I think she's waking up." I knew that voice. It belonged to my baby Zeyonna.

"Mom?" I knew Zander's voice also.

I struggled to answer him, but my throat was as dry as the Sahara. My tongue came out in a feeble attempt to moisten my dry cracked lips but it did no good. There was no moisture anywhere. "Sit her up so she can drink a little of this," I heard the Baby say to her brother. I felt Zander's strong arms around me, as he lifted me up to a seated position from what must have been my bed .

"Here Mommy, drink this." Zeyonna held a straw to my mouth and I opened my lips to welcome it. I took a sip of the cooling coconut water. After a few more sips, she took the blessed beverage away and Zander laid me back on the bed.

I finally pried my eyes open to see both of my kids hovering over me with worried eyes. "What day is it?" I croaked out.

"It's Tuesday," Zeyonna said.

Tuesday? Something about that wasn't right but in the haze of my mind I couldn't work it out. I looked at both of my children. Did they look like this the last time I saw them? Zander looked to be a good six feet tall with a solid build. His skin was a sun-kissed golden brown, his hair was cut close and wavy and he studied me with worried slanted chestnut-colored eyes. The Baby was of average height and slim build like her father. She was sun-kissed and golden brown too, but her skin had red undertones to it. Her thick long hair was in a messy bun on top of her head, and she studied me with her slanted midnight eyes. Tuesday. What month? What year? Why couldn't I remember anything? Did I have a stroke? "Tuesday when? What month, what year?"

They shot worried looks at each other. Zander answered. "It's July 19, 2016. Are you OK?"

I was struggling trying to remember the missing details locked away in my mind. I studied the faces of my children who were staring at me quizzically. They were just as confused as I was. I glanced past my daughter's shoulder and saw my closet door was open and it looked pretty empty. That's right. I remembered I wanted to clean out my closet and give some old things to the Goodwill. I peered over at the closet again. The closet was darn near empty. Where the heck were all my clothes? And that was last week, wasn't it? Last Thursday I believed.

What happened between then and now? Why couldn't I remember? Did I have an accident? Did I hit my head "What happened?" I asked my kids.

Zander and Zeyonna glanced at each other and then looked at me. "We don't know Mom," Zander said, "We just don't know."

Here's what transpired during the manic episode.
.

Thursday Night

I couldn't sleep. I had been tossing and turning for hours. Usually, after taking my nighttime regimen of medication, I would be asleep within twenty minutes but not that night. I peered over at the clock seeing twelve thirty. I gently got up out of bed so I wouldn't disturb Jericho and went downstairs for a drink of water. After I got some water I decided I would have a few Townhouse crackers for snack. Maybe I was a little hungry and that's why I couldn't sleep. I had my crackers, washed them down with the refreshing water, and went back upstairs.

1:40 am

I was still awake, what the heck? I couldn't get up and go downstairs to watch television because Jericho would get up and sit with me just to keep an eye on me to see what I was doing. I know. I could read a book I thought. I had a book light that wouldn't disturb Jericho and I could start reading one of the books I had piled up by my recliner. That was guaranteed to put me to sleep. I slipped out of the bed and reached into the side cabinet of my nightstand for the book lamp. Once I found it, I turned it on and made my way over to the pile of books. I wanted something good but not anything too deep or heavy that would get my mind going and keep me awake.

I came across Mitch Albom's Tuesdays with Morrie. It looked like a nice short read and I loved his books. I settled back against my pillows and dug in. It was three fifty now, I had just read the last page, and I was crying like a baby. I'm not going to give any spoilers, but what a great book. I was wiping tears and snot off my face. I tried not to blow my nose so I wouldn't wake up Jericho. I noted the time was four o'clock. I grabbed another book.

Friday

Up the steps. Down the steps. Up the steps. Down the steps. All morning long.

"Mom!" Zeyonna yelled.

"Yeah," I answered on my latest trip down the steps, my arms full of clothes.

"What are you doing?" she asked.

"Oh, I'm just cleaning out my closet, rearranging stuff, decluttering. Why?" I asked dropping my load on the floor next to the storage bins I had lined up near the steps.

Zeyonna came over to inspect the items I had just deposited on the floor.

"Mom, these are your good church suits. I hope you're not giving these away. You paid a lot of money for this stuff."

"Oh, of course not! These are all suits that are too big for me now since I've lost so much weight. So what I'm going to do is buy a sewing machine and take one of those sewing classes at the community college to learn how to do alterations so I can alter all this stuff and be able to wear it again," I explained.

Zeyonna gave me a *yeah-right* look. "That's your plan?"

"That's my plan," I said with full confidence.

"OK Mommy, good luck with that," Zeyonna said and went upstairs.

After I got done emptying my closet, I decided I needed to put some time in on the treadmill. I got my sneakers on, headed down into the basement, and did three miles on the treadmill to start.

As I came back upstairs and scrutinized my living room, I saw a spider web in the corner of the ceiling. I decided my walls could use a good cleaning. I jumped in my car, went to the dollar store, and got a few of those dollar sponge mops. I came back home, put some soapy water in a bucket, and wiped down all the walls in the living room, dining room, and kitchen. That was better. It was time to hit the treadmill again and get another three miles under my belt!

"Hey Mom, what's for dinner?" Zander inquired.

Dinner? I saw the time was six o'clock. Gee, what happened to the rest of the day? It didn't matter really because now it was dinner time. I ordered dinner, Chinese food, I think, because I didn't eat much. Then I sat back and admired all my hard work.

Saturday 1:00 am

I couldn't believe I was awake again! I got up, got my water and Townhouse crackers, and grabbed my book light and another book. It was good old Mitch again so I settled in for another good cry.

5:30 am

I got up and boiled two eggs to eat after I got done on the treadmill. I got my three miles in to start the day off right!

"Es, are you feeling alright?" Jericho asked as he came up behind me and started to massage my shoulders.

"I feel fine, great even. Why?"

He turned me around to face him and looked me right in my eyes. It was like he was seeing through me. "Esmene, don't think I haven't noticed you haven't slept for two nights. The kids said yesterday you were mopping the walls. Do I need to call someone?"

I knocked his hands off my shoulders. "Oh, so because I decided I don't want to live in a filthy house something has to be wrong with me? What, do you want to be on the next episode of Hoarders? Will that make you happy? I thought you'd be happy that I was actually getting some work done so you didn't have to do it for a change. But suddenly that's a problem?"

I turned to walk away but he pulled me back. "Es, it's not a problem that you're doing things. I just want to make sure it's NOT a problem, OK?"

And I couldn't stay mad at him because he was being so sweet. I wrapped my short arms around his waist. "Babe, everything is golden. I'm just trying to get stuff done while I have the energy to do it," I assured him.

My cousin Kenneth and his wife were coming into town with their kids the next day. They were both career military personnel and we had never met their children. We were so excited to meet them. "We can host them at my house!" I offered to Mom. My hospitality was met with shocked silence. I never invited people to my house with the exception of one time every year, my annual Christmas Eve party. There were no birthday parties, no barbecues, no anything. Something was up.

"Esmene, are you sure you're up for it?" Mom asked.

"Of course Mom. It's going to be fun."

Sunday, 1:00 am

I thought I fell asleep, but I was awake. My heart was pounding in my chest and I was sweating. I felt like something had happened. Something scared me. Did I have a nightmare, I thought. I took some deep, calming breaths and told myself I was safe. Was I safe? I listened for any sounds that would indicate otherwise. I heard nothing. I got up and got some water and Townhouse crackers. The routine was the same, yet different. The rhythm was off.

My heart was still beating fast. I went for my book light and a book. Tonight I picked up John Green. But I don't think it would have mattered what author I picked. I couldn't concentrate. I couldn't make sense of the words on the pages. I couldn't think straight. I gave myself a headache.

3:00 am

Two hours and I was still on the same chapter. I threw the book and light on the floor. Who the heck wanted to read John Green anyway?

2:00 pm

My cousin called. They were just five minutes away! Everyone was so excited. My excitement was so great that my head was beginning to hurt and a low buzzing had begun in my ear. I ignored it. I wasn't going to let that ruin this moment. The pizza was warming in the oven and my parents' entire extended family was crammed into my house or across the street at my parents' house.

My parents and all the siblings with their families were in attendance. Mom, Dad, our paternal Grandmother, who was now living with my parents, and Delilah. Kenny's sister Veronica came with her sixteen year old twins, Vance and Vanessa. Vance had a light complexion and looked like his father. Vanessa had a darker complexion and was the spitting image of Veronica. My oldest brother Braxton was there solo. He and Deilah weren't married and didn't have any children. My baby sister McKenna was there with her husband Cedric with their three girls, Lyndsey, Sydney, and Bailey. Cedric was a sturdy built guy who used to wrestle in his high school days. Lyndsey was fourteen, Sydney was eleven, and Bailey was eight. The girls were literally clones of my sister. And lastly, my youngest brother Lyam was there with his wife Monica and their son Carter. Monica was a pretty girl with a mocha complexion and thick long hair. Carter, who was three, looked just like my brother with a mop of curly hair covering his head. Add Jericho and my kids to the group and that made for a full house!

It was so good to see Kenny and Debbie again. Kenny had come a long way from the little troublemaker he was when we were little. Now he was a career military serviceman with a family. Aunt Marie would have been proud of her son. Debbie was also a career military woman. She was a beautiful, petite girl with cocoa colored skin and pretty dark eyes. She had two children from a previous relationship, Mario aged sixteen and Keyla aged thirteen. They had one child together, a little girl who was just a year old named Kaya who looked just like her mother. We had met Debbie briefly during a previous visit. And we were finally getting a chance to meet their children! There were hugs and kisses, hand shakes, introductions, pizza, drinks, chips, and dips. Everything just flowed perfectly and everyone was having a great time.

4:30 pm

I walked into my dining room, sat down in a chair, and made this announcement: "You all have to leave now. I'm tired."

"What?" said Lyam.

"What did she just say?" Braxton asked Veronica.

"We have to leave?" McKenna questioned

Jericho came and knelt down next to me. "Baby, what's wrong?" he asked, rubbing my back. What was wrong was that I barely had the energy to get those words out. I was completely and utterly exhausted; and it happened in a matter of seconds, like flipping a light switch. My limbs felt like they were made of lead. I had started to drool. Jericho stood up. "Hey, everyone, how about we move this party across the street? Esmene isn't feeling well. You can go ahead and take all the food with you."

"Esmene, you OK Baby?" Mom asked.

"She's OK Mom," Jericho explained. "I think she's just gotten a little overwhelmed. I'm going to take her upstairs to lie down."

"Alright. Call if you need me," she said, as the rest of the family started gathering up their things to go across the street to my parents' home.

Once the house was empty, with the help of Zander, Jericho got me up the steps into the bed. That's where I had apparently been since Sunday.

I tried to search through the murk and through the fog of my mind for the truth of what had happened to me. I got nothing. I studied the worried faces of my children as they continued to hover over me, waiting for some sign, some signal that I was OK. I once again scanned past my daughter's shoulder towards the vast emptiness of my closet.

"Zee", I croaked out, "where are all my clothes?"

Four years have passed since that manic episode and the mystery over my clothes has yet to be resolved.

JCPenny Doin' It Right

Leaving my job at the mortgage company was one of the hardest things I ever had to do. It made me feel useless, like a burden, a waste of space. I had always hoped to one day be well enough to re-enter the workforce. I had been stable on my meds for about a year and decided to make a real effort at getting a part-time job. I thought it would be a good idea to consult my doctor before actually gaining employment, so on my next visit with Dr. Diane, I broached the subject.

"So, what do you think"? I asked Dr. Diane after telling her my plan.

"Esmene, I really see no reason why you can't re-enter the workforce. You've been pretty stable for the last year. I definitely wouldn't advise you going back to work full-time into your previous profession, but a part-time job working fifteen-twenty hours a week would be good for you. Do you have any places in mind?"

"Well, I've applied and have been turned down by a few places. Not sure why. Is there a list out there that informs employers about who's disabled and why?" I asked.

Dr. Diane did her head tilt thing. "No Esmene, there's no such list. Is that why you think you keep getting turned down for jobs?"

"Yes. I can't think of any other reason why. They keep telling me my qualifications aren't a good fit for their workplace. How am I not qualified enough to work at The Dollar Tree? I gave them my resume and everything!"

"Esmene, you gave Dollar Tree a resume?" she asked incredulously.

"Yes. What's wrong with that?"

"Esmene, that's probably why they didn't hire you. The manager probably thought you wanted to take his job. Most likely they feel you're overqualified," she explained.

"What kind of nonsense is that? How can I be overqualified to work at a dollar store?"

"It happens to people with college degrees, Esmene, trust me. Have you tried anywhere else?"

"I put in an application at JCPenny in the mall where my son works. I'm hoping they'll call me."

"And how do you think that's going to work out, working with your son?"

"Well, I don't anticipate really working with him because I put in for day shift hours. Zander works at night because of school. I wouldn't want any conflicts to arise with us working together."

"How does Zander feel about you working there?"

"He said he doesn't care, just as long as he gets the referral bonus."

"Are you going to inform them about your condition?"

"Do I have to?"

"No, you don't have to. However, if you do start to have some issues, you'll have to let them know if you find that you require any accommodations."

"I don't think I'm going to need to tell anyone anything. I've been doing really well over the last year, the best I've been in years. Believe me, no one will ever know."

So, I went home after my morning appointment. I received a call that afternoon to come in for an interview on Thursday at noon. On that Thursday, I was there at eleven forty-five. I took a seat and waited past noon.

"Esmene Munroe?" A very petite blonde called in the reception area.

I stood up. "Hello, I'm Esmene Munroe. I have an interview with Amanda today."

The woman smiled at me and held out her hand to shake. "Hi, I'm Amanda. Sorry I'm a little late. Come into my office so we can talk." I followed her down a short hallway into a small office and she closed the door. I continued to stand because you don't take a seat until you're offered one.

"Please have a seat," Amanda offered. I sat when she did.

"So Esmene, it says on your application that you're related to Zander but it doesn't say how," Amanda stated.

"Zander's my son," I answered, praying that wasn't going to be a problem.

"Oh, OK. It's just that I saw your year of college graduation so that makes us the same age. I just didn't put it together that he was your son."

"Is that going to be a problem?" I asked.

"No, not as long as neither one of you makes it a problem. For example, if he were to be reprimanded by a superior for something he did, are you going to go all mom on his supervisor or are you going to stay out of it?"

"Zander's a big boy. He doesn't need his Mommy to fight his battles for him." But his Mommy most certainly would if he was treated unfairly, I thought.

"Well that's good. We have a position open for our support team. The start time is six am and you'll usually be working until eleven am. When there's a big event or around the holidays you may have an occasional day when you work until two pm but you won't ever work past two pm. Does that sound like something you're interested in?" she asked, looking up at me.

This was exactly the type of position I was interested in. I was a morning person. I was my sharpest in the morning. As the day wore on, I lost my energy, concentration, and focus. This was the perfect position for me. I said a quick thank you to Jesus before responding. "Yes, that sounds absolutely perfect for me."

Amanda made some notes in my file, and then she looked up and smiled. "Great! I'll go ahead and get the background check done; and if everything comes back fine, you'll be hearing from me."

"Sounds good. I look forward to hearing from you," I said as we stood and shook hands.

Amanda led me back out to the reception area and we said our goodbyes. I was feeling really confident about getting the job until she said background check. Background check? What about my background did they want to check? And just like that, my thoughts hopped on a runaway train.

When I checked with them, Nancy and Dr. Diane assured me that there was no list or record potential employers could access that would alert them to my disability and the nature of it. But I'd been turned down by so many other potential employers. What if they'd done background checks too and they DID find out something? Maybe that was why I didn't get the jobs. Nancy and Dr. Diane were smart, but they didn't know everything. Maybe something did come up on the background check, something that made me undesirable as an employee.

I began to wonder what it might have said. Would it just say that I was disabled or would it list my disability? Could it say that was the catalyst behind me leaving my last job? No, no. They wouldn't know that. Or would they? Oh my goodness, would they find out about that incident with the police? I didn't commit a crime or anything but the police were involved. Was there a record of that? And if there was, now all my son's co-workers would know that his mom was crazy and they'd look at him with a jaundiced eye because of it. Have I screwed up before I've even gotten the job? I should just go back in there and tell Amanda to tear up my application and forget about it. I'm just one big screw up, I thought. I wanted to cry. Here was my one good shot at getting a job and I'd ruined it. I ruined everything. Why did I have to be such a loser all the time?

Two days later, Amanda called and offered me the job as a seasonal employee.

So the incident with the police didn't come up on the background check. I wonder why? They took my name, address, and phone number. You'd think they would make a record of that. I wonder if there was even an incident report made down at the precinct. Why am I so concerned about it? I'm being offered a job!

But my mind wouldn't let it go and I drifted as we spoke. She's not going to question why I've been out of work for ten years? That doesn't seem like good business practice. Do I really want to work for a company that doesn't question such a large gap of employment? If I have no criminal record, what have I been doing for ten years? Doesn't she want to know? Or maybe something DID come up, but there are laws preventing them from discriminating against me. But I know the stigma against mental illness, especially Bipolar Disorder. They'll be watching me closely. The first time I get angry, they'll think I'm going to come to work with a duffle bag and a gun. Maybe I should just turn down the offer, I thought. I don't want pity employment just because the government says they can't discriminate against me due to a disability. I want to be treated like everyone else, because I'm essentially like everyone else.

Wait, what were we talking about again? I was trying to bring my mind back into focus. "Esmene, are you there?" Amanda asked.

"Yes, I'm here."

"So do you accept the offer of employment?"

"Yes, I do."

Family Reunion

In 2017 we had a family reunion. Family reunions were a time when the past, present and future generations came together and became familiar with each other, the younger generations benefiting from the wisdom and experience of those who came before them. Well, not all the time.

I personally didn't like family reunions. I didn't care to be around so many people in tight spaces and I was sensitive to a lot of noise. And then there was always the issue of eating. I didn't like to eat in front of people because I could never gauge what was an appropriate portion size. I always felt like I was eating too much; and, of course, if I felt like I had eaten too much, I would want to get rid of it. I wouldn't disrespect my aunt's home like that. I had never purged outside the comfort of my own home and I wasn't going to start now.

However, I had made an exception for this family reunion. It appeared that it was going to be on the smaller side as far as attendees and there were people attending that I really wanted to see. So, much to the surprise of my family, I sent an RSVP for four. For once, I was actually excited about something family related.

So, the 2017 Family Reunion was in full swing; and I had to admit, I was having a great time. There was plenty of room to move around in my cousin's backyard so I didn't feel overwhelmed by people. Unfortunately, Jericho and Zander had to back out because of work, so Zeyonna and I attended with Mom and Delilah. Although she was getting to know some of her cousins that she never met, Zeyonna stuck by me the whole time. Surprisingly, even food wasn't being much of an issue for me. I couldn't believe how great the day was going. I shouldn't have expected things to continue that way. I suddenly heard a group of people closer by the road shouting exclamations.

My Uncle Joel called out "Oh my God. I can't believe you're here."

"When did you get out?" My cousin Shayla asked.

"Why didn't you tell anyone you were coming?" My Aunt Mallory asked.

I wondered who it was and Mom asked the same thing I was thinking from her place across from me at the picnic table "Who is that?"

"I don't know," I said, standing on tiptoe trying to see over the crowd of well wishers to learn the identity of this stranger. "Everyone is too tall. I can't see over them."

Zeyonna then stood up to try to get a look. She was taller than us, standing at five foot four. Her head was moving back and forth as she tried to get a glimpse of the mystery guest. Then she sat back down. "Whoever it is, it's a man," she said, shrugging her shoulders.

And just when my curiosity had gotten the best of me and I was about to go see for myself who was causing such a ruckus, Uncle emerged through the crowd to stand directly in front of our table. Uncle had not aged well in the twenty years since I last saw him. Gone were all his youth and virility; and what was left behind was a tall, thin, old man with thinning gray hair that was fashioned into a ponytail and a thin mustache over lips that were too prominent for his face. He had on a jogging suit as usual with matching sneakers and hat but his accessories now included a cane at his left side. Mom squealed like the rest of the women in my family and got up from the table to give him the biggest hug she could. Delilah followed right behind her.

"Oh, it's soooo good to see you! We've missed you!" Mom said.

"When did you get home, Uncle?" Delilah asked. Mom swatted at her. Uncle had been in jail about ten years. I don't know what he did and I didn't care. I was glad he was in jail.

Uncle smiled. "It's ok, Bella. Dee, I've been home a few months now. I heard about this little family reunion and thought I'd come by and shake things up!" He hugged Delilah again and dropped a kiss onto her forehead. Then his eyes zeroed in on me.

I was still sitting in the same spot, stunned. Actually, stunned doesn't even justify what I was. Stupefied is better. My heart was thundering against my chest like a battering ram. My mind switched into overdrive. He was going to come to me, I thought. He was going to touch me. Oh God...think darn you...pray, I said to myself. God you are my refuge and strength, an ever present help in trouble. Uhh...The Lord is with me...I will not be afraid. The Lord is with me. He is my helper. Oh God..cast your cares on the Lord. I need you right now God, I prayed.

"Esmene," Uncle said my name, the same way he said it all those years ago. It was ninety-seven degrees out and I was shaking with cold. It felt like ice was crawling through my veins.

"Esmene?" Mom called to me, "What's wrong with you? Aren't you going to say hello to your favorite Uncle?" That's right, according to her and everyone else, he was my favorite Uncle and I was his favorite girl. Of course I would want to say hello. I was always such a good little girl. I stood up as if in a trance. I didn't know who was controlling my limbs. It wasn't me. My focus was on not vomiting.

He held his long skeletal arms out and opened towards me. "Come on Esmene, I know you don't think you're too old to give Uncle a hug and a kiss do you?" He flashed that smile at me. Everyone laughed. I felt myself moving along the moist grass, inching closer to him, until at last our bodies were flush together. I did not hug him, nor did I give him a kiss; but he wrapped his long arms around me and kissed me on my forehead. "You're beautiful," he whispered.

I backed out of his embrace, not caring who noticed. He gave me another smile and then looked over my shoulder. "And who is this little beauty right here?" he asked, talking about Zeyonna.

The ice in my veins was replaced by flames of fire. My body was now moving under my own command. I stood right next to Zeyonna and took her hand. "This is my daughter. I was just about to take her to the bathroom." I hoped I said it with enough ominous warning in my voice that he would stay away from her.

I didn't know how to protect myself as a child but I would damn sure protect my baby. "Come on Zee," I pulled her up to standing and she followed right behind me. Zeyonna was a good baby. Even though she was taller than I was and almost an adult, she still held my hand wherever we went and I still took her to the bathroom. I could feel his eyes on us as we disappeared into the house.

I knew Zeyonna didn't have to go to the bathroom, so I took her straight through the house and out the front door so I could talk to her alone. "Zee, I need you to do Mommy a favor and not ask any questions right now, OK?"

"OK," she said easily.

"I need you to stay by me the rest of the reunion. I mean right by my side. If you have to go in the house, you take me with you. If you want to go to the basketball courts, I go with you. If you want to sit somewhere different, I sit with you. Not Mom-Mom or DD. Me and only me. Also, if anyone, I don't care who it is, tries to hug or kiss you, you tell them no! If they have a problem with it, tell them to come see me," I told her.

"Mommy, that's mean," she said with a confused look on her face.

"No, it's not. You've already hugged these people. You don't have to do it again unless I tell you to. You understand?" There was no answer. "Zee, do you understand?"

"Yeah, Mommy. I understand."

"Good," I went to give her a little peck on the lips.

"Nope Mommy. No kisses, remember?" she said with a grin.

She actually made me smile. "You're right Baby, no kisses."

Entanglements

Two months had passed since the family reunion and I was finally putting the whole episode behind me. I was getting ready for bed one evening when my phone buzzed, notifying me I had a new text. I assumed it was Mom texting me goodnight, so I finished my preparations for bed before picking up my phone. It wasn't Mom. I was about to have a long text exchange with the Devil.

Hi Baby girl. It was good seeing you again. You look like you did the last time I saw you.

I'm sorry, who is this?

Come on Baby girl. Don't do me like that.

Oh, you. How did you get my number?

Wasn't hard. After all, I'm Uncle. I get whatever I want. Don't tell me you forgot.

Leave me alone.

Now how am I supposed to do that? Listen, I'm in town for a few days. Why don't you come visit Uncle.

Come visit Uncle? Are you some kind of psycho? No I'm not coming to visit you, you sick bastard!

Whoa Esmene. When did your mouth get so filthy? What happened to the good little girl I remember?

You're sick, you know that? The little girl you destroyed grew up, despite what you did to her; and now I'm a woman. I wasn't strong enough to tell you no then but I for damn sure know how to tell you no now. If I were you, I'd rethink inviting me to spend any time alone with you. I've gotten a lot more comfortable with knives over the years…

You threatening me Little Girl? I think you forgot who you dealing with. I still hold the power in this relationship. I still pull the strings. You do what I say.

You have NO power over me!

Really? Who have you told? Did you run and tell your beloved Mommy that big bad Uncle soiled you on her

*precious sheets? Did you? Held you, caressed you, loved
you the way you wanted to be loved?*

I DID NOT! I did not want that!

*You craved the attention. You couldn't stay away from
me. I just gave you what you wanted Baby Girl. But you
didn't answer my question. Who have you told? Who? You
tell that boy you married?*

*He's not a boy. He's a man, a man who doesn't go
around raping little girls.*

*That's how you see it Esme? If that's what I did, then
why wouldn't you tell anybody? If I'd raped you, I should've
been in jail for it. But you saw how the family still loves me.
You're a smart girl. You know why you kept your mouth
closed all these years.*

Screw you!

*Lol, you already did that now, didn't you. But if you'd like
to do it again, I"ll let you know where I'm staying. You could
come for that visit.*

*Listen, let me tell you something. I'm not coming to visit
you. Lose my number and don't contact me again. Don't
call me, don't text me, don't email me, and especially don't
come to my home. Stay away from me and my family,
specifically my little girl. If I see you anywhere near her, I
swear I'll cut your balls off and stuff them down your throat.
I'm not that scared child anymore. I'm not scared of you.
You can't hurt me, and you won't hurt my baby. You'll die
first. And that's not a threat. It's a guarantee!*

I turned my phone off after that. I didn't want to hear
anything else that sick bastard had to say. I thought about
blocking him; but then in some weird way I thought if I
blocked him, I wouldn't know where he was or what he
was doing. I wondered if anyone would understand my
reasoning; but then I thought, who cares? I was angry
someone had given him my phone number; but, then
again, why wouldn't they? He was Uncle. It was probably
my own mother who did it. And of course that piece of crap

had to text me right before bedtime so my anxiety was at a ten. I took my nighttime meds, went downstairs, and got one of Jericho's wine coolers. I knew better than to drink while taking my meds but I didn't consider a wine cooler really drinking. It was just enough alcohol that would ease me into blessed slumber.

I had work the next day. I was a little groggy from the mix of medication and alcohol; but I slept, and my shift was only five hours, so I would be OK. I had gotten my equipment to do my work for the day and was headed for the office when I saw my team leader, Ms. Dora, coming towards me down the hall. Ms. Dora was great. She was an attractive African American woman in her mid fifties who acted like everyone's mother, regardless how old you were. She was married to the most adorable man, Mr. Kevin, who treated her like a queen. "Good morning Ms. Dora," I greeted her, looking down at the pricing libby in my hand as I was putting in my password.

"Baby, come with me, we need to talk," she said as she continued to move in the opposite direction.

What the heck? This sounded serious. We went around a little corner near the supervisor offices. "What's wrong Ms. Dora?" I asked with concern in my voice. We had gotten quite close over the year that I had been working there. She had some health issues I knew about and I was praying she wasn't about to give me bad news.

She took a deep breath and looked me right in the eye. "Baby, I got your text message last night."

I looked at her totally lost. I had no clue what she was talking about. "Ms. Dora, I didn't text you last night. In fact, I turned my phone off. It's actually still off," I told her with confidence.

Her look was very serious. "No Baby, I got the text you sent. It wasn't supposed to be to me but I guess you hit my name by accident. It went "*Listen, let me tell you something...*"

Oh my God. She looked at me as I realized what she was telling me. She knew. I slid down the wall that my back was against and plopped right down on the floor, legs outstretched like a rag doll. She knew. My vision became watery. "You know," I said, my voice hoarse with emotion. I couldn't even look at her.

"Yeah Baby, I know. I'm so sorry," she said with sympathy in her voice.

I brought my knees up and put my head between them and silently weep. I was so very tired, tired of this man who no matter what I did kept ruining my life. I lifted my head up a little. "I'm so embarrassed. I can't believe I made that mistake. I'm sorry."

A gentle hand landed on my shoulder. "Baby, does anyone else know?" Ms. Dora asked. I shook my head in the negative. She inhaled deeply, "Well maybe this happened for a reason then. Maybe God wanted someone to find out so you could finally have someone to listen to your story. You have nothing to be embarrassed about. It wasn't your fault."

I looked up at her, full on crying now. "How can you say it wasn't my fault when you don't even know what happened?"

Ms. Dora reached down for my hand and helped me get up off the floor. After I stood up, we went into the supervisor offices and she closed the door. She found some tissues and handed them to me so I could wipe my face. When I'd had a few moments to get myself together she asked, "How can I say I know it wasn't your fault? You were a child. There is absolutely nothing you could have done to make anything he did to you your fault."

"Nothing?" I repeated.

Her look was serious and sincere."Nothing!"

"Please, don't tell anyone."

"No, I promise and I swear. I"ll tell no one."

And I usually didn't put much trust in people when it came to stuff like that; but on that day, in that office, at that moment, I trusted her. We became something more, more than a superior and a subordinate, more than just co-workers. Ms. Dora became a confidant, something I had never had before outside of doctors' offices, someone with an insight into my soul and secrets. I looked at Ms. Dora, standing there smiling at me, much like my Mom would; and I thought this crazy woman has no idea what she's signing up for.

I hoped she wouldn't regret this later; but, now, right now, I needed to hold steadfast to her earnest offer of support. I had nothing else that could compare.

Biggie "The Mini-Series"

After I started part-time at JCPenny, Grandmom returned to my life in a big way. Kathleen Weston, better known as Biggie, was a cantankerous woman to put it kindly. Her son was my Dad. She grew up in one of the most rural areas of Virginia and lived there her whole life up until she was eighty-five. When she was eighty-five, she received a diagnosis of cancer: and since the closest medical facility was an hour away in a different state, her doctors suggested it would be best for her to go and live with her son near the city.

Yes, Biggie was my paternal grandmother and she was like no grandmother I had ever met before. While other grandchildren may have had memories of baking cookies with Grandmom on Sunday afternoons or snuggling up with Grandmom when they were sick, I have memories of holding Grandmom's liquor bottles as she watered them down before she opened the doors of her speakeasy on Sunday after church. There was nothing more fun than having her make me jump out on the side of a country road while she was driving and crawl down in a ditch to gather some aluminum cans so she could turn them in for change. And there was absolutely no problem Grandmom couldn't solve. No white milk for my Frosted Flakes? No problem. Use chocolate milk: problem solved.

Grandmom had grown up and lived in Accomac County, Virginia, the youngest of nine children. My Grandpop, Lee "Buster" Weston, had died in 1986. Since then, Grandmom had lived alone. Grandmom had never learned to read or write but she managed to take care of herself just fine. Grandmom was independent, shrewd, and wise. You weren't going to fool her easily. She was so wise, I just couldn't understand why she didn't know how to read or write. I thought she just didn't go to school, which wouldn't have been uncommon for a black girl from the segregated south. So one day I asked her about it. "Grandmom, did you go to school when you were young?"

"Yeah, I got schoolin' when I was a youngin'. I was schooled 'til the fif' grade when I had ta leave ta take care o' Mama 'cause she was sick," she answered in her southern drawl.

"Fifth grade? Well Grandmom, if you went to school until the fifth grade, how come you never learned to read or write?" I was confused. Surely things didn't move that slowly in the south.

Grandmom sat back in her recliner and looked up to the ceiling. She rested her hands on her belly. I knew that pose. I was about to hear something profound. "Well Baby, I'll tell ya'. I had dis teacher, Ms. Lulla Mae Johnson, in da third grade. She made me so mad one day in school, I decided ta git back at 'er. I was gon' ta set dere and learnt nothin'. So fer tha next two years, I just set and did nothin'. Dat taught 'er a lesson." Self-satisfaction was clear in her voice.

OK, so maybe she wasn't so profound or so wise. Grandmom obviously didn't know a lot about revenge back then. "Wow Grandmom, you sure taught her not to mess with you," I said while rolling my eyes on the side. Then came the next obvious question. "So Grandmom, what did she do that made you so mad?" This had better be good, I thought.

Grandmom put her head back again and let out a long sigh. A minute filled with anticipation went by as I waited to hear about the egregious wrong that had been done to Grandmom by Lulla Mae. Grandmom turned to look at me and said…. "I on't rightly 'member now. But she got what was comin' ta 'er," she said with a self satisfied click of her teeth.

I was going to have to have a serious talk with Grandmom about revenge. She must have also skipped that class too. There are tons of anecdotal stories to tell about Grandmom. But there was another side of her, a side that wasn't so sunny and bright, a side that was downright malicious, hateful, and spiteful. Biggie could switch in the blink of an eye. One minute Grandmom was serene as could be, having a peaceful conversation and laughing over stories from her youth. But, in the next moment, she would condemn you to hell because you needed to check her blood sugar and you were interrupting her trying to watch her Spanish novelas which were soap operas. She didn't know any Spanish, by the way.

Grandmom, being a product of the segregated south had some serious issues with color. She had always held an animosity against my mother strictly because of the color of my mother's skin. She frequently referred to my mother, Bella, as "dat white woman dat think she betta' den ever'one else" and referred to me and my four siblings as my parents' half-breed children. She had also taken the time to come up with colorful nicknames for most of us. I was "the Mexican," my little brother Lyam was "Julio," Delilah was "Pocohantas," my son was "dat white man Jim," and my daughter was "the lil Indian girl". When I was little, my Grandmother told me on more than one occasion that when I had children, I better have children by a white man because my mom wasn't going to love any dark babies.

Grandmom was a little crazy. And that was the flame that drew me closer to her. For the last three years of her life, she lived with Mom and Dad. I took over primary responsibility for her medical care and running her errands because I only worked part-time. It was NOT easy. Grandmom's moods were unpredictable. One minute, I was the only grand who loved her and cared about her and she loved me soooo much. The next minute, without any provocation, I deserved to die alone in the street like a dog.

Yeah, thanks for those kind words, Grandmom, I often thought.

And the things she would say to my Dad, her son, I could never imagine saying to my beloved son. She would tell him how she wished she never laid eyes on his father and how she never wanted my Dad. I couldn't imagine how that made my Dad feel. But Dad gave as good as he got, because he said some pretty nasty things back to her, things I could never imagine saying to Mom.

Yes, Biggie drove me to the edge of my remaining sanity. When she first came to live with my parents, I was seeing my psychiatrist once every three months and my therapist as needed. Within a year, I was seeing my psychiatrist every three weeks and my therapist every two weeks. I never disclosed to my family that my psychiatrist and my therapist suggested I turn the care of Grandmom over to someone else. But there was no one else. So despite the toll it was taking on me, I continued to care for Biggie for one reason, I loved her. And Biggie loved me in the only way she knew how to love. So, I popped more pills, went to more appointments, and even started drinking a little bit, just to do what I needed to do for Biggie.

Biggie and I shared a connection in other ways and she knew it too. Sometimes we would be sitting silently in the room together watching her Spanish novelas and she would turn to me and look me in the eye. "Yer nerves is bad, ain't they Baby?" she would ask me.

"Yes ma'am."

She would grab my hand and say, "Grandmom's nerves is bad too, Baby."

That's when I knew I couldn't leave Grandmom. She knew my secret and I knew hers. I saw in her some of what was wrong with me. Grandmom couldn't control her emotions. She was bitter, angry, and malicious; but she was also sensitive, sad, and empty. I assumed she was bipolar and I may have even inherited it from her.

Sometimes we would find Grandmom crying for no apparent reason. Dad would ask, "Biggie, what are you crying for?"

"I 'on't rightly know," Grandmom would whisper.

"Well people don't just cry for no reason, so something's wrong," Dad would say exasperated.

I thought, yes, some people do cry for nothing Dad. I understood my Grandmom loud and clear, for I too often found myself in the throes of tears for reasons which I was unaware. And just like Grandmom, I would become angry when someone wanted an explanation, because there was no way could I answer that question when I didn't know the answer.

So despite the bedlam that was BIggie Weston, we all persevered because she needed us. Grandmom slowed down the beginning of 2018 and celebrated her eighty-eighth birthday. One morning in February, I gave her a sponge bath in her bed, put fresh clothes on her and Dad put fresh sheets on her bed. "Grandmom's tired Baby," she said

"I know Grandmom. Dad's almost finished making your bed. You can lay down and take a nap," I told her gently.

"No, Grandmom's tired," she repeated.

"I know Grandmom. I know." I knew what she was saying but I just didn't want to accept it.

When Dad was finished making her bed, I got her all settled in. I asked her if she needed anything and she said no. She thanked me for the bath, telling me it felt good. I told her to get some rest and I would check on her later. That was the last time I heard my Grandmother's voice.

Grandmom's blood sugar and blood pressure dropped while she was asleep, and she had gotten a septic infection from gallstones that couldn't be removed. Although Grandmom regained consciousness, she was non-verbal and paralysed. Her body couldn't fight off the infection. We made her comfortable for the rest of the time she had with us.

Grandmom died on a snowy Monday morning, a week later.

My first emotion was not grief, though I cried. It was a relief. It was over. Then I felt guilty. What kind of granddaughter was I to feel relief that my grandmother was dead? Later, I began to feel grief that she was gone. I blamed myself for a long time. Sometimes I still do. I often wonder if there was something I could've done sooner that would have prolonged her life? Was she suffering that week because she was non-verbal and couldn't let me know? Did I do enough to make sure she was comfortable? Did she blame me?

The answer is I did the best I could with what I knew, with the best of intent in mind. If I didn't know what to do, she certainly didn't make it any easier to understand. My actions were motivated by the love I had for my grandmother. I just prayed to God she knew how much I loved her, that I tried my best, and that I was sorry if my actions caused her any pain.

I miss you Grandmom. Rest well, My Dearest Biggie
Sunrise, January 19, 1930 - Sunset, February 12, 2018

<u>Masquerade</u>

When Jericho had me admitted to Lincoln Hospital's Psychiatric Unit in February of 2019, I didn't tell anyone else in my family except for my sister Michaela. Michaela actually worked in this field so I knew she had a better understanding than most of what I was dealing with. It wasn't until the day after I was admitted that I called her, saying "Hi Michaela. It's Esme."

"Hey Sis. How are you?"

I didn't know how to tell her, so I just blurted it out. "Rico had me admitted to an Intensive Outpatient Program (IOP) at a psychiatric hospital. I start tomorrow."

"What? Why? What happened?" Her voice was full of concern and confusion.

I took a deep breath. I was exposing more about myself than I'd ever done before, but I needed someone who could help Jericho through this. "I was ready to die. I am ready to die. I finally told Rico and he took me to my psychiatrist. She told him where to take me to be admitted."

"Es," she said with tears in her voice, "I love you so much. How long have you been feeling this way?"

"Maybe five or six months. It's gotten worse over the last month."

"I'm here for you and Rico. Please tell me, what do you need from me to help you through this?"

I was full on crying now. "I need help with Rico and Mom. Mom doesn't know yet but I'm going to tell her this weekend. I just can't find the words to explain everything to her. It's too much and I know she's going to have so many questions that I just can't answer."

"What do you need me to do?"

"I did a two hour intake today. I put you down as a contact person." Then I went on to explain to her that I arrived at the facility at five pm and didn't walk out until a little after seven. The counselor with whom I did the intake,

Rebecca, asked about ten pages of questions. She asked questions about my birth, my childhood, my parents, siblings, pets, friends, boyfriends, husband, children and everything in between. I felt totally exposed when I left her that night. "Could you call my caseworker, talk to her and tell Rico and Mom the truth about what I've been hiding from them and everyone else for years. Explain to them that I wear a mask, I fake being well, and now I have to take the mask off."

"I'll do that for you. What's her name and phone number?"

I provided Michele's phone number. "Sis," I said, "I'm sorry to bother you, I know you're busy. I just...I have no one else."

"Stop. You stop right now," Michaela interrupted me, "Don't apologize. You're my sister and you need me. I want to help you. You're never a bother. I'm always here for you. I'll call Michele; and, then, after I talk to her, I'll call Jericho and Mom Bella and talk to them. In the meantime, please reach out to me or anyone else if you need support. You're not in this alone. We all love you Esmene."

And I cried even more at that, because I could feel the love in her voice, a love I felt I didn't deserve. "Thank you, Sis," I said through my tears. "I love you too."

"Get some rest. I'll talk to you soon. Goodnight."

That was on a Friday. I knew I needed to tell Mom before Michaela spoke to Michele. I called her on Sunday night. "Hi Mom."

"Hello Esme. How are you?"

"I'm OK." I took a deep breath. "Listen, there's something I need to tell you."

"I didn't do it," she joked but I could hear the nervousness in her voice. I gave a fake laugh in an attempt to ease her worries.

"You know that 'class' I've been going to every day?"

"Yeah, what about it?" she asked hesitantly.

"Well it's not a class, not in the way you think it is. Rico had me admitted to a psychiatric hospital last week because I was...I AM suicidal. That's where I go every day after work and on my days off," I finished. There was silence. "Mom?"

She cleared her throat. "How long have you been feeling this way?" I could hear the emotion in her voice.

"It's been building up for a while. It was something I thought about fleetingly; and, over the months, the thoughts became more persistent to the point where that's all I've been thinking about."

"Do the kids know about you being in the hospital?"

"No, they think I'm taking a psychology class at the local college."

"So you're going to stay at work and do this program?"

"Uh, yeah. At least that's the plan right now."

"That's not going to be too much for you? Why don't you take a leave from work?" she suggested.

"Mom, work makes me feel normal. It's one big bit of normalcy in my life and I want to keep it. I'm terrified that if I take time off, I'll lose the one thing that makes me like everyone else. I already lost my career because of this disease and I'm not willing to lose my job too. I know this is just a part-time retail job, but I worked hard to get it and I take pride in my work. It's all I have, apart from my family."

"It's not all you have Esme but I understand what you're saying. I don't understand how you managed to hide this from everyone, from Rico and from me for so long. Why would you hide this? If something happens to you, don't you know your family would be devastated? This whole family would be lost without you."

I took in a long, wet breath. "I just..Mom, I don't know. Listen, I talked to Michaela. She's going to speak to my caseworker at the hospital, get all the details, and then call you, OK? I just can't explain everything right now. I just wanted to prepare you before she calls."

"OK. Thank you for being honest with me. I'll wait for Michaela to call. If you need me, just call me. Don't be afraid to reach out. I love you."

"I will. I love you too, Mom."

I nervously waited to hear from Michaela. I got a call from her two days later. "Sis, is it all true?"

"Is what true?" I countered.

"Everything Michele told me," Michaela said, her voice laced with concern.

Oh God, what did Michele tell her, I wondered. She wasn't supposed to tell her about Uncle. I thought I had made that clear to Michele when I gave her permission to talk to Michaela.

"About how long you've been having suicidal ideation. About how long the binging and purging has been back. About how bad your depression has really gotten. How has no one else noticed this? How have you continued to get up, go to work, and live life like everything was fine without anyone having the slightest clue of the hell you were going through?"

"It's the mask," I said sadly.

"The mask?" she repeated.

"The mask."

There was a moment of silence between us. "Es, tell me about the mask," she requested gently. I hesitated for a few seconds. I've never revealed the secrets of my alter ego before. This was a big step, I thought to myself. Did I dare? "Es, I please, tell me about the mask."

I sighed. I couldn't deny her. I explained dejectedly "Every morning when I wake up and start my day, not only do I put on my clothes, socks and shoes. I also put on my mask, the one that tells the world I'm OK. The mask says to the world, I'm fine, nothing's wrong. The people around me don't know how to react to my illness, so I put on a mask. I hide the pain inside behind a veil of false happiness to make everyone else comfortable. And it works. But my mask is made of iron and wearing it is exhausting. People still aren't equipped to deal with my brand of sickness. So I wear the mask, the veil of wellness, for the greater good. I'm always sick and I fake being well."

"You fake being well every day?"

"Seven days a week."

"You're amazing Sis," Michaela said in awe.

"No. No I'm not amazing. I'm ill."

Michaela did as she said and spoke to both Jericho and Mom. I could tell they were both trying to be supportive, but they were still at a loss as to what that really meant in terms of what they needed to do to help me. I never asked for help before, so I wasn't about to offer them any suggestions on how to help me out. Over the next few weeks it was an awkward dance between the three of us, as I worked my way through the IOP program at the hospital.

Michele insisted on a family meeting, so Michaela came to the facility for the meeting. Jericho was supposed to attend also, but he had a big job that day and couldn't get off. Once again Michaela offered to fill him in on the proceedings. On the day of the meeting I was nervous. I hadn't spoken about this situation with Michaela face to face since I told her about the hospitalization. I was embarrassed and ashamed, and I didn't know what would be asked of me in the meeting. Even though it was cold that day, I waited for her outside. When Michaela arrived she came over and gave me a hug and a kiss. "Why are you waiting out here in the cold?"

"It's not that cold," I mumbled. Bull crap, I thought. It was freezing, but my nerves were getting the best of me so I had started sweating.

"Are you ready?" she asked me, trying to catch my eyes to gauge my feelings.

"No," I replied quickly.

Michaela grabbed my hand and pulled me close to her. "Come on. You're going to be fine."

So we walked back into the facility and had a seat in the hall to wait for Michele. We didn't have to wait long. "Hi ladies. You can follow me into this meeting room," Michele directed. Michele followed us into the room and closed the door. She then turned to my sister with her hand outstretched. "Hi, I'm Michele, Esmene's caseworker. We spoke on the phone."

Extending her hand, Michaela said, "Hi, I'm Michaela, Esmene's eldest sister. It's nice to meet you." I really wanted to get the heck out of there. I was starting to sweat again.

"Please have a seat," Michele gestured towards the seats on the opposite side on the table. Michaela and I sat on one side next to each other, Michele on the other side.

I thought OK, nothing bad yet. So far so good. Michele started off. "So today I wanted to talk about Esmene, how she's feeling, and what the people around her can do to support her while she's getting treatment. I also want to find out what Esmene feels she needs from others in the form of support to help her during recovery." Now, I thought, it's not going so well. Saying what I needed wasn't going to be so easy. Michele looked straight at me. "Esmene, how are you feeling today?"

Michaela was watching me too. "I'm fine," I said, with my customary answer to the routine question.

"What does that mean?" Michele asked.

I thought what DOES that mean? I took in a deep breath. I was already getting frustrated. I didn't deal in feelings: feelings were messy. Confusing and complicated, feelings never felt good. I was either fine or not fine and that was the extent of my feelings. "It means I'm not bad. I'm fine," I said, with a hint of annoyance in my voice.

Michele and Michaela glanced at me with compassion in their eyes. "Esmene, do you still feel like your family would be better off without you?" Michele asked. I looked down at my freshly painted fingernails. I got mood changing polish this time. It went from a burgundy to a burgundy/ black color. My nails were burgundy a minute ago. Now they were nearly black. Michaela had also observed the change. "You have mood changing polish on don't you?" she inquired.
"Yeah, why?"

"Because I just watched them go from red to black within seconds of Michele asking that question. Your nails are telling on you." she said with a grin. I pulled my sleeves down over my hands.

"Esmene," Michele continued, "Tell me about your children?"

Immediately I brightened up. My hands came from under my sleeves and I could feel a small smile beginning to play on my lips. "My children are my everything. They're the one good thing I've done in life. My son Zander is a film major in college and my little one Zeyonna is a senior in high school. They are awesome kids. They have never given us any kind of trouble. They are smart, respectable kids with a great sense of humor. I love them dearly," I concluded. My polish was a fiery burgundy again.

"And what about your husband?"

"Jericho? I love him. We've been together over twenty years now. He's a wonderful husband and father. He always puts me and the kids first and never thinks about his own needs or comforts. He works hard to support us. I never have to worry about him being in the street or hanging out with his friends. I've never even met one of his friends. He comes straight home from work every single day. He does chores around the house. If I've had a bad day, he'll come home from work and cook or buy dinner. He spends quality time with the kids and with me. He's sweet, funny, loveable and supportive. He accepts me for me and I never imagined I would ever be lucky enough to have someone like him in my life." I was on the verge of crying now and it was making my nails dark again. Michaela rubbed my back.

Michele inquired, "So Esmene, if you feel this way about your family, why would you want to hurt them by taking your life?"

The smartest people have no common sense. Wasn't it obvious? "My kids are grown up and they've made it to this point unscathed by my issues. They don't need me anymore. If I keep hanging around with my problems, I'm going to do something to screw them up or embarrass them. Then they'll hate me because I ruined their lives with my illness. I'd rather be dead than have my kids hate me. And Jericho deserves a better wife. He's turned down so many opportunities to further his career just to stay close to home, close to me, because he can't trust what his psycho wife will do while he's gone. That's not fair to him. He's great at his job. He should have the opportunity to advance, not be held back by me. He's going to wake up one day, realize all the opportunities he has lost, and resent me for it. I can't live with that.

I'm just a burden. I bring nothing to the table. I don't even work a real job anymore. I go to work just to have something to do. My kids make more money than I do. I'm a waste of space. They don't need me. Besides, with the insurance money from my death, the kids' education would be paid for so they won't have to graduate with a bunch of student loans. Now that I think of it, I should ask Jericho if there is a suicide clause in my policy, right?" I look over at Michaela to confirm that would be an appropriate step, only to find her mouth wide open in shock. Then I looked down at my hands. My nails were black again.

Michaela shook her head. "Do you think Zander and Zee would rather have insurance money than have their mother?" my sister asked.

I looked over at her and saw a mixture of hurt, anger, and disbelief as it played out on her face. "I didn't say that," I corrected her.

"Then what are you saying?" she demanded.

"I don't know." I was tired now. I didn't want to answer any more questions. I wanted this meeting to be over. I was tired of defending something that they would never understand. I just sat there and tucked my chin into my chest. I was done talking. My nails were as black as night. They said everything I couldn't.

My sister continued. "Es, would it make you feel any better if Jericho started to explore some of the job opportunities he has turned down over the years? Would that make any difference for you?"

"Yeah, it would." I nodded my head in affirmation.

"And what do you need from me?" Michaela wanted to know. I shrugged my shoulders. I was really being quite childish. Michaela turned her whole body towards me and grabbed my hands in hers. She ran her fingers over my black nails. "How about I just make myself more available to you to listen when you need someone to talk to. I can be there to give you the support you need when you're struggling and just need someone who won't judge you to be there. How about that?" That sounded nice. I'd never had that before. I nodded my head yes.

"That sounds like a great starting place for you, Esmene," Michele said. I forgot she was in the room. "Now the last thing I want to talk about is based on some things you expressed today. If you're still dealing with a lot of suicidal ideation, I really think it's time for you to be bumped up to our full day program."

I immediately started shaking my head no. I had thus far resisted the full day program. How was I going to work and do a full day program five days a week? It couldn't be done. "No, sorry, I can't do it. I have to work and I'm not giving up my job. I told you that on intake. No." I was gripping Michaela's fingers now.

"Well, would there really be much difference? You already come three days a week. It's just two more days you would need to leave work early. And it won't be forever. Just until we feel that you're in a better place, mentally and emotionally. Then you would go back down to half day sessions. Your insurance company has been recommending it from the beginning; and with what you've expressed about feeling like a burden, I think you need it. You need the support of a group." Michele explained.

I finally looked up and made eye contact with her. What I saw in her eyes was empathy, not pity, which is good because I wanted pity from no one. I looked to my sister for guidance "What do I do Sis?"

She gave me a little smile. "You do the full day program so you can have support and get the tools you need to help yourself. Your job isn't going anywhere," she advised.

I was outnumbered and out of steam. I had no more fight left in me for the day, so I gave in. "Fine. When do I start?"

"Tomorrow," Michele said.

"TOMORROW?"

"Tomorrow," Michele repeated calmly.

I shrugged my shoulders and nodded my head. Of course I would start tomorrow, I thought to myself. "Fine." I said. "Tomorrow it is."

The session was wrapped up in a neat little bow and before I knew it Michaela and I were back out in the cold. Michaela said, "You did good Es, I'm proud of you for being so honest about how you felt."

"Yeah, well all my honesty did was get me more time in the program, so I don't know how proud I should be about that." I mumbled.

She came over and hugged me. She was taller than I was, so my chin fit perfectly on her shoulder. "You should be very proud. What you did today took a lot of strength. I'm proud of you," she said as she rubbed my back.

And between the warm words and the rubbing of my back, the tears I tried so desperately to hold onto began to flow.

"It's OK Esmene. Let it out. Let it out," she encouraged.

And I did, right there in the parking lot, my tears dropping to the ground, forming their own little intricate patterns in the snow.

It's OK Not to Be OK

Finally, the most hellish workday I had ever experienced had come to an end. It was hellish because that was the day my employer discovered they had a mental case on their payroll and I could already feel the judgement. Or was that pity? Or perhaps fear, Whatever it was, I was about to escape when Ms. Dora pulled me aside.

"OK lady, what's going on?" she demanded, looking me straight in the eyes.

"What do you mean?" I tried to play dumb. Silly me, Ms. Dora was a smart woman.

"Baby, I know something's wrong. I mean really wrong. You're not yourself today. Now come on. Tell me the truth. What's going on?" she pried gently.

I could feel the burn of tears building up behind my eyes. I didn't want to cry here but she was being so kind, I couldn't help it. The tears began to flow. "Jericho had me admitted into an outpatient program at a psychiatric hospital yesterday because I'm suicidal. I check in tomorrow," I explained to her, looking down at my shoes because I was too ashamed to look her in the eye.

"Lord have mercy," she exclaimed. "Now why didn't you tell me this earlier? You've been walking around here all day on the verge of tears and I could've been supporting you the whole time. Why'd you do that to yourself?" she demanded to know.

I sniffled so she grabbed a tissue and handed it to me. "I'm embarrassed. Ashamed. Who wants to tell her superior and friend that they've been admitted to a psychiatric hospital?" I explained.

Ms. Dora sighed, then came over to give me a hug, "Baby, I have no idea what you're going through but I want you to know that you don't have to go through this alone. It's OK that you're not OK. It's not just you. Most of the people in here probably need to be in a hospital." I laughed at that because she was right. "What you're doing is brave and I admire you for doing it. I'm going to be there to support you anyway I can. Now what's going to happen as far as work?"

"Umm, I have to be there three days a week from ten to one. I talked to Karla already and she just went in and adjusted my schedule for me to leave every day at nine thirty. She said if Karen, Amanda or Donna had any problems with it, she would let me know."

Ms. Dora nodded her head. "Good, good. I'm glad she didn't give you any trouble. You see. Everyone's willing to work with you so you can get the help that you need. We want you to be OK. Now you just let me know what you need from me to support you through this." She gave me her motherly smile.

I felt so guilty. I had no right putting her under such obligation. She was my team lead, not Iyanla Vanzant; yet she was always there to encourage me and lift my spirits. I was lucky to have her in my life. "I'm sorry," I told her through fresh tears. I was sorry to burden her with the nightmares of my past.

"Hey now, you stop that. You have nothing to be sorry about. This isn't your fault! You hear me! Esmene, look at me." She lifted my chin up with her finger, bringing my eyes to meet hers, "Esmene, I told you before, none of this is your fault. OK? So no more apologizing. I'm supporting you because that's what I want to do. I'm a big girl; I can handle it. Don't worry about me," she assured, giving me a smile.

And in that moment, I truly believed that I had her support unconditionally, that she was OK with me not being OK, that my past wasn't going to scare her away, and that she would see this through until the end. It was I who initiated the hug this time, which was rare for me. "Thank you, Ms. Dora," I whispered, hoping she could hear in my voice how grateful I was to her.

I sensed she was smiling against the side of my face. "You're welcome, Baby. You're welcome."

I Feel It Coming

Lincoln Hospital's Psychiatric Unit wasn't too far from my home. I put up a hell of a fight the first week. I couldn't believe this was what my life had come to. I was a wife, mother, and a Christian. Now another adjective was added to the list: psychiatric patient.

However, as it had forever been in my life, I quickly realized that the one place where I despised being was the primary place I truly felt accepted by my peers. It was a place where I belonged. Without saying a word to each other, we patients just got it. We understood our complicated language and communicated our support with simple head nods and grunts of understanding. No long monologues or diatribes were needed.

I was in a group made up of about fifteen people, men and women from all age groups and all walks of life and every psychiatric diagnosis in the Diagnostic and Statistical Manual of Mental Disorders 5th edition aka DSM-V. However, we all had one thing in common: we either had suicidal ideations or actually had attempted suicide. My diagnosis read like a menu at Chick- fil-A:

Bipolar 1 w/ psychotic features
PTSD
Obsessive Compulsive Disorder
Generalized Anxiety Disorder
Bulimia
Primary Insomnia

It was quite an impressive list if I do say so myself. But my list was not unique amongst my fellow patients. There was Ricky, a sixteen year old high school drop-out who was on his fourth trip to the facility. He had no job; and, according to him, every week he was going to be discharged. He had plans to enroll in culinary school to become a bakery chef with aspirations to then go to law school. Despite being unemployed, he insisted on showing us different apartments he was looking to rent when he got out. Some were even more severe cases. There was Evelyn, twenty-nine, who lived with her husband and four kids. She tried to commit suicide by taking pills to permanently end the argument she and her husband were having. She had a wicked sense of humor with a temper to match. There was Terry, thirty-five, a wife and mother of three girls, whose boss drove her to a nervous breakdown. Jerry, forty, lived alone. He sliced both his arms open from wrists to elbows. He spent two months in the hospital before being released into the program. He kept having dreams of being in bed with a man when he was a child but he refused to believe that it was anything more than a dream. And then there was Jordan, thirty-three. She had an issue of becoming sexually aroused by her dog but she assured us nothing inappropriate ever went on between them. We were a diverse group but we became close and we didn't let anyone come between us.

When Danielle joined our group, we knew it was going to be trouble. Danielle boasted about how much money she had; how many famous people she knew; how her children worked with celebrities; how her siblings were doctors and lawyers; and how they had multiple homes in California, Las Vegas, and New York. Every day it was a continuation of "Danielle: The Life of a Diva." She was stressed because celebrities were calling her to cater parties for them in the Hamptons at three am. Rachel Ray had to send a car to come pick her up because she lost the key to her Mercedes and couldn't make the drive to her studio. Oh, the humanity! It was ridiculous. It got to the point that every time she started to talk, most of us would roll our eyes or look out the window and try not to throw ourselves out of it. Evelyn got totally disrespectful and put her earbuds in.

For those of us who were full day patients, we were served lunch at noon. One day, Ms. Diva (Danielle's new nickname) was telling Jordan, who seemed to be the only one who was ever interested to hear what she had to say, about another adventure in her ongoing saga. Ricky, God bless him, interrupted them. "Hey Danielle. Why you here?" he yelled down the table.

Danielle took her finger to swoop nonexisting hair out of her eyes and said "What do you mean why am I here? I'm here for the same reason you're here."

"No, I don't think so. I know why I'm here. But all we ever hear you talk about is your kids, your brother and his wife, or your other brother and how he tries to diagnose you. We done heard about your business, your clients, your YouTube channel. We heard about your ex. But like why are you here? What's wrong with you?" he insisted.

Danielle rolled her eyes and gave him a look of exasperation, like how dare he ask her such a thing. "Well, not that it's any of your business but I'm stressed and depressed. It's not easy being a caterer to the stars." Jordan looked at Ricky and nodded her head as if co-signing on Danielle's assertion. Ricky immediately started banging on the table while he dissolved into a fit of laughter. One of the facilitators came in to see what all the noise was about.

"Everything OK in here?" Shelby asked.

"We all good," Ricky responded, still laughing. "Danielle got jokes," he said, continuing to laugh.

Danielle's nostrils flared out and she put her hands on her hips. Shelby looked around the table. "Just keep it down, Ricky," she said and left.

Danielle spoke through gritted teeth. "What's so damn funny?"

"You are." Ricky looked over at her, "Yo...are you serious? Ma, you kidding me right? You here with us because you stressed and depressed? I was depressed in kindergarten!" He turned towards the rest of the table. "Did you guys hear that shit?" He turned back to Danielle. "Danielle they must've told you, you gotta have at least three debilitating disorders to be in this group. You talkin' about stress. Shit, I eat stress with my Cheerios in the morning!"

Danielle looked like she was about to blow a gasket. "Ricky, it's not funny! Who are you to judge how I feel and how my condition affects me. You're just some punk kid who can't even graduate high school!"

That was a cheap shot but Ricky wasn't even phased. "That was cute, sweetheart, but you gonna have to come better than that to get at me. But for real though. You don't believe me? Hold on, check this out," Ricky pointed to Jordan. "Jordan, what you got?"

"Bipolar disorder, Borderline Personality Disorder and PTSD," Jordan answered like she was ordering a sandwich from Subway.

"Yo Ez, you next. Don't be shy."

"Bipolar with psychosis, PTSD, OCD, Bulimia...I think that's enough," I mumbled while picking through my salad.

"Jerry, my man!" Ricky yelled down to the end of the table, "What's up?"

Jerry looked over at Ricky and held up both arms showing the deep scars running the length of his forearms. "Does this answer your question Little Buddy?"

Ricky gave him two thumbs up. "Loud and clear Captain!" Ricky turned back to Danielle. "I may be off my shit, but I know what I'm talkin about. I'm gonna be a lawyer. Stressed and depressed? Please, those are daycare problems. Sorry, you gotta have your own table. You can't sit with us. Not today Ma!" And with that Ricky stood, picked up his lunch and moved down the end of the other table with Jerry.

Jordan looked at Danielle, stood up, shrugged her shoulders and said, "Sorry," grabbed her lunch and moved too.

I moved as well. I wasn't sorry. I was just glad not to listen to her voice anymore. In the end, poor Danielle sat at the far end of the table all by herself. I couldn't believe what happened. Someone actually got bullied inside a psychiatric unit for not being disturbed enough to fit in with the group. I couldn't stop smiling over it. What the heck was happening?

I guess Danielle got tired of eating alone because she quickly got her act together. A week later she threw a chair across the room at a facilitator and the crisis team came through the double doors and dragged her away. We all stood up and applauded her theatrics. Ricky even whistled and told her it was about time she released the beast. As they took her away kicking and screaming, Ricky yelled down the hall that when she got out, we would have a seat at the head of the table waiting for her.

You can't make this stuff up.

Dim All the Lights

It started out like any other morning that I had to go to work. I got up, gave myself "the talk," and put my mask firmly in place. I took my shower and got dressed. I went into the kitchen to take my medication and heat up my coffee. I grabbed a few Townhouse crackers because my stomach was feeling a little upset; but, other than that, I felt fine. I looked at the clock and saw it was time to go. I had to stop to pick up my co-worker Jasmine. Jasmine was a single Caucasian woman in her early thirties who lived down the street with her father, step-mother, and brother.

While driving my truck to Jasmine's house, I started to feel shaky, like I was nervous or something. I knew I didn't have time to stop at Wawa, so when I got to the stop sign, I dug around in my bag and got a piece of candy. I thought maybe I needed some sugar. Confident that I took care of the problem, I continued on my way. "Hey lady," greeted Jasmine as she got in the truck.

"Hey girl. How are you doing?"

"Oh, I'm good. Queenie almost tripped me this morning…" Then Jasmine launched into a recap of her morning escapades with her five cats. While she was talking, I was starting to feel worse. I was starting to sweat. I was shaky and my left hand was starting to go numb.

I drove on for another five minutes before I realized I was driving slower. I had to alert Jasmine. "Jasmine, listen, I don't feel well. I'm not sure what's wrong, but I feel like I'm going to be sick. I'm shaky and sweating and my whole left side is starting to go numb. I'm going to try to get us to work," I told her in a calm voice. I didn't want her to panic.

Jasmine looked at me with wide eyes. "What do you want me to do?"

"Just be prepared to take the wheel if necessary and pull over to the side. But we're going to be OK," I assured her.

By the grace of God, we did make it into the JCPenny parking lot. By that time, my foot felt like lead and I was drooling out the left side of my mouth. I could barely speak and there was no way I could get out of the truck. "Jasmine," I mumbled," you're going to have to go get some help. I can't get out."

Just then, other employees started pulling into the parking lot. Naomi was the first to get out of her car. She was one of our co-workers, an African American woman in her fifties. Jasmine called over to her. "Naomi. NAOMI!" Jasmine screamed across the parking lot.

Naomi turned around. "What? What's wrong?"

"We need help. Something's wrong with Esmene!"

Naomi hurried over to the truck. "Esmene, what's wrong? What happened?" she asked me urgently. I really couldn't respond. I was drooling. My head felt full of static. Our location was right around the corner from a hospital. I just needed to get there.

Jericho was still home. I needed him to come get me so I grabbed for my phone and pointed. Naomi looked down at my hand. "You want me to call 911?" she asked. I shook my head. "You want me to call Jericho?" I nodded my head.

Naomi took the phone and scanned my contacts, looking for the number. While she was doing that, another co-worker, Jessica, had made her way over to the truck. Jessica was a Caucasian woman in her mid thirties, married with two sons.

Jessica grabbed my hand. "Esmene, I'm going to pray for you, OK?" I nodded my head because right then I needed a prayer. Jessica held my hand as she prayed for me. While Naomi was on the phone with Jericho, another co-worker,

Breonna, walked up to the car. Breonna was an older African American woman in her fifties.

By this point, I couldn't speak. Breonna asked Jasmine what was going on and Jasmine filled her in on the details. Breonna offered to go into the building and fill in the supervisors on what was going on outside. Jessica gave my hand an affectionate pat and went with her. Jasmine and Naomi waited by my side in the parking lot until Jercicho came flying in there in his minivan. After getting an update from Naomi and Jessica, he pulled me from my truck, deposited me in the mini-van, and whisked me off to the emergency room. I kept trying to mouth the words thank you to my friends but nothing except drool seemed to come out of my mouth. I hoped that my eyes told them how grateful I was for their help.

When we got to the ER, I was quickly taken to a back room. I was terrified, thinking that I'd had a stroke. Jericho looked as scared as I was. When he gave them my driver's license and they pulled up my information, my records from Lincoln Hospital came up. The triage nurse read through the notes and then got to work. "Hi Esmene. I'm Tanisha," she told me. "I'm going to be your nurse for today. I need to check your blood sugar. Have you had anything to eat today?" she asked as she put gloves on.

"I had some crackers and candy," I murmured, while my tongue was refusing to cooperate.

She nodded her head that she understood and went over to my right side to do the blood sugar finger stick. As Tanisha was preparing for the glucose test, the doctor came in to talk to me. "Hi Mrs. Munroe. I'm Dr. Lisa. I'll be taking care of you today. Why don't you tell me what's going on today?"

With my troublesome tongue, I relayed the details of my eventful morning. She seemed to comprehend everything I said. "Your blood sugar is at 79," Tanisha said. "Didn't you say you had crackers?"

"Yes, and a piece of candy."

Tanisha nodded her head. "OK, I'm going to draw some blood so we can get some lab work done." Tanisha tried to draw blood, but when she stuck the needle in my arm, my blood wouldn't flow.

"I think you may be dehydrated," Dr. Lisa suggested. "Tanisha, give her a few glasses of fluid and wait about fifteen-to-twenty minutes. See if that gets her blood moving." Then she looked at me. "Mrs. Munroe, after Tanisha draws your blood, I'm going to have a tray of food delivered for you. I need you to eat it. I'm also going to schedule you to get a CAT scan just to make sure nothing else is going on. For now, just sit here, drink your fluids, and try to relax."

So, I drank my water; and, within a half hour, Tanisha came back and was able to draw my blood. I was actually starting to feel better after drinking the water. I was getting the feeling back on my left side. As Tanisha was leaving, someone else came in to take me down to get my CAT scan. They were very efficient at this hospital.

The CAT scan was over within minutes and I was back in my room with a tray of food in front of me. Jericho was watching me eat. "You know, you don't have to sit there and watch me eat," I said to him.

"Apparently, I do."

"Touche."

So I ate, he watched, and we waited for the doctor to come back and render her verdict. About an hour later, Dr. Lisa reappeared. "Mrs. Munroe, did you finish your breakfast?"

"Yes I did."

"Good. Very good. OK, well I got the result of your blood work back. Just as I expected, you are dehydrated and your blood glucose is low. It's only at seventy-three and you said you ate crackers and candy this morning, correct?"

"Yeah, I did. I ate about twenty crackers."

"I can't imagine how low your blood sugar must have been. Thank God you didn't pass out behind the wheel of your car." I looked over at Jericho who looked like he was ready to spit nails. I was in trouble.

"The results of your CAT scan were normal, so there was no stroke or anything like that. How do you feel now?"

"I feel tired, but the numbness, shakiness and sweating are gone," I told her.

"That sounds about right. You're probably going to sleep the rest of the day. I need you to make sure you're drinking enough fluid during the day and you need to eat. Are you still seeking professional help for your issues?"

"Yes, I'm in a program now."

"Good. I would definitely let them know about this episode. Well, if you have no questions, I'll go print out your discharge papers so you can be on your way. Do you have any questions?"

I chanced a look over at Jericho. He wasn't in the mood for talking. I turned back to Dr. Lisa. "No. No questions. Thank you for everything."

"It was my pleasure. I'll be back shortly," she said with a smile. She left the two of us in the room.

I decided to confront Jericho now that there were witnesses around, hoping to prevent an eruption. "Jericho, why are you so angry?"

He turned to look at me like I had lost my mind. "Es, I thought you were making progress, that you'd gotten this under control. Now I'm sitting here finding out that you haven't, and it was so bad you could've killed yourself and another person by passing out behind the wheel of your truck! For God's sake, they couldn't even draw your blood!"

"Rico, you just don't understand..."

"Damn right I don't understand. Not when it comes to your life. No, I'll never understand. I don't care how many different ways you try to explain it to me Esme," he said angrily.

I dropped my head back onto the bed, too tired to continue arguing with him. We waited in a heavy silence for Dr. Lisa to set me free.

A Life Worth Living

I was admitted to Waterford Behavioral Center just two days after being discharged from Lincoln Hospital in April. I was sent to Lincoln to deal with the immediate issue of suicidal ideation, but at Waterford they were going to address the trauma I had experienced as a child that was the cause of my PTSD. They intended to give me positive coping skills to replace my negative ones, bulimia and self harm.

Waterford was a sizable place. From the outside, it looked like your typical office building. Unlike Lincoln's, Waterford's programs were separated into men's, women's, mixed, and children's. I was in the women's program. The women's program was broken down into smaller programs, each class limited to ten people to keep patients from getting overwhelmed. The first two hours were dedicated to your particular program. So if you were in the Trauma track, you would work on the Trauma program for the first two hours. For the third hour, you had to choose from a variety of classes: Anger Management, Stress Management, Music, or Art. If you were a full day patient, you would have lunch; and then after lunch, there would be two more random classes that would change daily, chosen by the facilitators .

On my first day, I was introduced to my caseworker, Casey. Casey was a young Caucasian woman, probably in her late twenties or early thirties. Casey smiled a lot. As I said before, I don't trust people who smile a lot so I didn't trust Casey. "So Esmene," she said with much sincerity, "one of the most important things we need to establish is your life's worth living goal."

"My what?" I asked.

She smiled again. "Your life's worth living goal. What would be your reason to continue living?"

What WOULD be my reason to continue living, I asked myself. Why was I alive at that moment? I thought about the people in my life. I loved Jericho with all my heart. However, I always felt he could do better and deserved a better wife. I was definitely holding him back from achieving his true potential as far as his career was concerned. He wanted to be an over the road truck driver; but, because of me, he was stuck doing local jobs for hourly pay. Besides, there was no guarantee we would be together forever anyway. There was always a chance for a divorce. In my mind, if I were to die today, I would be doing him a favor. But, my babies definitely made my life worth living. My babies would mourn for me. I was their mother and no one would ever replace me in their lives. They'd be so hurt. With the thought of them standing over my casket to say goodby to me and the indescribable pain that I would cause them by the actions of my own hand, I wouldn't deserve the peace I sought in death. I couldn't abandon them.

"My children, Zander and Zeyonna. They're my life's worth living goal," I answered, my eyes glossy with unshed tears.

Casey nodded her head. "I think that's a perfect life's worth living goal, Esmene. Now, you were going to be placed in our Trauma program; but after talking things over with Dr. White and your care team, we decided it would be best to place you in the DBT program. DBT stands for Dialectical Behavioral Therapy, which is a behavioral therapy that will provide you with the skills you need to manage your emotions and decrease conflicts in your relationships. We believe that DBT will give you the healthy coping skills needed to deal with both your bipolar and PTSD symptoms, therefore reducing the bulimic and self harm behaviors. We feel that's really important, especially after your latest trip to the emergency room. How does that sound to you?"

"That's what I'm here for, so I'd say that sounds fine," I responded. What else was there for me to say?

Casey made a few notes in my file before looking up at me again. "Good, good. OK, so just to recap. You are starting out in our full day program, nine-thirty to three, Monday through Friday. Lunch is provided every day. You can sign up for one of the three options offered daily. You can't miss more than three days of program in a row. If you miss more than three days in a row, regardless of the reason, you will be discharged from the hospital. It's just the way we keep tabs on the people that we are treating. If we haven't laid eyes on patients in three days, we aren't sure what they've been doing. Some people here struggle with substance abuse issues. You'll have two sessions of DBT in the morning with your core group, and every afternoon you'll have two classes picked by the staff. They'll differ every day. Now you'll be moving to different rooms throughout the day, so it's very important that you write your name on the board outside whatever room you're in so staff can know where you are. When you have counseling sessions with me and Dr. White once a week, we'll come looking for you. Now, do you have any questions?"

No, I never had questions when it came to these things. I just went with the flow and asked questions when they came up. I didn't make things overly complicated by asking questions. "No, no questions yet," I assured her.

Casey smiled again and nodded. "OK, great. Now, I have your binder here with all the hospital phone numbers, crisis numbers, and my number in it should you need them, along with all of your lesson plans. Our class facilitators rotate, so every day someone different will be running a group. If you have any questions, any one of them can answer them for you. Now, please follow me..."

I Love You Too

Other than Michaela, none of my other siblings knew about me being in the hospital. It wasn't so much that I was keeping it a secret, I just really didn't know what to say to them. The time did finally arise when I felt I needed to address the issue. My parents were hosting a small family BBQ, and I was not feeling up to it. I knew the question "what's wrong with you" would come up, so I figured I would address it ahead of time.

A phone call was just too much effort for me, so I sent a group text message to Delilah, Veronica, Braxton, McKenna and Lyam. It read: *Hello everyone. I just wanted to tell you all something. Jericho had me admitted to a psychiatric hospital in February because I was suicidal. I'm still in the facility. I'm not feeling my best today, so if I'm not really engaging with the family, you'll know why. If you have any questions, I'm open to discuss this with any of you.*

For a time, my phone remained silent. Then I received this response from Veronica: *Esme, I'm sorry to hear about what you've been going through. Thank you for sharing with us. I know that was hard for you to do. I want you to know that I'm here to support you with anything you need. I love you and want you to be well.*

Veronica's response was expected; but Lyam's wasn't, not because I thought Lyam didn't care, it was because Lyam was the poster boy for annoying little brothers. I never expected to receive serious support from him. He wrote, *Esmene, people leave this world every day because they think no one loves them. I want you to know that I love you and my life would not be the same without you. I'm here to support you through this. I love you.*

And just about every night since that day, I received his text: *Good night I love you.* Most of the time when he sends it, I am already asleep; but I always respond the next day with *Good morning. I love you too.* It has been that way with us ever since my first text and he'll never know what it means to me to see that text first thing in the morning. Some nights I go to bed feeling so insignificant. I felt like a burden, worthless, a waste of space. But to wake up in the morning and know that someone was thinking of me, motivates me to go on another day. Apparently my life did mean more than I thought to the ones I always loved.

Good night I love you.
I love you too.

Don't Leave Me This Way

Back at Waterford Behavioral Center, our facilitator Shanon greeted us on a Tuesday morning in May. As with any other day, Shannon came in and wrote her name and the date on the white board and then sat down and waited for everyone to arrive. I actually liked my group here better than the one at Lincoln. It was a lot smaller and better controlled. I also liked the fact that it was all women. It made it easier to talk about female things.

Shannon glanced at the time on her cell phone. "Alright, it looks like mostly everyone's here. Good morning again. I'm Shanon, today is Tuesday, May 7, 2019, and this is DBT," she announced with enthusiasm. We all gave fake cheers and hand claps like we were at a sporting event. "Ladies, today we're going to be talking about distress tolerance skills. Now when do we use those?"

"To decrease the intensity of a feeling so you don't feel consumed by it," I answered.

"Good Esmene. Anyone else?"

Elaine, a fifty year-old mother of three who had been assaulted at work and suffered with PTSD as a result called out "To gain self-control."

"That's right, Elaine," Shannon said. "To gain self control and not just react impulsively. Now can anyone give examples of what kinds of behaviors we would want to target with distress tolerance skills?"

"Suicidal ideation," Amalia said softly. Amalia was a twenty year-old college student who was on sabbatical after being raped at a campus party by a "friend."

Shannon looked over at Amalia trying to make eye contact, but Amalia was hiding behind her golden veil of hair. "Amalia, have you been struggling with suicidal ideation again?" Amalia peaked out from under her veil of hair to look at Shannon and nodded her head. A sympathetic look crossed Shannon's face. We all felt like

Amalia's mother. "Amalia, has something recently happened to bring this on?" Shannon prodded.

Amalia started sniffing. "People at school who I thought were my friends are on social media calling me a whore and a slut. They were so supportive of me when I was still on campus; but now that I'm gone, they're saying that what happened was all my fault, that I'm a liar, and that I wanted it. They're all in his corner. I just feel so worthless. I can't take it anymore!" Amalia collapsed in a fit of tears.

I lifted her head up from the table and rested her head on my shoulder, just like I would if she were Zeyonna. Elaine began rubbing her back in gentle circles as sobs wracked her petite body. And it was sad that even though we were all going through the program, none of us had words of comfort for her. Most of us in this group were burdened with the same feelings from assaults, so all we could do was hold her while she wept.

Suddenly, Rachel, a tiny Caucasian woman in her early twenties, burst into the room. "I'm so sorry I'm late again. I swear it won't happen again. I Swear. Seriously." Rachel pledged almost every day since she started. She stood exactly five feet tall. Her hair looked like an accident at the Crayola factory. It was purple, green, blue, and I think pink or faded red. Rarely did it look as if it had been brushed. Rachel's clothes were often on backwards, inside out, or in some form of disarray when she came barging into the room. Rachel had been diagnosed with Bipolar II, Borderline Personality Disorder, and ADHD, all of which were evident in every aspect of her life.

Shannon sighed. "Rachel, you're going to end up being kicked out of the program if you keep being late. This isn't a game. You're missing vital information to help with your recovery."

"I totally get it, I do. I just..." she stopped to look at Amalia, "Aww, Mali, what's wrong Kiddo?" she asked. She was only a year or two older than Amalia; but because

Rachel was married and in a really strange love triangle, she always referred to Amalia as Kiddo.

Shannon gave her a pointed look. "You'd know if you'd been here on time."

Rachel, a tangled mass of bags and latte, let out a sigh. "Oh my God, guys, you have no idea what I've been through the past few days." Rachel was on a three day schedule now, so we only saw her Tuesdays, Wednesdays, and Fridays. "So, last time we were together, I told you that I'd decided I was going to work things out with Chris and stay with him since we are married and made a commitment right?" she said while brushing random hair out of her face. "But then guess who blows into town on a weekend leave without notice? You guessed it, Samantha!"

Here's a quick rundown on the Rachel-Chris-Samantha situation. Rachel and Chris had been married for two years. A year before our time at Waterford, Rachel met Samantha who was in the Army Reserves. They fell in love and started having an affair. Rachel swore to leave Chris to go be with Samantha. But when she was confronting Chris, he easily convinced her to dump Rachel to stay with him. When she went to dump Samantha, she just as easily convinced Rachel to stay with her. A year later, the saga continued.

Tracy, another member of our group, who was familiar with the affairs of the heart when it came to another woman, jumped in. "No, you didn't try to end it, Rachel, did you?" We all knew the answer.

Rachel put her right hand up like she was about to swear on the Bible. "Girls, I'm telling you. This time, I was serious. I told Chris that when I went to see Samantha, I'd break it off once and for all. I love my husband and decided I want to be with him. We even discussed having children together. So Friday night, I went to Sam's apartment to see her and she was just so happy to see me. We ordered in takeout, Chinese. I love Chinese food and we sat around the table and talked. Then I told her. I told her 'Sam, I can't do this anymore. I love Chris. So I can't see you anymore. She looked at me with her beautiful blue eyes and said 'Rachel, I love you more than Chris does; and to prove it, I'm going to let you go.' Then she got up and walked away! I couldn't believe it! How could I walk away from a love like that! So I ended up spending the weekend with her. And when I got back to my apartment this morning, things didn't go well with Chris, let me tell you." She shook her head in disbelief.

We all sat there in complete silence and in awe of the story we just heard. You'd think after a month of hearing such stories I'd be accustomed to them but they seemed to get more and more wild as the weeks went on. The only good thing was that it got Amalia to stop crying. Shannon decided she had to take control of the room again. "OK ladies. We've heard Rachel's colorful story. So let's use it as a teaching opportunity. What DBT skill do you recommend she use to deal with her dilemma?" She looked to each one of us for answers.

"Interpersonal Effectiveness, definitely," I answered.

"You might want to throw in some DEAR MAN too," Tracy offered.

"Rachel, your group mates are giving you some great ideas to help work out your issues. I suggest you start exercising these skills before your situation gets out of control," Shannon said, looking at her pointedly.

Rachel took a sip of her latte and shrugged her shoulders nonchalantly. "I guess you're right; but really, what's the worst that could happen?

Can You Hear Me Now?

Every patient was required to see his or her assigned psychiatrist and caseworker once a week. Dr. White was my psychiatrist at Waterford. She was a beautiful African woman who oozed peace and serenity. "Hi Esmene. How are you today?" Dr. White greeted me in her calming voice as I walked into her office.

Dr. White's office always had a calming effect on me. There were no windows in her office and she didn't use bright lighting which made me more comfortable. She used flameless candles and accent lights and the room was scented with essential oils. The atmosphere of her office combined with the melodious tone of her voice soothed my anxieties. "Esmene, last time we met, you were complaining about still hearing voices and how they were interrupting your sleep. I increased your Latuda hoping that would cut down on the chatter. Has it helped any?" she asked.

"Whoa, whoa. Hold on Dr. White. I never said I heard voices. I did say there was a lot of chatter going on in my head. But it's inner dialogue. I don't hear voices. I haven't heard voices since I was a child."

"Are you sure about that?"

"Absolutely. I'd know if I was hearing voices. This is inner dialogue. Everyone has inner dialogue. Mine just won't stop. When I'm ready to sleep, it just wants to keep engaging. I need it to shut up so I can sleep."

Dr. White sat back in her chair and crossed her legs. "Tell me, Esmene, does your inner voice sound like your own?

"No. I know the voices because I've heard them for so long. But is it my voice? No. Depending on the conversation, the voices change; but it's still inner dialogue because we're communicating back and forth. When I heard voices, it was just one-sided."

Dr. White nodded her head. "How long have you been engaging in this inner dialogue?"

I shrugged my shoulders. "For as long as I can remember. It's always been there. Sometimes it's more prominent than at other times but it's always been there in some form. That's why I don't have issues spending so much time alone. I don't feel alone. But sometimes the chatter gets incessant. That's when I can't hear people talking to me over the chatter in my head. It exhausts me. I just need it to quiet down so I can think."

"I see. And has the increase in Latuda helped?"

"I haven't been waking up as much at night, so I think it's helping with my sleep. I can't say I've really noticed much of a difference during the day."

"Well, it's only been a week since the increase, so let's give it another week to see what happens. Now about this inner-dialogue that you have. Tell me more about it."

"What's there to tell? What do you want to know?"

"Well, you said it's not your voice. Who do the voices sound like? What do these inner voices say to you?"

I wondered how I could explain my inner thoughts to someone else. It was such a complicated "relationship" between us. During the day, my inner dialogue could be most helpful. We were friends. When I first encountered the voice, I thought it was the Devil, so I actually ran to my abuser to hide from it. But this inner voice was something different.

In order to help her understand, I recalled the detailed conversation with my inner voice for Dr. White's edification...

<u>Killing Me Softly</u>

Well, I told Dr. White that sometimes I would find myself laughing at the things I would hear. Zeyonna might look at me oddly and say, "Mommy, what are you laughing at?"

"Nothing." I would tell her. For it was truly an inside joke.

It was at night that things would change for me and the voice. The tone of our conversation would become sinister. These are the inner demons I fought with...

I told the voice "I hate you. I'm sure you already know that. Why won't you just leave me alone?"

Come now child, I know you don't mean these words you say...

"Yes I do. All you do is destroy everything. You have robbed me of my happiness, health and sanity. You have even stolen my sleep, hijacked my dreams, and disturbed my peace. This relationship must end."

I take offense to such accusations. You opened the door for me. You invited me in. I have been an honored guest at the table, a trusted companion on your journey. How can you say I stole what you so freely gave?

"I am not that same child. I am a woman now and your services are no longer needed. Can't you see that you're no longer welcome? You are a squatter in my life. I wish you a thousand deaths."

Ahhh, you see, we are one. Great minds really do think alike, for I have such wishes for you also...

"Our minds are nothing alike. Your wishes mean absolutely nothing to me. All you do is steal, kill and destroy. I am not that person. I want to live a life of abundance, a life of joy and happiness, a life that doesn't include you."

I see. I've become the scapegoat for all the troubles in your world? Am I the one who stole your innocence? No. I have different means of seduction that you're far more familiar with. Did I kill your trust with my deceit? No. I've never lied about who I am. I'm the same yesterday, today, and tomorrow. Yet you still welcomed me with open arms and engaged in my bondage. Am I the one who destroyed your faith? Faith in love... Faith in humanity...Faith in YOUR God? As I recall, those things were already destroyed when I arrived. You were a pitiful mess, yet it was I who gifted you the tools you needed to function in your mess. Was it not I who provided you the map to navigate these flaming halls of Hell? And after all I have done for you, my dear sweet child, this is how I'm repaid? I regret to inform you that your compensation is inadequate. I demand much more than your incensed words. I'm disappointed in you. But you are well accustomed to disappointment, are you not? That's another old friend...

"Your disappointment matters not one bit to me. I have plenty of my own, for as you say we are well acquainted. But our relationship is over. I'm giving you your notice to quit. I no longer need nor want your interference. Leave just as swiftly as you came. The door from which you entered is still open..."

What happened to cause such animus feeling between old friends? Ahh yes, I remember a crying, broken child, begging between her gut wrenching sobs for someone, ANYONE to come, pleading for someone to rescue her. Refresh my memory dear. Who was it that came for you...who? You know! It was I, your black knight in coal armour. I plucked you out of your own personal hell. I gave you your liiiifffeee... the same life you are accusing me of destroying. What more could I have given you? What more do you desire of meee..?

"What more do I want from you? There is only one thing you can do for me. Tell me when I will be free of you."

Tsk, tsk... You should know better than to ask questions for which you already know the answer...

"Just tell me! I'm tired of playing this game."

But is this not part of the game that we've played so many times before? We are both aware that you already know the answer which you seek...

"WHEN will you go?! WHEN! When will this end?"

Hahaha! You silly, delightful girl! When will this end? Oh my dear! The answer to your question is really quite simple. This will all end... WHEN YOU DO!

"So, Dr. White," I asked, "does that help explain my inner voice?"

For a long time, Dr. White was speechless.

Undercover, No Longer Underwraps

I was sitting on the couch in the living room enjoying a documentary about the Damsel of Death, Aileen Wuornos. Zander was in the kitchen making a sandwich. "Mom, did you have class today?"

"Yeah." I felt like such a fool. I'd never told my children that I'd been admitted to a psychiatric hospital. When I was admitted to Lincoln, I told them I was taking a psychology class at the local community college. As far as they knew, I was still taking it.

He nodded his head while he continued his sandwich prep. "How much longer are you going to be in school? I'm surprised your class is still in session. It's June." Zeyonna, who was also in the kitchen, co-signed on his observation.

I should have been honest with my children from the beginning. I had long ago disclosed my diagnosis of bipolar to them because I suspected the disorder was hereditary; and I didn't want my children to be in the dark about it like I was, not knowing that they could be at risk for having the disorder. They also knew I had OCD but they didn't understand why I had PTSD. I was forever questioned about the source of my PTSD and they were continually denied an answer. They didn't know about the bulimia as far as I knew, although, according to Nancy, after all these years, they probably knew. I hated to admit it, but she was probably right about that too.

But how could I explain to my children that I had to go to the hospital because I wanted to take my own life? I didn't want them to be burdened with that. I didn't want them to internalize that, to make it about them when it had nothing to do with them. They'd never know I thought my death would give them a better life. I wasn't being fair, though; and I wasn't giving them enough credit. I should have told them. They deserved to know. It was time to put an end to my clandestine activities.

So I got up from my spot on the living room sofa and went into the kitchen to join them at the island. I inhaled deeply and went for it. I said, "Listen kids, there's something I need to tell you, something I should've told you a while ago; but I didn't know how to tell you. I didn't want to hurt either of you and I was embarrassed about it as well."

I was standing next to Zander who looked down at me while chewing on his sandwich like it was a steak and he asked, "What is it?"

I took another deep breath and looked down at the floor. There was some spacing between the tiles I hadn't noticed before. It may have been time to put new flooring down. I'd have to remember to tell Jericho about that when he got home. I looked over to the opposite side of the island where the baby was sitting, her dark eyes wide with innocence and anticipation. Why would I want to ruin that kind of innocence by telling her this?

"Mom, can you get on with it? I have to get ready for work," Zander said with a mouth full of sandwich.

So I got on with it. "I'm not really taking a college course. I was…" My voice trailed off. I didn't want to say the words. I could feel their eyes boring holes into me.

"Mom," Zander said with more patience, "you were what?"

I took a moment to get my thoughts together before I continued on because I knew Zander had to get ready for work. "I was suicidal. I was suicidal and your dad found out. He had me admitted to a mental health facility. I was discharged from there in April and two days later I was admitted to another one. That's where I am now. That's where I go during the day." I looked down as I finished and again wondered when the spacing between the tiles got like that.

After what seemed like an eternity, Zander put his hand on my shoulder to get my attention and said, "Mom, I knew you weren't taking a class. I didn't know where you were going but I guessed it was serious so I didn't say anything."

I looked up at him with eyes as big as saucers. Then I turned to look at Zeyonna.

"Yeah Mommy, I knew you weren't taking a class also, but I figured it must be something serious if you had to lie to us like that. I was kind of scared to know the truth, so I didn't say anything either," she said.

And here I thought I had been so clever! These two had me figured out the whole time. I turned to Zander. "How did you know I wasn't in school? I left here every day with a bookbag. I did homework. How could you have known?"

He shrugged his shoulders. "Easy. You were coloring," he said nonchalantly.

"I was coloring?" I said confused.

"You were coloring," he repeated.

"And how did coloring help you figure out I wasn't taking a college course?"

Zander turned toward me then. "Mom, I've known you all my life. I've never seen you pick up a crayon, marker, or colored pencil to color anything. Even when we were little, you didn't color with us. Now all of a sudden you have these adult coloring books with markers and colored pencils and you're coloring. I knew something was wrong," he explained.

Zander was right. I was never encouraged to color as a child. It was seen as beneath me. I was too intelligent to waste my time on coloring. And it was something I never encouraged in my children, although my daughter had somehow become a fabulous artist. Her talent was natural. Art therapy at the hospital is what encouraged me to color. It helped me to relax, to relieve stress. And here as I thought I had covered my tracks, I had given myself away with a coloring book and some markers.

I looked over at my baby. "And what about you Little Miss?" I asked with a smirk on my face.

"You were really sad and Daddy seemed scared. I knew something was wrong. I just didn't know what, but I knew it had nothing to do with a class. I mean, you're a nerd. Nerds don't get sad about school," she said softly.

It was a proud mommy moment. My kids were so smart. But now I needed to know something. "Well Zander, now that you know, how do you feel about it?"

Zander stood to his full six feet and took a big gulp of his cranberry juice before answering. "I'm glad you reached out and got the help you needed," was all he said but that was all he really needed to say. Zander wasn't much for words but I heard in his brief conclusion everything he didn't say. He tossed his empty juice bottle in the recycle bin, patted me on the head, and went to get ready for work.

Zeyonna was still sitting at the island. "And what about you Baby? What do you have to say about it?" I asked Zeyonna.

Looking me straight in the eye she said, "I think what you're doing is very brave. A lot of people have problems and they don't reach out to get help. You did and I know that was really hard for you. But you did it and I'm really proud of you for that," she said seriously.

And that's when the tears began to flow. It was a beautiful thing to be told by my children that they were proud of me. I no longer regretted waiting until that moment to tell my children the truth. It happened just the way it was meant to. I went over and gave my little one a hug and a kiss, silently letting her know that I was going to be OK and for her not to worry. She hugged me back. "Come on, you want to help me color?" I asked my little Picaso.

Zeyonna gave me a bent up face. "No offence Mommy; but now that everything's out in the open, your coloring needs some work. It's so flat. No depth or dimension to it. You really need to learn how to do some shading too. You work with just one color. There's no creativity there. Where's the pop? Where's the wow factor? You know, art really needs to…"

Oh lord what had I just done? Coloring was about to get stressful!

Reality Checks and Balances

Back at Waterford, Bree, who always appeared to be in a good mood, was starting a class. "Ladies, I am Bree, and today is May 29th, 2019. How is everyone today?" We collectively mumbled an unrecognizable response which all the facilitators were accustomed to. Bree carried on. "Girls, let me tell you. I went to Target last night, you know, just to get some dog food; and guess what I found? Esmene you're going to love this!" She said with a gleam in her eyes. Bree loved Target. No session was complete without one of her Target stories.

"What is it?" I asked.

She could barely contain her excitement. "A set of Golden Girls refrigerator magnets! As soon as I saw them I was thinking Oh my God, I have got to get these. Wait until I tell Es about these babies. I wanted to give you one; but we have rules here against that, so I took a picture for you," she said as she passed over her phone so I could see the magnets.

Bree and I shared a love for all things Golden Girls. I used to watch Golden Girls on Saturday nights with my Aunt Marie and Delilah when she lived with us. She, in turn, would watch the Facts of Life with me and Delilah. It was a special time for us with our beloved Aunt. Both shows still hold a special place in my heart. My spirits were lifted. "Bree these are cool," I said. "On break I'm going to see if they're at my local Target. I've got to get a set to add to my collection of Golden Girls memorabilia." I slid her phone back over to her. That gave me something to look forward to.

"Absolutely. No collection would be complete without them. Now, back to business ladies. Her voice took on a serious tone. Today we are going to talk about what may be one of the most difficult skills in DBT, radical acceptance." But just then hurricane Rachel breezed through the door. Bree looked at the time. "Well you're only a minute late today. I guess that's an improvement," she said, teasing evident in her voice.

Rachel didn't look like she was in the mood for teasing. Her skin was all red and blotchy like she'd been crying all night. Her hair was in a wet, messy bun and she had her glasses on, not her contacts. And if I wasn't mistaken, those may have been her husband's inside out sweatpants she was swimming in. Bree wisely decided to let Rachel be and moved on with the lesson. "So, as I was saying, we are going to talk about radical acceptance. Who can tell me what radical acceptance is?" Bree looked around for volunteers.

Tracy spoke up, "It's accepting something in your mind, heart, and body, accepting it totally and completely."

"That's right Tracy. It's when you stop fighting reality because it's not what you want and accept reality for what it is. Tracy, can you think of anything in your life that you need to radically accept?" Bree asked.

Tracy sat quiet for a few moments. But then she started to nod her head yes. "My girlfriend, Amy. I love her, but I don't think she's good for me mentally. When things don't go her way, she threatens suicide and that gets me scared because I don't know if she's serious or not. I think I need to radically accept that we shouldn't be together anymore but I keep holding onto her." Tracy ended on a sad note.

Bree nodded her head in understanding. "Tracy, do you know why you won't let Amy go if you know she's not good for you?"

"Because I'll be sad and lonely and feel guilty for hurting her. I don't want to sit with those feelings." She began to cry then. Elaine moved her seat over to offer her comfort. Elaine was good at that.

"That was good Tracy. We're going to come back to you. Thank you for sharing," Bree said sympathetically.

"OK, anyone else wants to share something they need to radically accept?"

"I need to accept that I can't keep both my husband and my girlfriend, even though I love them both," Rachel said in a soft voice.

We all nodded our heads in agreement. "Go on," Bree encouraged.

"My girlfriend, Sam, wants to move to Texas; and she wants me to go with her. As soon as she asked me, it felt so right to say yes without hesitation. But when I went home to tell my husband, he was so sad and upset. And my heart was breaking because, honestly, I didn't want to leave him. I was going to miss him and wished there was a way I could take him with me. He begged me not to leave him. He cried. And while he was crying on my shoulder, I realized I can't keep them both. I have to let one go. But who do I choose?" Rachel lamented, looking towards us as if we had the answer.

Bree shook her head. "Rachel, only you can make that decision. It sounds like you need to make it soon. Maybe today's lesson will help you." Bree turned towards me. "Esmene, what about you? What do you need to radically accept?"

I looked down at the table. The list of things was so long. How to pick just one? However, there was an issue that had bubbled to the surface now that Uncle had reappeared in my life and that was causing me much distress. "I guess I would have to say that I need to accept that I still care for my abuser. I think about good times that we shared in the past and I miss that person. I still love that person but I hate what he did to me and how he hurt me. How can I love someone who violated me the way he did?" I asked, still not looking up.

Bree leaned over towards me and stretched her hand out so it was near mine to get my attention. "Esmene, what you're feeling is very common when it comes to abuse of a child by a family member. It's called trauma bonding. I want you to know that you can have feelings of love towards the person who did those things to you and at the same time have feelings of hate towards that person. That's what's called a dialectic, the interaction of conflicting ideas, that two opposite things can be true. You can both love and hate someone but that doesn't lessen you as a person. It just means you're a human being; and, yes, it's something that you need to radically accept," she finished. I finally looked up at her and she offered me a smile.

"Elaine, what about you?" Bree asked. Elaine blew an errant hair out of her face, "I know I need to radically accept that my husband is gone forever and there's nothing I can do to change that. I'm still alive and I don't have to feel guilty about living." Elaine's husband Darren was tragically killed two years ago by a drunk driver going the wrong way down a one way street.

Bree gave an encouraging smile, "Good Elaine. And Amalia, what about you sweetie? Is there anything you need to radically accept?" Amalia, hidden behind her golden hair, shrugged her thin shoulders and then shook her head in the negative. I reached over and moved her silk sheath of hair away from her face. She settled her sad, green eyes on me. "Amalia," Bree tried again, "there has to be something you need to work on accepting."

Amalia, still looking at me, nodded her head in the affirmative.

"What is it?" Bree encouraged.

As one solitary tear made its way down her angelic face. She said, "I have to accept that I'll never be the same girl I was ever again. My life is forever changed, all because I trusted the wrong people." Amalia was pledging a sorority and went to a party with the other pledges at a fraternity house. One of the fraternity brothers was actually someone she knew. He gave her a drink and not too long after she started to feel ill. He offered her his room so she could lie down and rest. He waited until she was almost out of it, came in, and raped her. The door was left open a bit, so people, including some of the pledges, walked by and saw what was happening; but no one intervened.

I brought Amalia's head to rest on my shoulder, saying, "Baby girl, you know what happened to you wasn't your fault, don't you?"

"We both know that's not how it feels, Esme," she whispered softly. I couldn't argue with that.

The class continued and was coming to an end. Bree looked at her phone. "OK, ladies, before we break, just a few things about radical acceptance. Radical acceptance is not approval or compassion. You're not making light of what happened. I hear that a lot. Continuing to reject reality doesn't change it. Pain can't be avoided. Pain is a part of life. However," she said, looking at my scarred wrist and lifting her eyes up to meet mine," life can be worth living even with painful events in it. "

"It's break time ladies. Meet you back here in ten minutes."

From the Ridiculous to the Sublime

On Thursday that week, I was on my way to see Dr. White for my weekly session. I had been struggling with my feelings recently and I wasn't sure what to do about it. I was hoping Dr. White could give me some insight. When I got to her office the door was already open. "Hello, Esmene, how are you doing today?" Dr. White greeted me in her soothing voice. She wasn't fooling me. I was on to her.

"I'm really sad. I'm having a hard time adjusting to life without bulimia," I explained.

"Life without bulimia. What does that mean?"

"Ever since you implanted subliminal messages in my head to stop me from binging and purging, things are different. I don't even have the urge to do it anymore, no desire to do it. It's like my best friend died. I feel like I'm in mourning," I sobbed.

"Wait a minute, Esmene," Dr. White said. "Why do you think I used subliminal messages to get you to stop binging and purging?"

"Well, you said you were going to start me on a new medication that *may* have the side effect of stopping my bulimic behavior. I took one dose of this so-called medication after leaving your office and bam! Gone after one dose. I haven't had the urge to engage since then. Trust me, I've tried. No medication works that fast. You had to have implanted some kind of a message when you said you were going to give me the medication. The medication was just a placebo, right?"

"Esmene, I didn't implant any subliminal messages to stop you from engaging in bulimic behaviors. That would be unethical," Dr. White assured me. "However, I'm glad to hear that you're not engaging in those harmful behaviors anymore. But you're upset about it, so talk to me about how you feel," she encouraged.

My tears began to flow. "I feel abandoned. No matter what I was going through in life, food has been there. It's been my constant, whether I was binging it or purging it. Now, it's not there. The desire for it is gone. There's a hole that's been left that nothing can fill. I feel the emptiness deep down in my soul. I feel the loss. It feels like I lost a dear friend, like an actual person. It's gone. You took it away and there's nothing I can do about it!"

"Esmene, the binging and purging was causing you medical problems and could have possibly killed you over time. You know bulimia or any eating disorder isn't really about food. It's about all the issues you don't really want to deal with. Is that what this is about? Now that you don't have the bulimia to run to, all the things that you've buried are starting to come to the surface and you don't like that? You don't want to deal with them? You don't want to acknowledge the truth? How long are you going to let your past steal your future?" she asked.

"You don't understand. You don't know how much it hurts to think about what was done to me, how I did nothing to protect myself. I let him do what he did and I never said anything to anybody, even when I knew better. I have to live with that guilt!" I exclaimed.

"Esmene, you were a child, a child who was confused because someone you loved was hurting you and taking advantage of you. He was the adult. He was wrong for what he did. Stop punishing yourself for what he did to you. Let the memories, the feelings, come to the surface. Confront them, acknowledge them. Accept that it happened and they can't hurt you anymore. You can move on with your life. No more guilt. No more condemnation. Haven't you punished yourself enough?"

I was full on crying by then. "I just don't want any of it anymore. I want peace. For once in my life, I just want some peace..."

"And what does that mean?" When I just shook my head, Dr. White pressed on. "Esmene, what do you mean by you just want peace? Are you talking about eternal peace?"

I sighed. "My mind, Dr. White. I want my mind to be at peace. You have no idea what it's like to be inside my head. It's so loud sometimes."

Dr. White nodded her head in understanding. "Esmene, please believe me that I didn't plant some subliminal message in your brain to stop your bulimic behaviors. The medication worked and it worked fast. Let's take this opportunity to deal with the emotions that are coming to the surface now that bulimia is out of the way. We'll go slowly. Can you work with me on that?"

"Yes. Yes, I guess so," I agreed.

"Esmene, do you feel that you're safe? You have no plans to harm yourself, do you?" she asked in all seriousness.

"No, Dr. White. I have no plans to harm myself." And for once I didn't .

"Alright Esmene. I want you to keep a journal of the things that come up in the next week that you would like to talk about in our next session. If it's something really distressing, you can always put in for a special session with me or Casey, OK?"

"OK Dr. White."

She smiled at me. "No more subliminal messages, alright?"

I had to smile at that. "No more subliminal messages."

<u>When Doves Cry</u>

It was a steamy Friday at Waterford in June and we were well into the second half of our session. I was hot, tired, and distracted by the fairly large group of the facilitators gathering in the hall, along with Dr. White. They looked nervous or upset. Every now and then, one of them would make eye contact with one of us in the room and then quickly look away. Casey was our facilitator that day and she was sitting with her back towards the door. She was missing all the action. "What's going on that has you all so focused on the hallway?" she asked as she finally turned around in her chair.

Elaine spoke up. "They started gathering out there about ten minutes ago. First it was just two of them. Then more joined in. Then Dr. White and the director came out. Something's wrong. We can tell," Elaine explained.

We could tell Casey was now intrigued also but it was her job to keep us calm. "I'm sure it's nothing. Let's focus back on our lesson for today." She tried to redirect us back to our lesson.

Just then the door opened up and Dr. White popped her head in. "Good Morning ladies. Casey, may I speak to you. It's urgent," was all she said. Casey got up to go into the hall, but before she left, she gave us a mindfulness exercise to do. We had to pass the soccer ball around and name a celebrity whose name started with the letter our finger landed on. None of us was really very mindfully doing the exercise. We were too busy trying to pick up clues about what had happened. We knew it was something bad. After speaking with the director, Casey turned the color of a tomato and walked away from the group. We gave up on tossing the ball. I felt like I had a brick in my stomach.

"I'm scared Esme," Amalia said. "Why would they stand out there like that and keep looking at us and not say anything? They're making me angry" she exclaimed. Her small hands balled up into fists. I held her fist in my hand to try to calm her down. After a few minutes, I felt her fingers uncurl and wrap around mine. She, in turn, grabbed Elaine's hand and Elaine grabbed Tracy's hand. We all just sat and waited.

Casey eventually made her way back to the group in the hall and within a few minutes Casey and Dr. White made their way into the room. It was evident Casey had been crying. Whatever it was, it was bad. "Ladies," Dr. White addressed us in a shaky voice, "I have some upsetting news to share with you. I received a call this morning from the local police. There was an incident involving Rachel. Apparently, when she and her husband returned to their apartment last night, Rachel's friend Samantha ambushed them and shot them both. Then Samantha turned the gun on herself. All three were pronounced dead at the scene.

We didn't believe her. Casey turned and fled the room. She just couldn't stay. Elaine spoke up. "Rachel's dead?"

I moaned. "It just can't be. She was just here yesterday. No. Not Rachel."

An anguished cry escaped from between Amalia's lips, as sobs wracked her small body. I held her as she cried, too stunned to do anything else. I looked over at Elaine and Tracy, who were leaning on each other, trying to hold back tears.

Dr. White silently slid into the seat that was formerly occupied by Casey. I thought I saw tears on her face.

It was of no use. We had to radically accept that our beloved Rachel was gone.

Breathe Again

I was on my way to one of the conference rooms to meet Casey. It would be our last meeting. The door to the room was cracked when I got there, so I tapped on it lightly to get her attention. She turned and smiled and waved me in. "Are you excited about today?" Casey asked with a bit of sadness in her voice.

Today was my discharge day; and although I was excited to finally be discharged after seven months of hospitalization, I would be lying if I said I wasn't going to miss this place and miss her. "I am excited but I'm really going to miss you and Dr. White. I'm going to miss being here and all of the support everyone here has given me. It's a different world outside of these walls. I always feel safer in here," I said honestly.

Casey gave me an understanding look. "Esmene, you know we're always going to be here to help you. And we're going to miss you so much. You've been one of the most entertaining patients that we've had in a long time. Watching your progress has been amazing. I am so proud of you," she said with a smile.

"Thank you Casey."

Casey took a deep breath and sat back in her chair. "Well, as you probably already know, I have a stack of paperwork to go over with you. Then you'll have your final session with Dr. White. But before we get into that, I have something for you," she said with a gleam in her eyes.

"Really? What is it?"

Casey moved forward towards me and opened her hand that had been held in a fist. In it was a beautiful black stone that had the word "Breathe" etched in white on it. "It's beautiful," I sighed.

"I'm glad you like it. I saw this and immediately thought of you. When you first arrived, you were so reactive to situations. Your anger consumed you and that caused you lot of problems in your life. Now when situations happen, you use your skills. You literally STOP, assess the situation, and consult with yourself before you react or respond. Esmene, now you take the time to breathe. You had never done that before and what a difference it's made in your life. I want you to know we're all so proud of you and the progress you've made over these fifteen weeks," she said softly.

"Thank you," was all I could croak out without dissolving into a mess of tears as she gently placed the stone into my open palm. The stone was cool and smooth against my hand. Casey was right. I'd learned how to breathe under stress for the first time since early childhood and it HAD made all the difference.

"OK, so I know you can't wait to go over this paperwork so..." she said trying to lighten the heavy emotion in the room.

I smiled at her effort to make things less awkward for me. "Yeah so, come on. Let's see how many times you're going to make me sign my life away to you this time," I joked with a smile. We both laughed as Casey pulled out my pile of freedom papers. And, at my final meeting with Dr. White, I was so relieved she didn't tease me about subliminal messages.

All in Your Mind

I had been out of Waterford for a little over a month. I thought things would be different for me now, that I would finally be normal. But as I sat waiting for my appointment with Nancy, I could feel the bile churning in my belly. I was sweating despite the coolness of the day. My jaw hurt from the constant clenching of my teeth. My hands were indented with the imprints of my nails digging into them. I was on the verge of tears. I had to get help. I could stay silent no longer.

"Esmene, come on back, "Nancy greeted me with a smile. I weakly nodded my head and followed Nancy into her office. I plopped down on her usually comfy sofa. Today it felt like a stone slab and I sat ramrod straight. Nancy settled in her chair across from me. "Is something wrong with your hands?" she asked me.

I was once again digging my nails into my battered hands. I could withstand it no more. "Nancy, you have to help me. It's Dina. She's not who we think she is. She's not a psychiatrist."

Nancy looked at me confused. "Well who is she then?"

"Dina's a government plant, put in place by the hospital to keep tabs on me; and I know that at my next appointment she's going to try to have me put back into the hospital!" I blurted out. Tears started streaming down my face and Nancy collapsed back in her chair with her mouth open.

Dina was the psychiatrist Waterford Behavioral Center referred me to after discharge. Dr. Diane had retired while I was in the program at Lincoln. I really liked Dina...at first. But then I began to notice some things, things that didn't add up in my mind; and extreme paranoia started to take over. So I started putting the pieces together and then I figured it out. The reason why the hospital sent me to her is because she was an agent working for Social Security. It wouldn't look good for the government if they let a disabled patient leave the hospital and become a liability. They needed to keep an eye on me and they sent Dina to do it. I'd been having some issues the last few weeks, so I anticipated that at my appointment on Monday they were going to be waiting to take me back. I couldn't let that happen.

Nancy was still looking at me in awe. "Esmene, what makes you think Dina is some kind of government plant? What evidence do you have?"

This was the big chance for Detective Esmene. "Nancy, it's supposed to be a psychiatrist office, right? But it's at the top of a long flight of steps on the side of a building. What real psychiatrist would have an office there? Suicidal patients could easily throw themselves down the steps or over the side onto the cement below. When you go to the office, there's nothing permanent. There's no computer on the desk, just a laptop. There's no office phone. The receptionist uses a cell phone. The office is very generic. It could be any kind of office really. And why do I never see any other patients there? I've never seen another person in the waiting room, never even heard another person's voice. And whenever I call the office for anything, I always get the voicemail. Then, miraculously, I get a call back in ten minutes, like the receptionist is screening her calls."

Nancy continued to look at me with interest. Good, I thought. I really had her attention now so I continued. "Then there's her office. Again, there's nothing that says that's 'her' office. She never uses the desk, there's no computer, just her laptop, no pictures, no pens, pencils, nothing. And the office phone is in a weird place. The desk is on the side by the door, but the office phone is all the way on the other side of the room by the window. Why wouldn't you have the phone on the desk?"

"I don't know," Nancy said.

"But here's the kicker. Are you ready?" Nancy nodded and I continued. "She told me to watch a movie titled <u>A Beautiful Mind</u>. She said when I watched it, she thought that I'd be able to relate to the main character. We had a lot in common. Have you ever seen the movie?"

"Yes, I have," Nancy answered calmly.

"So OK, you see what I'm getting at, don't you?"

"No, Esmene, I don't actually," Nancy answered.

"How can you not...oh wait! I forgot to tell you about the emails! My bad. So yeah, every time Walgreens fills my prescriptions, I get these emails saying there's a problem filling my script because they can't verify the prescriber. SHE'S the prescriber! They can't verify who she is because she's not real! Then the government fixes it so I can get my meds. In the movie John Nash interacts with all these people who aren't even real. They're people his mind has created. I think that was her way of telling me that she wasn't real. That's what Nash and I had in common. She told on herself, not realizing I would figure her out. Or maybe she was warning me because she likes me. I don't know. Nancy, you have to help me!" I pleaded, completely exhausted from my diatribe.

Nancy sat silent for a few moments, then moved her chair closer to me and looked me in my eyes. "Esmene, how long have you thought this about Dina?"

"Maybe the last three weeks."

"Why didn't you say anything sooner?"

"I needed evidence. No one would believe me without evidence."

"Where are the emails you've been getting from Walgreens?" she asked.

"I tried to print them out, but I couldn't find them this morning. The government must have them on some kind of self-destruct timer so they can't be traced."

"OK, Esmene, OK." Nancy turned to her computer and then started typing, something she never does when I'm there.

"Esmene, I just typed in Dina's name and all her credentials came up on the physician's search. She's a real person, a real doctor."

"Ha!" I laughed. "Like the government can't plant that information. They had to know I would figure it out and they were ready. During my first appointment, she told me I was smart, brilliant even. She told them that so they probably knew I would figure her out and they had to get a dossier ready,"

"A dossier ready? Esmene, honey, you know me. You trust me, right?"

"Yes," I said because I did trust her.

"I'm going to call Dina. I'm going to bring up all these concerns you have and I'm going to make sure that she's real. No one is going to take you away to the hospital on your next visit. OK?"

I started to cry again. "Nancy, you don't believe me do you?"

"Esmene, I believe that you believe everything that you've told me. So yes, I believe you. I also believe you're experiencing some psychosis and that has me very concerned. I would prefer for you to see your psychiatrist as soon as possible; but since your psychiatrist is the cause of your concern, that wouldn't be the best option right now. Maybe a phone call will have to do. Do you think you could talk to her on the phone? Would you be OK with that?" Nancy asked gently.

"Yeah, I guess so. As long as it's really her," I mumbled in agreement.

Later that day, my phone rang from a private number. I ignored it. I didn't do private numbers. If a person wanted to remain private, I respected their privacy. Within a minute the phone rang again from a private number and I thought this might be the call I was waiting for.

"Hello," I answered hesitantly.

"Esmene? Esmene it's me, Dina," came the cheery voice over the phone. It was too cheery. She was trying to get me to lower my defenses.

"This is Dina? Dina the psychiatrist?" I asked.

"Yes sweetie, this is Dina, your psychiatrist. Listen, I just got off the phone with Nancy and we're both really concerned about you. Will you do something for me?" she asked.

That depended on what it was. "What do you want me to do?"

"Honey, I need you to go get some blood work done. I want to see where your Lamictal levels are. I'll send the order over to the lab for you. Can you do that for me in the next day or two?"

"I can go first thing tomorrow morning," I assured her. I never had a problem getting blood work done.

"OK, Esmene, thank you. I don't want you to worry about anything. Nancy and I are going to take care of you and get this all worked out. We just need to find out what's going on with you. OK?" she tried to assure me.

"I'll get the blood work done tomorrow," I responded. That was about all the assurance I could offer her at the time.

I heard her sigh. "OK, Esmene. I'll call you with the results. Call me...no, call Nancy if you need anything." And with that she hung up.

It looked like Dina got the message loud and clear. Three days later my phone rang from a private number. I assumed it was Dina so I answered this time. Dina greeted me. "Good Morning Esmene, it's Dina. How are you feeling?"

"I'm alright," I didn't ask her how she was, not really caring how she was doing. I wasn't in the mood for being polite.

"Well Esmene, right now I'm really alarmed. I just got your blood work results back and your Lamictal levels are zero percent. There are no traces of the drug in your system. Are you taking your meds?"

How dare she, I thought. She set me up! This was another part of her plot to get me put back in the hospital and I wasted no time in telling her. "What kind of games are you playing, Dina? I knew this was a setup. You may have Nancy fooled but I have you all figured out. That's why you wanted to send the lab request electronically so I couldn't see what you were testing for. They probably didn't even test for Lamictal! I got out of that hospital fair and square and there's no reason why anyone should be trying to take me back," I yelled into the phone.

"Esmene...ESMEME!" Dina said sharply to get my attention.

"WHAT?" I yelled back.

"Esmene," she said more mildly, trying to get a hold of the situation, "Esmene, can you please do me a favor?" she asked.

I took a deep breath to try and calm my erratically beating heart. "What?"

"Good, thank you. Can you get your bottle of Lamictal? Tell me the date you got them and count how many pills are in the bottle. Can you do that for me?" she coaxed gently.

"Yeah, I can do that. Hold on second." I went to the kitchen cabinet which held all of my daytime meds and pulled out the bottle of Lamictal. As I was looking for the date the script was filled, I noticed all these lines someone had drawn on the bottle like they were keeping score of a game or something, along with little notes like smells funny, look diff and taste nasty. What the heck, I wondered. I grabbed my Prozac and saw the same thing. I grabbed the Latuda. It, too, was also the same. Why had I never noticed this before? I touched these bottles every day. I know I did. I remembered it clearly as anything. Then I remembered the phone.

"Dina, I have the bottle. The prescription was filled August 24th," I told her.

"OK," she said, "today is September 12th. Go ahead and count how many pills you have left in the bottle."

"There's something wrong with this bottle, actually with all my medicine bottles," I told her.

"What do you mean something is wrong with your bottles? What's wrong with them?"

"They have lines on them, like someone was keeping score of a game; and they have little notes written all over the labels,' I explained.

I heard her inhale deeply. "What do the notes say Esmene?" she asked.

I cleared my throat. "Taste nasty. Look different. Smells funny. Different color. Wet," I rattled off.

"Wet?" she repeated.

"Uh huh, wet."

"Count the Lamictal, Esmene," Dina directed.

"OK." I counted out the pills in my bottle, one by one, very slowly. Then I counted them again. "Dina, I have twenty-one pills left." This, even with my terrible math skills, meant I hadn't been taking my medication as prescribed.

"Now we're going to repeat this same process with your other meds, one by one, OK?"

"OK." And so I did, emptying each bottle and counting out each pill. The results all came back the same. I hadn't been taking my medication.

I heard a deep inhale and then a long exhale. "Esmene, I need you to take the top off of the Lamictal and Prozac. I need you to take one pill from each bottle and place them in your hand," she told me gently.

I was scared now and I had started to panic because now the realization had dawned on me. Something wasn't right and that something was me. "Esmene, do you have three pills in your hand, one out of each bottle?"

"Yes," I said between sniffles.

"Everything's going to be OK, Esmene. Stay with me. Now Esmene, I need you to get something you like to drink and take those three pills. All three," she directed me over the phone. I got my water and quickly washed the three pills down. They were nasty and wet when the water mixed with them.

"Esmene, did you swallow all three?" Dina asked.

"Yes," I answered honestly.

"Good. Good," she said, sounding relieved, "About what time do you usually eat dinner?"

"Maybe five-thirty or six o'clock."

"I need you to set an alarm on your phone for every night at six o'clock to remind you to take your Latuda. It's very important that you take that every evening and you have to take it with at least three hundred and fifty calories. So that's why I'm telling you to take it with dinner. Every day Esmene. Now is Jericho still managing your nighttime meds?"

"Yes. He fills up the pill box a week at a time so I don't get confused but he lets me do the day meds because I leave for work before he does. I thought I could handle them." I started to cry.

"And you can Esmene. You just got off track. You take a lot of medication in one day. You need help keeping track of it. Do the same thing with your morning meds that you do with your nighttime ones. Put them in a pill box for a week at a time and keep them where you can see them. Set reminders or put notes up to remind you to take them. Get the family involved in reminding you. Your children aren't babies. There's no reason why they can't step up and help you with this."

"My kids shouldn't have to remind me to take my meds," I said adamantly.

"Stop 'shouldn't' on yourself. You need help. Let them help you. They want to help you. Look at where you are right now? Is it worth it?" I had no answer. "Esmene, you're experiencing psychosis. I know what you believe seems real. I know you believe it. I'm not going to try to convince you I'm not a government agent. I'm just asking you to take your medication. It's the same medication the hospital was prescribing you and you were doing well. Please, please, please...take your meds. Morning, evening and night. Can you do that?"

"I can do that for you," I said.

"No, do it for yourself, not me," she said. "Now one more thing. Do you feel safe?

"Yes."

"Do you feel like you might harm yourself or anyone else in any way?"

I answered honestly, "No."

"In the event that you did feel unsafe or that you might want to hurt yourself or someone else, would you commit to calling the Crisis Hotline or 911?" I said nothing. "Esmene, please don't make me escalate this."

"Yes, I commit to call Crisis or 911. Yes," I assured her.

"OK, thank you. Now I'm going to get in touch with Jericho, just to let him know what's going on because you don't have the best track record of keeping people informed of what's happening when it comes to your health. Now we have an appointment on Monday. If you have any issues before then, call me or Nancy immediately. Do you understand Esmene?" I hated when she talked to me like I was deficient.

"Yes, Dina, I understand," I said, enunciating every word to get my point across.

Another sigh. "Alright, Esmene, I'll see you Monday."

<u>Memories</u>

One afternoon I was confronted with this Facebook post:
ABUSE IS NOT RIGHT AT ANY AGE.

Normally it wouldn't have been a problem because I
wholeheartedly in agreement with that sentiment. My
problem was Uncle was the person who posted it. Uncle, it
seemed, had a convenient case of Alzheimer's disease
when it came to the atrocities he committed in his lifetime. I
was seething with rage. How could he? How dare he? But
of course he would. He was Uncle. He could do whatever
he wanted to do.

I tried to let it go. I tried to use my DBT skill from the
hospital and "ride the wave" of emotions that threatened to
overtake me and drown me but my OCD kicked into high
gear. The button was stuck on my mental tape player and
the words just kept running over and over in my head,
blending in with the distortions he had sown and cultivated
so long ago. I decided there was only one way to deal with
this. I needed to confront him. I didn't have his number, so I
called Mom to ask her. I was praying she wouldn't want to
know why I was calling him.

"Mom, do you have Uncle's number?" I asked her.

"Oh that's so nice. You're going to give him a call and
check on him. He's been asking about you."

I bet that sick bastard has been asking about me, I
thought. "Yes, I'm going to check him." I said, knowing my
mother wouldn't catch on to what was on my mind.

Mom gave me his number and I promptly hung up. I
went over to the cabinet and got my Vistaril. I usually didn't
take it during the day, even though I could take it up to four
times a day. I was always afraid I was going to get
addicted to something. But today was different. Today I
needed it. I took two and gave myself a half hour for them
to get into my system before I made the call. Who knew,

maybe I would talk myself out of it. Maybe I wouldn't. I didn't.

"Well this is a pleasurable surprise," Uncle said when he answered the phone. He had no need to say hello or inquire who was on the other end. Uncle probably had caller ID and probably memorized it when he got my number two years before.

I didn't bother with making small talk. I got right to the point. "I have a question to ask you. I saw that post you put up on Facebook about abuse not being right at any age."

"Yeah. What about it?"

"If abuse isn't right at any age, what about what you did to me?" I asked angrily. I heard him chuckle. My blood ran cold.

"What about it?" His voice was just as cold.

"What do you mean what about it? That was abuse and you didn't seem to have a problem with it," I pointed out to him.

"Baby Girl that wasn't real abuse. People who go through real abuse usually end up committing suicide. You're still here, so it couldn't have been that bad."

"Couldn't have been that bad?"

"Exactly."

I took a deep breath and counted to ten. I reminded myself I needed answers and pushed forward. "Why me? You didn't do this to my other siblings, did you?" recalling the incident with Braxton so long ago. I didn't know if I wanted the answer to be yes or no and I felt guilty about that.

"No, no I didn't. I only liked them. You were different. Besides, you were just right for me. Not too young, not too old." This bastard was proud of what he had done.

"But what would possess you to do that to me in the first place?" I wanted to know.

"Well Baby Girl, as Prince said, maybe I'm just like my father. He was a bastard. So am I," he said solemnly.

"Don't you feel any kind of remorse for what you did?"

"No, not really. Things were different back then. It wasn't called abuse. Besides, you lived through it and look at us now having a conversation like two old friends."

This man had lost his mind. "What made you stop?" I desperately wanted to know. My voice, though, was devoid of any emotion.

"You got too old. Was being hard headed. Wasn't appealing any more." I hated to admit it, but that hurt my pride for some reason and that made me feel sick. "Listen Baby Girl, if it makes you feel any better, it was nothing personal, OK. I think the problem here is that you need to work on your forgiveness. The Lord's Prayer tells us 'And forgive us our debts, as we have forgiven our debtors.' Having strife in your life gives place to the devil. I'm surprised at you. I would think you of all people would know better."

"I…you...forgive? What?" I was dumbfounded. I couldn't even put a sentence together.

"I think instead of wasting your time on Facebook, you could spend that time working on forgiving me. I know you go see those shrinks, so talk it over with them and see what they think. I'm sure you've told them plenty about me as it is. When you're ready to forgive me, I'll be waiting. But it's been too long for you to keep obsessing over this. Maybe it's because you've got mental problems. Could that be it? Or are you going to blame me for those too? Regardless, I bet if you forgave me, you wouldn't even have those problems anymore. And while you're at it, forgive yourself too."

"Forgive myself?" I screeched incredulously.

"Yeah. Don't act like you didn't play a part in all of it. If what I was doing was so bad, why didn't you ever tell anyone? You were a big girl, a smart girl. You knew the difference between right and wrong. You could've easily gone to your mom or Delilah and told them. Sometimes they were right there in the house. You never made a sound. Here we are thirty years later and you still pointing fingers. Now what you got to say about that?" he laughed into the phone.

    I hung up.

<u>Puppy Love</u>

For months, the kids, Jericho, and I watched the same little matted pup run through our front yard just about every day. Despite its unkempt appearance, he was a cute little Yorkie who looked like he desperately needed some TLC. We watched him roam the neighborhood all summer but I began to get concerned when the weather turned colder. So one day, I tried to lure him into the house with some bologna. "Come on puppy. Come get the food," I said in that voice that is reserved for people who talk to dogs. The puppy was untrusting, so he would only get close enough to grab the meat quickly and then run off.

Zander called from the doorway, "Mom, give it a rest. The dog doesn't like you."

"Be quiet. He's just scared is all. Come on puppy," I continued to coax, but then a cat appeared across the street and I lost my audience.

A few days later, I saw a Facebook post by a former classmate who lived down the street stating that she actually caught the dog and was returning it to the owner who was her neighbor. I was glad. It was getting colder and the puppy was small. It was too cold for him to be outside.

About two weeks later, I saw what looked like the same puppy in my front yard again. I wasn't sure because this dog didn't look as matted and was in better condition. I sent my friend a message via Facebook. *Hi Nita, did you return that puppy to its owner? There is a dog in my yard right now who looks like him.*

Yes, I returned him but he's out again. My husband just texted me because he was in our backyard. When I returned him, the owner swore he would keep him in the house. I'm going over there when I get off of work.

Later that evening, I received a message from my friend. *Mama, I have the dog. I took him back to the owner and his wife doesn't want the dog. She told me I could keep him. I brought him to my house but I have three dogs and they're beating him up. Can you come get him?*

I didn't know how this was going to go over with Jericho but I couldn't just leave this puppy out in the cold. *I'll be right there.* I wrote

Jericho protested. "You're going to bring some dog in this house that's been on the streets for months! The thing could be flea infested or have rabies! I don't want that thing in this house!"

"I'm with Daddy," Zeyonna said. "You don't know where that dog's been."

I continued to put my shoes on as I listened to their concerns. "Listen, I'm going to bring him here and put him in the basement. When I get home from work tomorrow, I'll take him to the shelter, OK?" I got mumbeld responses from both of them, but Zeyonna got up to follow me out to the car.

It took thirty seconds to drive to the corner. My friend was out there waiting, her tiny four foot nine frame bundled up against the cold. "Hey Nita. Sorry it took so long. Where's the puppy?" I asked.

"Hey Mama," she replied. "George is bringing him out. I can't believe these people are just abandoning this dog. I'm going to go around here one more time to see if they're going to take care of him. After that, I'm done."

George came out with the puppy who was shaking against the cold night air. The poor baby looked scared. We walked three houses down from Nita and she knocked on the door. A middle aged Hispanic woman answered. "Hola!" she greeted Nita.

"Hola," Nita greeted back. "I just came by to be sure that you don't want the puppy," she said, not disguising the disgust in her voice.

The owner looked down at the puppy and sucked her teeth. "I told you before. I don't want that dog. He's more trouble than he's worth. He tears up everything in my house. He doesn't listen and he's always running away. I've had enough of him. I got my hands full with five kids. I don't need him stressing me out too. Just take him. If you don't want him, take him to the pound and put him down," she said with no remorse.

I looked down at the little guy as she spoke and I swear he could understand every hurtful word out of her mouth. My heart broke for him. She had called him a burden. He was worthless to her. She didn't care if he lived or died. He was untrusting because he'd been mistreated by those who were supposed to love him. I knew what it felt like to be unwanted and unloved, to feel like trash to be tossed away in the garbage, to be insignificant, to feel that no one cared about whether you lived or died, to be betrayed by those who were supposed to love you. My heart broke for the poor puppy. "What's his name?" I finally asked.

"Toby. He's five years old. He's not neutered. We were going to mate him with the Yorkie across the street for puppies." What? I thought. So you don't want to take care of this dog but you want to pimp him for puppies? "If you come back tomorrow," she continued, "I'll have all his papers for you. He's up to date on all his shots, but don't bring him back. He's not welcome here." Then she turned, went into her house, and closed the door.

Nita and I turned to walk back to my truck. "Can you believe her?" Nita asked in outrage.

"Actually, no I can't. But it doesn't matter. He's safe now," I said opening my back door and putting him in.

"Thanks for taking him, Mama."

"Of course. Glad I could help. Get inside. I'll let you know how he's doing."

"Alright Mama. Goodnight."

When I got back in the truck, Zeyonna had the flashlight on her phone pointed at the puppy who wasn't really a puppy. The poor thing was shaking. He was scared. We drove thirty seconds back down the street. I gathered him up in his blanket held away from my person. Zeyonna opened the side door that led right into the finished basement and we took him down there. I untangled him from the blankets and he just sat there taking in the environment.

He was so adorable. I didn't want to take him to shelter. I had to think of a way to convince the rest of the family to let me keep him. I heard Jericho's heavy footsteps descending into the basement. He sat on the couch next to me. "So this is the dog, huh?" he asked.

"Yeah," I answered. Then I recounted the conversation we had with the owner.

I suddenly heard, "Aww, he's so cute." I looked over and Zeyonna had her phone pointed towards him showing him to her friends.

When Jericho reached out and rubbed his head, I tested the waters. "Yeah, so tomorrow I guess I'll take him to the shelter," I said sadly.

"Why're you going to take him to the shelter? He's so cute. Can't we keep him?" Zeyonna asked.

Jericho was now rubbing his belly. "You don't have to take him to a shelter. He's a good dog. I like him. Can't we keep him?"

I looked at both of them wide-eyed. "Aren't you the two that didn't want a dirty dog in your house? What changed?"

They both denied that with "who us?" smiles on their faces. "What's his name?" Zeyonna asked.

"Toby."

"Toby?" Zeyonna made a face. "Yuck, Toby. He ain't no slave. We have to change that name. If my name was Toby I'd run away too!" We all laughed. "Nope," she said, "Toby just won't do. You're way too cute to be a Toby. How about...how about Kobe?" she said enthusiastically. Toby, now Kobe, actually looked at her when she said the new name and responded to it.

"Well Zee, I guess Kobe it is. After work tomorrow, we'll take him to get all cleaned up. But for tonight," I said to Kobe, "you'll have to stay in the basement my friend." I put out some food Nita gave me to tide him over until I could get to the store.

"I've got some blankets from work I can put down for him to sleep on," Jericho said.

So we got the food, water, and blanket set out to make Kobe comfortable for the night. When we were about to go up for the evening, Kobe sat at the base of the stairs watching us.

"Thanks for letting me keep the puppy," I told Jericho.

"You knew you were going to keep him anyway. You're such a softie," he said.

Kobie started crying when we were about to close the basement door. "Esmene, do you think I should sleep downstairs on the couch with him? I don't want him to be lonely."

"Who's the softy now?" I teased, closing the door behind us.

The Truth about Daddy

My parents had been married almost fifty years, yet my father was mostly a mystery. Barock Turner was a hardworking man. He worked constantly when we were younger. He went to work before we got up for school and he came home after we went to bed. He worked most holidays, so we didn't even see him then.

I remember once he told my Mom he was going to take us kids to an amusement park for the day. He dropped us off at the front gate, gave Delilah some money, and told her what time to meet him back at the gate. We met him at the appointed hour. He took us to McDonald's to get something to eat and that was our day out with our Dad. I don't even think he saw any of us graduate. He heard we graduated and that was good enough for him.

As a child, there was definitely some resentment there on my part and from my siblings. We lived with this ghost of a father no one ever knew existed. On the rare occasion when he was there, it was awkward because it was almost like there was a stranger in our home. We were uncomfortable with him going into our refrigerator, using our bathroom, or going into Mom's room. And just when we would get used to having him around, he would be gone again.

It wasn't until we became adults and started having our own families that we understood and appreciated what our father had done for us. My mother was able to stay home and be there with all of us all the time. We all went to private school. He paid for us to go to college. I didn't even get my first job until I was nineteen. He provided everything for me. He sacrificed a relationship with all of us to provide for us. We couldn't be upset about that.

One day I was at my parents' house asking my mom if I could borrow her truck because I needed to go to the doctor. "Mom, can I borrow your truck?" I asked. "I need to go to the doctor today. Zander's using mine."

"Sure. The keys are in my bedroom," she said.

"Thanks." I went to her bedroom, grabbed the keys, and made my way out the door; and that's when I realized I was being followed by Dad.

"So uh, what doctor you going to see? Your family doctor?" he asked.

I was a little taken aback by the question, so I hesitated a minute before answering "No, I'm going to see my psychiatrist." I wondered why he was curious. Why did he have a sudden interest in my doctor appointments?

My dad had looked down and found the driveway asphalt very interesting suddenly. "Does it help?"

"Does what help?" I was confused.

Dad looked up at me from under the brim of his sombrero. "Going to see the doctor. Does it help?"

I didn't know where he was going with this but I answered, "Yes. But mostly because she prescribes my medication. I do most of my talking with my therapist. Why are you asking?"

Dad looked down again, rubbing his beard and kicking at a non-existing stone. I looked at the time on my phone. If I didn't leave soon I'd be late. I opened the door to the truck and started to get in to give him a hint. "Come on Dad, spit it out."

"Can you get me one of her cards? The doctor at the VA hospital keeps saying I need to see somebody for my PTSD. It's getting worse," he said.

I stopped backing onto the truck seat and turned to look at him. "PTSD? You have PTSD?" I asked, completely stunned.

"Yeah, from Vietnam," he said gruffly.

"When did you find out?"

He put his head back in a thinking gesture. "Oh, let's see. '83 or '84. They denied me disability for it, so I just gave up pursuing it or doing anything about it," he explained like it was the most normal thing in the world.

My mind was totally blown. "Dad, are you telling me that you were diagnosed with PTSD over thirty years ago and you never said a word about it to anyone until now?"

He smiled. He actually smiled. "Yeah, well now you know. Whatever mental problems you have, you probably got them from me. You're not alone in this. Go on, go to your appointment. Make sure you get me a card." And he walked into the backyard to continue doing whatever it was he was doing.

I looked at my phone, noted the time, and started the truck. Did that just happen? I didn't want to think about it too deeply because I had to drive on the highway and I didn't want to get lost in my thoughts. How do you just casually drop that bomb on someone and then be almost proud that you may have passed it on to your child? I knew PTSD wasn't hereditary but, gee, thanks dad. You couldn't pass on a car or something? Still it got me thinking, what else might he have passed on to me? PTSD wasn't hereditary, but Bipolar Disorder was. I couldn't help but notice some similarities in the behaviors of my grandmother, my dad, and myself.

It felt a little strange knowing the truth about Daddy's mental issues.

Through the Fire

I relapsed in my recovery and I was binging and purging again. It hurt so bad, I couldn't even lay down to sleep. I had to sleep sitting up. I had three pillows on the bed propping me up so I wasn't lying flat on my back, hoping to relieve some of the pain I was in. It felt like someone was holding a blow torch aimed right at my chest. I had taken every OTC heartburn medication available and swallowed them like Tic Tacs with no relief. I even started swallowing baking soda mixed with warm water for some respite, but it was to no avail. What was the cause of all my distress? It started out as a one-time occurrence and then came back with a vengeance. I called my family doctor hoping he could offer some relief. But he was absolutely no help. "Esmene," Dr. Richards said gently, "you need to work with your therapy team to get this bulimia under control. There is nothing I can do to help you. I'm sorry." He didn't sound sorry to me.

Thankfully, I had an upcoming appointment with my new psychiatrist, Dr. Mya, the next day. I liked Dr. Mya. She was the first African American psychiatrist I ever had and she was very knowledgeable and thorough. She also wasn't a government agent. We were in the same age group, so that made me feel like she could empathize with what I was dealing with as a middle aged black woman. Maybe.

When the appointment began with Dr. Mya she asked "Esmene, how often are you binging and purging? When you had your first appointment with me, you said you had a history of bulimia. You never said that you were engaging again. Why didn't you tell me?" Dr. Mya asked, sounding a little confused.

"Umm, I never mentioned that to you?" I asked knowing darn well I didn't.

"No," she said matter of factly.

"Oh, I thought I did. Well yes, I'm actively engaging again. I have been since maybe December." It was now July.

Dr. Mya took a deep breath. "OK Esme. How often are you doing this? Please be honest with me."

I thought that it was pretty sad that she had to ask me to be honest with her; but considering the current conversation, I guess it was warranted. "Only once a day."

"Once a day! Esme, that's a lot. Once a day is considered a severe case that requires hospitalization!" Dr. Mya said. I thought she was being a bit dramatic.

"Dr. Mya, surely you're mistaken. Once a day isn't even that bad. There were times when I've done it two or three times a day." I failed to mention that on some occasions I still engaged twice a day.

"Esmene," Dr. Mya said, in a voice laced with concern. "you have a serious problem that needs to be addressed. Binging and purging once every day is a serious issue. It'll cause severe electrolyte imbalances that cause damage to your kidneys and heart. You're already showing signs of kidney damage. It's only going to get worse."

She was right. My kidney function was already off and my potassium levels were low. I'd been warned while I was in the hospital of the dangers of both; and if one more person told me about Karen Carpenter, I was going to scream. Yet still I didn't stop. Well, once I did. I was seven months clean when I was in the hospital, but then I fell off the wagon during the whole Dina situation. It started out with "just this once" and I swore that I wouldn't do it again. Now it was a daily occurrence.

"Esmene I need you to work with your therapist Nancy to get to the heart of what's driving you to engage in these behaviors. I also need you two to figure out what DBT skills you can use in times of distress instead of binging and purging. You spent eight months in the hospital Esme. You have the skills. Use them. They'll help you. Can you do that?"

"Yeah, I guess I can."

"I know you can. You're stronger than you realize, Esmene."

I didn't feel strong, not in that moment. I felt like a failure. How many times was I going to have to climb this mountain? I was beginning to feel like the children of Israel who wandered in the wilderness for forty years before getting to the Promised Land. But I had found my way once, so I knew I could do it again. And I knew who to turn to help me. Nancy had been my therapist for almost thirteen years. I had been through countless psychiatrists, but Nancy had been my rock through them all. Since my discharge from the hospital, we had a standing appointment, every Wednesday at three-thirty.

On Wednesday, I was sitting in the waiting room waiting for her to come get me. Nancy asked "Esmene, is there a reason why you didn't let any of us know you were engaging in this behavior again?" She had the patience of a saint. Apparently I didn't tell her either.

"I don't know Nancy. I thought I mentioned it."

Nancy laughed. "Come on now, Esmene. This is me, Nancy. Be honest with me. Be honest with yourself."

"I guess I was embarrassed and ashamed. I had seven months clean and then threw it all away for food. It's just food. It's not drugs or alcohol. It's food. Harmless, right? Yet, I threw my recovery away for it. Everyone thought I was doing so well. My family was treating me like I was normal, like the hospital had cured me. Jericho wasn't watching over me anymore. I had freedom to move around. How could I disappoint everyone because I couldn't resist the call of a krimpet?" I asked, my voice laced with tears.

"But it's not really about the krimpet at all, is it?" she asked patiently.

"No, no I guess not," I said sniffling.

"OK, so what's it about?" she prodded.

"I don't know! If I did, don't you think I would have stopped already?" I yelled.

Ever patient Nancy. "Actually, no. It goes beyond knowing, Esmene, and you know that. It's about breaking what you know apart and examining it. It's hows and it's whys. It's about getting your hands dirty and your heart breaking a little bit. It's about falling apart and then putting yourself back together the way you should be. That's the work you started in the hospital. That's the work that needs to continue. All is not lost, Esmene. You can get back to that place of recovery. You just need to put in the work. Can you do that?"

"I think so," I said, unsure of my answer.

"I'll take that. Esmene, I'm not going to ask you to stop binging and purging altogether. But for this week, if you engage, I want to know what you're thinking and feeling before the binge, after the binge, before the purge, and after the purge. You can do that, can't you?"

I hesitated in my answer. That time alone with my food was very intimate. I didn't like to share that with anyone. The ritual of getting rid of it was even more secretive to me. Now she was asking me to share the most cherished details of my day with her? But I gave in. "OK, I can do that," I agreed.

We discussed some other issues and Nancy told me my time was up. "OK, Esmene. Thank you. I'll talk to you next week. If you need anything, just call me."

So Later that evening, I found myself again sitting up in my bed, with that burning in my chest which almost had me in tears, wondering what it was that motivated me to continue to engage in an activity that caused me so much pain. The one thing I always had confidence in about myself was my intelligence. This had nothing to do with how smart I was. This was deeper than intellect, deeper than cravings or desire. This went to the very core of my being. As I lay back on my pillows and closed my eyes, I allowed my mind to ponder such things. If Bulimia were a person and I had the opportunity to confront him, what would I say?

Bulimia, my nemesis, my love. You're my enemy and best friend. What is it that continues to draw me to you like a moth to a flame? I feel an overwhelming sense of emptiness. Before we meet, I have a hunger, a hunger that echoes throughout my body. It's unnatural. I feel alone, vulnerable and weak, like Superman when he has been exposed to Kryptonite. I feel... unsafe. There's a roaring in my ears. I'm shaking. I'm sweating.

Bulimia, you know the routine. I'm shaking with a need. And my need is great. It's a need to feed. I'm feeding. I'm binging. We're together at last! The roaring is gone for now. The shaking has stopped. I feel secure, accomplished, satisfied, and safe. Moments later I feel guilty, gluttonous, disgusting, and out of control. I need to get my control back. I need to get rid of you. I've had my fun. I'm satiated but I don't deserve it and I can't keep it.

I start shaking again, but differently. Now I'm frantic. I hear the imagined ticking of a timer in my head: ten minutes...ten minutes to get rid of it is all I give myself. I rush to get my implements of purging: a soda and a chopstick. I use a soda because the bubbles help the food come up easier. I use the chopstick because it's long and I can get it further down my throat. I'll also avoid getting those scars on my hand. I take a couple big gulps of the soda. I feel the churning in my stomach and I take one more big swallow. Then I turn to the toilet, fold myself in half, stick the chopstick down my throat and up you come. Beautiful relief! Another swallow of soda, another use of the chopstick and euphoria, I am unburdened of my sin. I want to do it again, so I do. I do it until my liquid lover is gone. When I'm done, I feel lighter and lightheaded, accomplished. I feel good about myself for taking control when I was out of control. I flush away the evidence of my sin and then wash my hands and chopstick. I mix warm water and baking soda to rinse my mouth in an effort to minimize the damage done to my teeth by my stomach acid. My ritual is finally over.

I look at myself in the mirror. My eyes are cherry red. My nose is running. I'm coming down from my high. My throat feels raw and there's a burning in my chest. My stomach is making odd noises. This is what I am reduced to. I am no better than a crackhead. But even a crackhead can get clean. Bulimia, this is how you degrade me. However, I know there's a reckoning coming and you will no longer contaminate my life.

We Part Only to Meet Again

It had been about a month since the truth was revealed about my clandestine activities. No matter how hard I tried, more times than not, I found myself bent over the toilet bowl ridding myself of another binge. I had finally decided I needed some divine intervention.

So when my Pastor answered the phone and asked how I was, I said, "I...I don't know how I am. I'm struggling Pastor."

"OK, talk to me. Tell me what's going on," she encouraged with much patience.

"I'm not sure my prayers are sincere when it comes to me being delivered from bulimia," I admitted softly.

"What do you mean by that?" she asked.

"What I mean is..." I paused because it was hard to explain but I started again. "What I mean is, when I was in recovery from bulimia while I was in the hospital, at first I was devastated. I mourned its loss like it was a loved one. Dr. White was actually going to admit me full inpatient because she was so worried about my safety. That's how bad I was. But after a few weeks, I started to feel better; and although I still missed it, I knew I was better without it and I was glad it was gone. I was happy that it was over. I felt a new kind of freedom, a new normal. Did I think about it? Yes, but it was like thinking of a childhood friend, a memory, but not something I wanted back. Do you understand what I'm saying?" I asked.

"Yes, I do. Go on," she encouraged.

"OK, so now it's back, back with a vengeance. I never wanted it back, but here it is. And a part of me that wants it to be gone again like it was when I was in the hospital. But I'd be lying if I said that there wasn't another part of me that loves that it's back. Some part of me wants to hold onto it and never let it go. I'm praying every day for God's strength to conquer this mountain in my life. But how can my prayers be sincere if I'm openly admitting that there's a part of me that doesn't really want to let it go? I'm lying." I finished sounding defeated.

I heard her take in a deep breath. "Honey, your prayers are sincere. They're coming from that place that does want to overcome this addiction. The part that wants to hold onto it is just a feeling and feelings are fickle. Now's the time to push through those feelings and tell yourself that you can do all things through Christ who strengthens you. I've never been through this myself, but it's an addiction so I know this is hard for you. However, you're more than a conqueror. You can take control over anything that's trying to control you. Don't ever give anything or anyone control over your life. You can do it. I know you can," she said. I could hear the conviction in her voice.

"So I'm not lying to God? I've been feeling guilty every time I pray. Some days I don't even pray I feel so guilty," I admitted to her.

"Who do you think is behind that? Who do you think would put that thought in your head to keep you from praying? That's the trick of the Enemy. He's playing his games again and you're falling for them. He's relentless. You can't let your guard down. Ask the Holy Spirit to help you each day to put on the full armor of God to fight against the tricks of the Enemy. Your battle is not against flesh and blood. It's against the forces of evil in the heavenly realms. The battle is in your mind. You're going to win. You can do this."

"I don't know if I can. I don't like this. I've been three days with no binging or purging and I thought I would feel better but I don't," I complained.

"So what do you want to do?" She asked in all seriousness.

"What do I want? I want to feel 'normal.' I want to not have to take three different sets of medications each da just to function. I want to eat and enjoy my meal and not be anxious the entire time. And then when I'm done, I don't want to fight with myself over running to the bathroom to purge that meal. I want to know what it is that I did in my life to deserve all of this!" I cried.

A moment of silence hung between us. "Try talking to the Lord. Ask Him for His help and wisdom. When you pray, ask God to answer you like He did Noah, with clear instructions, not with vague impressions in Jesus' name. He'll answer you."

"I'm getting tired," I said.

"Now what does that mean?" she asked with alarm creeping into her voice.

"I didn't sleep well last night," I said, trying to lead her away from what I really meant.

I could tell she didn't believe me. "Let me get Pastor on the line with us for a short prayer, OK?"

"OK."

I waited for a moment and then heard the melodious voice of Pastor Langston come through the phone. "Sister Esmene, how are you today?" He greeted me enthusiastically.

"Hello, Pastor. How are you? I miss you both." I sidestepped his question.

"Well Pastor Doreen and I miss you too. Am I going to have to come up to that job of yours and have a talk with your supervisor about you working every Sunday? We want to see you too!" His rich laugh soothed something inside of me. "Now, I know you've been speaking to the Pastor about some things and she wanted us to have a moment of prayer. Is that alright with you?" he asked.

"Yes sir."

"Alright Dear. Pray this prayer with me. Father in the name of Jesus I bind every demon spirit that has been assigned to Esmene. In the name of Jesus, I render every assignment null and void over her life. She is the righteousness of God. And, Satan, we command you this day to leave her, her mind, and her home, in Jesus' name. We loose the angels of God to encamp around about her and bring God's peace right now in the name of Jesus. Thank you Lord for her freedom. Now, in the Mighty name of Jesus, Amen. Hallelujah!" he prayed.

"Amen," I agreed.

"And Amen," Pastor Doreen agreed on speakerphone.

"Yes, Lord, we say Amen," Pastor Langston said. "Every word you believe releases virtue for performance. Do you believe God will perform it, Esmene?" he asked.

I did believe God would perform. I still didn't believe in myself. "Yes, I do believe."

"Well praise God. I'm so glad to hear that! It was so good to talk to you and pray with you, Esmene. I want you to know that the Pastor and I are here for you anytime you need us. We're just a phone call away. You're not in this alone. We're with you. Most importantly, God is with you. He's with you and He's for you. Get Him involved in everything you do. Ask for His help and He will help you. He's just waiting for you to ask. Alright Sweetheart, peace and blessings to you. Here's Pastor Doreen," he finished.

"Esmene, are you still there?" Pastor Doreen asked.

"Yes, I'm here."

"Muffin, before you go, there's something else I want you to remember: your health. Dialysis is a part of damage to your kidneys. You must protect your health. I need you to take this seriously. I need you to take baby steps tomorrow. I'm counting on you. You can do it." Pastor Doreen was my accountability partner. Baby steps was code for no binging/purging that day.

"I understand. I'll do better tomorrow. I promise. I love you," I said because I honestly did love her.

"I love you too. Call me if you need me." Her voice was full of reassurance that I could do this.

"I will. Goodbye."

<u>Just Give Me a Reason</u>

It was a typical Tuesday evening. Jericho was unwinding from a hard day at work by playing <u>Call of Duty</u> and I was folding last week's laundry. Suddenly, I made a startling declaration. "I'm going to quit my job."

Jericho, clearly into his mission on the game, barely heard me. "Babe, you said something?" he questioned without ever bothering to turn around.

I huffed in frustration, threw down the towel that I had been folding, and said it again. "I said, I'm going to quit my job," louder this time.

"You're going to quit your job?" he repeated, turning around quickly to look at me before turning his attention back to the game, "Why, what happened? Did someone do something to you?"

"No," I answered honestly.

He chanced a glance at me again. "Did someone say something to you that you didn't like?"

"No," I said again to his back.

"Well I don't get it," he said while continuing to furiously press buttons on his controller and trying to hold some semblance of a conversation with me, "If nothing happened, why do you want to quit?" He turned to glance at me quickly.

But he wasn't quick enough though, he got ambushed. "Crap!" He threw the controller down. Now I had his attention. "Babe, I thought you liked your job. Now you want to quit. Why?"

"I don't know. It feels like the right thing to do," I said honestly.

"What do you mean the right thing to do?" he asked.

"Well, when I woke up this morning, I had this thought that I should quit my job today. I thought it was just that, a thought. But it's been playing over and over in my head all day, so it must be the right thing to do. I must really want to quit my job. So I'm going to quit. You don't mind do you?" I asked.

Jericho sat on the bed looking dumbstruck. He put his face in his hands and ran his large hands down his face. A long, weary sigh went past his lips. "Es, you fought to keep this job the whole time you were in the hospital. Now you just want to quit. Are you sure this is what you want to do?"

"Yes, I'm sure. It feels like the right thing to do. If you're OK with it, I'm just going to quit," I said as easily as if I were asking him to pass the salt.

He rubbed his hand down his face again and looked me right in the eyes. "Esme, you do feel alright, don't you?"

I threw down the towel that I was folding. "Why is it that every time I want to do something, everyone has to question if I'm OK? Can't I have a legitimate feeling, want, need, or desire without there being something wrong with me? Despite what people think, I'm capable of having regular emotions, just like everyone else. Now, I want to quit my job. All I want to know from you is if you're OK with that. I need a yes or no answer, Jericho. It's not that hard," I said, my chest heaving in anger.

Jericho shook his head, turned his back to me and picked up his controller. "No Esmene, I don't care if you quit, as long as you're OK with it. Just do what makes you happy." He grabbed his headset off the nightstand, put it on, and started up his game again.

"Thank you," I said, but I knew he couldn't hear me.

I knew I'd made him angry and that I'd hurt his feelings but I didn't know what to do to fix it. Jericho hated conflict, so whenever there was a confrontation, he usually caved pretty easily. I felt bad for taking advantage of him and I knew from past experience it was best to leave him alone. I gave up on folding last week's laundry, threw it back in the basket with this week's laundry, and left the room so he could have his space.

The next day at work, I finally got a moment alone with my direct supervisor Donna, so I asked if she had time to talk. "Sure, what's going on?" she asked. Donna was always so sweet and helpful. I really didn't want to tell her I was leaving, but it was what it was.

"Donna I wanted to let you know that I'm going to resign, effective in two weeks."

Her face was crushed. "Oh no. I don't want you to go. Did something happen?" she asked, with sincere concern in her voice.

Now I knew I couldn't just tell my supervisor that I woke up and wanted to quit my job, so I was going to take the politically correct route. "I just need to take the time to focus on myself and my mental health. Things have been going downhill since I left the hospital and I just can't dedicate time to my job anymore. I need to focus on myself one hundred percent. I appreciate everything you did for me while I was in the hospital and all the support you have given me, but it's time for me to go." As I said the words, the truth of them hit me harder than I realized.

Donna got up out of her seat and hugged me. "Esmene, I just want you to be OK. You do what's best for you. I'll miss you." And with that, the floodgates opened and the tears began to flow unchecked for both of us. I hoped I was doing the right thing.

When I got home that day, I knew I had to let someone on my care team know I had made such an impacting decision. Dr. Mya was still new to me. I had only been her patient since February. She probably wouldn't understand my motivation for doing such a thing. I decided to go with Nancy. I sent her a text: *Hi Nancy. I just wanted to let you know I resigned from my job today.*

Before my phone left my hand, it was ringing. "Hello."

"You did what?" Nancy asked.

"Well hello to you too," I said sarcastically.

"I'm sorry Esmene. Of course, hello dear. Now, tell me this again. You resigned? Why? What happened?"

Why did everyone think something happened? Couldn't I just not want to work anymore? That wasn't a "thing"? I was required to have a reason to quit my job? "Nothing happened Nancy. I woke up and decided I didn't want to work there anymore," I explained.

"OK," she said slowly, "so there's somewhere else you want to work. Is that it?"

"No, there's nowhere else I want to work."

A subtle sigh reached me through the phone. "So you woke up and decided you just didn't want to work anymore, anywhere. How do you feel about this decision? Do you feel sad, happy, relieved?"

"No." I answered.

"No? To what?"

"No, I don't feel any of those things. I don't feel anything at all," I said.

"Esmene, last year when you were hospitalized, you did anything and everything you could do to make sure nothing affected your job. That's all you talked about. It was the one piece of normalcy you had in your life and you were determined to keep it. Now you're telling me you woke up, what, yesterday and decided you didn't want to work anymore and you feel absolutely nothing about it? How is that possible, Esmene?" she asked.

"I don't know. The thought was in my head and it seemed like a good idea. It felt like the right thing to do, so I did it. I don't feel sad. What's there to feel sad about? I don't feel happy. What am I supposed to be happy about? Relieved? Relieved about what? My job really wasn't stressful. But if you think I should be sad or happy, tell me what I should be sad or happy about because I'm at a loss right now," I said, genuinely not knowing why I should be feeling any of those things.

There was a silence between us that was longer than normal but I didn't say anything. I was waiting for Nancy to tell me why I should be feeling things that I didn't. "Esmene, during our last few sessions, we've talked about how your energy levels have dropped and how it's harder for you to function later in the day. You said the feelings of worthlessness and being a burden to your family have returned. Do you still feel that way?"

"Yes. I feel like I have no purpose. I'm just taking up space."

"OK. Are you making any plans, Esmene?" she asked in a serious voice.

"Plans for what?" I asked but I knew what she was talking about.

"End of life plans. When people are ready to end their lives, sometimes they'll make end of life plans and that include quitting jobs for no reason and giving away their possessions. Is that what you're doing Esmene?"

I had to seriously think about that. Was that what I was doing? I didn't think so but I couldn't always be trusted either. I hadn't given anything away and I had no plans to give anything away. I just resigned and didn't feel anything about it. "No. No end of life plans. Just me being a loser, probably making a bad decision. It's what I do best," I said.

"Esmene, stop it. You're not a loser, you're depressed. Listen dear, I have to go, I've got a client in a few minutes. I'm going to send a message over to Dr. Mya. I want her to talk to you about this, OK? See what she has to say about it. Then we can discuss it further during our appointment next week. In the meantime, if you need me, just reach out like you did today, OK?" I told her I would.

Who knew that leaving a job would cause such a ruckus? Later that day I received a call from Dr. Mya's secretary. Jackie asked if I would be available for a Zoom appointment with the doctor at ten o'clock the next day. I told her I would. The next day, soon after I logged on for my appointment, Dr. Mya asked "You resigned from your job?"

"Yes. Yes, I did," I affirmed for what seemed like the hundredth time.

"And how are you feeling about that decision?" she asked.

Here...we...go...again, I thought. "I feel nothing about that decision. I woke up. I didn't want to work anymore. I went to work. I resigned. I came home and ate a sandwich. I took a nap. I'm not sure what you and Nancy want me to feel about this decision," I said, getting annoyed. "It's not a big thing."

"Esmene, this decision just came out of nowhere. People don't just get up one morning and decide, 'hey I want to quit my job,' and then actually do it and feel nothing about it. I need to make sure that this isn't a part of something bigger that..."

"You mean an end of life plan?" I asked, cutting her off.

She sighed. "Yes, I mean an end of life plan or maybe a problem with your medication. What do you think, Esmene? Please be honest with me."

"I've thought about whether it's part of a plan or not. I'm ninety-eight percent certain I'm not making end of life plans. I don't know why I wanted to quit my job. It just seemed like the right thing to do. It's so much effort trying to be normal every day. It's exhausting, especially now that my co-workers know about my condition. I know they're watching me for any signs of trouble. Some days, I just don't have the energy to fake being well," I told her.

"I see. Let me ask you. What do you do on your days off?" she asked.

"Let's see. I get up with my puppy and drink coffee. I go across the street and see my parents. If it's Tuesday or Thursday, I go meet Ms. Dora at the gym for Aqua Aerobics. I shower, eat lunch, sleep until 3:45, get my nephew Carter off the bus, and watch Judge Judy while making dinner. I'm usually in bed by six or six-thirty," I rattled off.

"Why're you in bed so early?"

"I'm exhausted."

"Even after sleeping during the day?"

"Yes."

"What do you do on the days that you don't go to Aqua Aerobics and don't have to work?" she asked.

"I lay on the couch all day and watch serial killer documentaries."

"Wow. OK then," she said, "Do you talk to anyone on the phone?"

"Not really. My mom if she calls. All my siblings work. I have a few friends but they all work too so they're busy. I don't bother them. I hear from people when they want something."

"Is that how you feel? That people only reach out to you when they need you for something?" she asked.

"That's not how I feel, Dr. Mya. That's a fact. If we are strictly discussing my family, with the exception of my mother, Michaela and Lyam, I only hear from them if they need something. And as far as friends, yes, I hear from them; but I don't have that many to begin with, so it's not like my phone is blowing up. It could go all day without a text or phone call," I said honestly.

"So let me tell you what I heard you say. Besides work and going to an Aqua Aerobics class on Tuesday and Thursday, you spend the majority of your time isolated. Now you've quit your job, the one thing that gave you the most interaction with the outside world. Now you're going to be isolated even more, therefore making your depression worse. That's not good Esmene. That's not good at all."

"So what am I supposed to do?" I asked.

"Esmene, we need a plan. We need to set some goals for you," she said firmly.

"Goals?"

"Yes, goals. You can't isolate completely, especially if you're only going to watch murder and mayhem all day. Now let's think of three goals that'll get you moving and out of the house during the week."

"Three!"

"Yes three. That's not many, Esmene."

"Fine," I agreed reluctantly.

"How has your hygiene been? I know that's been an issue for you in the past," she said bluntly.

"I shower when I have to be around people," I answered honestly.

"How many days did you go to work last week?"

"One, but I did aerobics two times."

"So you showered three times last week?"

"Yeah."

"So goal number one is to shower and put on fresh clothes every day. That includes brushing your teeth."

"I have to change my clothes every day? You know how much laundry Jericho will have to do?"

"How much laundry you'll have to do. Jericho won't be doing your laundry. That's not one of your goals. That's something you should be doing to care for yourself."

"Whatever," I mumbled.

"I can hear you. Goal number two. How about you get to the gym four times a week instead of just two? You can do aerobics two times a week and the other two days you can do a different workout. How does that sound?" she asked.

She was asking for way too much. Maybe I could ask Ms. Dora to do it with me. She needed motivation to work out more too.

"OK, I'll try that. And the third goal?" I asked, hoping the appointment would be over soon.

She looked at me through the screen with her hands folded on her desk. "You tell me. What goal can you set for yourself?" she challenged.

I looked up at the ceiling, knowing this would not end until I gave her something. What could I do that would not be a lot of effort on my part? I knew. My mom had a daycare. I went to see my mom every day. I could help her with her daycare for a few hours in the morning. She would appreciate that and I wouldn't have to get dressed up or anything. She lived right across the street. "I can help my mom with her daycare. She has six kids there, five under the age of four. She could use my help during the day."

Dr. Mya clapped her hands. "That's an excellent goal. I love it! So now we have three very solid goals to get you moving during the day. If you get tired later in the day, it's OK to take a nap; but I need you up doing something. Isolating yourself in the home is not good for you. You need to be off your couch and out of your house. I'm also going to increase your Prozac by 20mg because I don't think it's holding you throughout the day. Other than that, I'm not going to make any other changes to your medications. Is there anything else you need from me today?"

To get off the phone, I thought to myself. "No, I think that's everything," I said instead.

"Great. I'm going to let Nancy know about the goals we set for you and she can check on your progress during your weekly sessions. If you have any problems, just call my office." Finally, she bid me goodbye and the chat disconnected.

After I thought about it a little, I realized the goals weren't that outrageous. I wrote them down on an index card and posted them on the side of the fridge so I could see them when I made my morning coffee. I called Ms. Dora and she said she was willing to go to the gym with me for the additional two days. And since I would be sweating at the gym, I knew I would shower on those days.

I was all motivated to start my new goals. But then COVID-19 shut everything down. Stay at home orders were put in place, the gym closed, and I couldn't go anywhere. Even Mom's daycare was closed with the exception of my nephew Carter and his baby sister Caydence. However, the shower was still available. Now the real isolation had begun.

<u>Pandemics and Life's Other Inconveniences</u>

COVID-19 "aka" the Coronavirus, had wreaked havoc upon the United States, causing everything that was considered non-essential to shut down; and stay at home orders were issued. If you did have to venture outside for essentials or to go to work, you had to cover your face with a mask or a shield. It was a very challenging time for some.

My poor son Zander was a senior in college that year. The last few months of his senior year were stolen from him as well as graduation. Sydney, my niece, was being promoted from the eighth grade and we did a drive by graduation parade for her.

Senior citizens were particularly vulnerable to the virus which meant that we wouldn't let my parents out of the house. Of course Dad, being Dad, went out anyway; but we refused to let Mom out for any reason. Mckenna and I did all her shopping for her so she wouldn't have to risk infection by going out to fight over toilet paper and soap, both of which were in short supply. Once the infection rate started slowing down, Mckenna would come pick Mom up and take her to Mckenna's house to spend time with Mckenna's family and then bring her back home. We couldn't help being overprotective. We didn't want Mom to get sick.

Jericho was considered essential personnel, so he worked during the whole pandemic. Every day we prayed that he be covered from the crown of his head to the soles of his feet by the Blood of Jesus. Zander didn't seem to be bothered by the lockdown. He got to sleep all day and stay up all night playing video games, and he was getting paid to do it. He was living the life.

The shutdown didn't bother me either. I was the queen of isolation. However, isolation had not been good for my mental health. When it first started, I made three new goals since I couldn't go to the gym and my mom really didn't need me at the daycare. The first goal was to go to the local soccer field and walk four times a week. The second was to shower at least every other day, but I had to brush my teeth every day. The third goal was I had to write a journal. I am a writer, so journaling was my way of expressing what was going on inside of me when I couldn't give voice to it. I did well the first few weeks. But getting up, getting dressed, and leaving the house was draining, mentally and physically. Then I started walking three days a week and missed an extra day of showering. Soon I was walking maybe two days every other week. The showering was sporadic. The journaling was more consistent, but not by much. Pretty soon I was just parked on the couch with Kobe, drinking coffee and waiting for the appropriate time to take a nap. By the time the stay at home orders had been lifted and life was returning to some sense of "normalcy," the damage to my psyche was evident.

I had a computer video appointment with Dr. Mya coming up and I already knew she wouldn't be happy. On the day of my appointment I logged in right at ten o'clock. "Good morning, Esmene. How have you been?" asked Dr. Mya.

"I'm still here. How are you?"

"What does that mean, you're still here?"

"I'm still here, doing OK," I corrected quickly. "How are you?"

"I'm doing good. Got a little bit of heartburn going on. I shouldn't have had that oatmeal," she bemoaned.

I loved Dr. Mya. "You should drink some baking soda in warm water. It works," I suggested.

"You know what?" She pulled out a huge bottle. "I have my baking soda tablets right here. Give me a second while

I take two." She shook two tablets into her palm and deposited them into her mouth. The faces she made were hilarious. She reminded me of a little kid taking cough syrup. She washed the pills down with a swig of water and was all done. "Sorry about that Esmene. Those pills are so nasty, but they work so I take them," she apologized.

"No problem. We all got something going on," I said.

"So, last time we talked, you were doing better with the binging and purging, using mindfulness techniques for the intrusive thoughts; but you were sleeping during the day and not really getting out much. How are things now?"

"Well, I'm not doing as well with the binging and purging, but I still get a day or two without engaging. I still sleep a lot during the day. I pretty much stay to myself. I don't reach out to anyone via phone or text except my mom; and no one really checks on me because I'm annoying and a burden and they don't have time for my BS anymore, so I just sleep my day away," I explained.

"How do you know that people think you're a burden and that you're annoying? Did they tell you this?"

"Yes," I affirmed.

"Esmene, are you telling me that people, your family, actually told you that you were annoying and a burden?" she asked with her voice full of doubt.

"Yes. Well they didn't say it with their mouths but I still heard them. They probably think I didn't hear them," I told her.

"What exactly do you mean they didn't say it with their mouths but you still heard them. Explain that to me, Esmene."

"Dr. Mya, you know when you're having a conversation with someone and you stop talking and that silence drops between you? You're both looking at each other and you can hear what that other person is saying but their mouth isn't moving?" I asked.

"So let me get this straight. You hear what the person is thinking, but they aren't actually saying anything out loud. Do you hear it in your inner voice?" she asked.

"No, why would I hear it in my inner voice, I didn't say it? I hear it in their voice. They're the ones saying it," I said incredulously.

"And it's during these silent moments that you hear people say that you're annoying and a burden. Are you sure you aren't projecting your own feelings about yourself and attributing them to these people?" she suggested.

I was getting quite annoyed with Dr. Mya. It wasn't like her to be this dense first thing in the morning. Maybe she should have had coffee with that oatmeal. "Dr. Mya, are you telling me you have never had the experience of speaking to someone and then having the silence fall between you? Then that person gives you THE LOOK and you can HEAR them, that you clearly hear every word as if they were saying it right to your face? That's never happened to you?" I asked her.

She was giving me a poker face through the computer. "No, Esmene, I'm sorry. I don't have those kinds of superpowers," she said and began typing something on her computer. I hated when doctors did that, I thought.

"When was the last time you were out of the house to do anything?" she wanted to know.

That was a good question. When was I last out? Then I noticed my wrist. "Oh, I was out about two weeks ago. I got a tattoo. See?" I held up my wrist to the camera so she could see.

"Oh my goodness. What made you decide to get a tattoo?"

"Well, my baby wanted one, though I really didn't want her to get one. She's nineteen now, so she was going to get one whether I liked it or not. She was a little scared so I went with her. And well, since I was already there and I was paying for hers anyway, I just said what the heck, tattoos for everyone."

It was at this point that Dr. Mya's forehead went to rest in her folded hands. She needed a moment. Dr. Mya sat up momentarily and looked at me through the computer. "Esmene, is it possible that we're dealing with some manic symptoms right now? Hearing conversations, randomly getting tattoos? What do you think?" she asked.

"I think I was at the tattoo shop anyway, so why not get my baby's name put on my wrist to cover the scarring there. What's the chance of me going back into a tattoo parlor any time soon?"

"Is that what you were thinking when you decided to get the tattoo?" she asked.

"No, it just seemed like the right thing to do at the time. But looking back, that was probably my motivation. It's what makes sense."

After a silent pause, she asked "How are you sleeping?"

"Oh, I sleep. No problems there."

"Did the pharmacy fill the prescription for your anxiety meds?"

"Yes."

"And are they helping you?" she asked.

"Yes, I sleep much better during the day with them."

"Esmene, I didn't give them to you to sleep during the day. I gave them to you to help manage your anxiety," she sighed. Oops, I thought, I'm telling on myself. She continued, "Are you still having feelings of worthlessness, feeling like you're a burden to your husband and children or that you embarrass them?"

"Yes, every day."

"If I asked your husband and children, would they agree with your assessment of you?"

"No, but that's because they don't want to hurt my feelings. They feel sorry for me. They see I'm already pathetic. They aren't going to kick me when I'm down. You know what happened yesterday? I was home all day. I simply got up but I didn't shower or brush my teeth, nothing. I laid on the couch most of the day. Jericho got home around five. He washed dishes, put dinner on the grill, and did a load of laundry. He had to work and then do all the things I should have done. If that's not the definition of pathetic, then I don't know what is," I said with tears in my eyes.

Dr. Mya gave me a look of understanding. "Esmene, you're not pathetic. Far from it. You're depressed and this pandemic didn't help you. It's made things worse. Now that things are opening back up, I want to get you moving. How about I give you one goal until I see you next time which will be in four weeks instead of six. Your goal will be to shower, brush your teeth and go grocery shopping. Just once. If you do it more than once, that's great. But your goal is to just do it once. And I want you to write in your journal about how that felt to do that for your family. OK?"

"I guess I can do that. OK," I agreed.

"I'm looking over your meds and I don't see that I need to make any adjustments. Explain to Jericho what manic behavior is. If you or Jericho see any more evidence of manic behavior, please contact the office before things get out of hand. I know mania can feel good, but you know it usually doesn't end well," she warned. "Is there anything else you need from me?"

"No Dr. I think I'm fine," I said.

"Good. Keep up with your appointments with Nancy and I'll see you in four weeks. Call if you need anything."

The Awakening

As summer transitioned into fall and the leaves changed colors and fell from the trees, I began to notice some changes from within myself. I was leaving the house to run errands more than usual. My daily naps had gotten shorter. Some days, I wouldn't even fall asleep. Some nights, I stayed up that extra half hour working on my various art projects. I was bathing more during the week and changing my clothes. I had done the laundry, cleaned the kitchen, and cooked dinner.

The awakening had begun. Slowly but surely, the depressive mood I had been in for so long was finally lifting; and I could see the dawn ahead of me. Nancy noticed the change during our next appointment. I was even logged in early this time. "You sound better Esmene," she said.

"I feel better. This is the best I've felt in months. Probably since I left the hospital," I said truthfully.

"And what does that feel like? Can you explain it to me in words?"

I searched my mind for the right words in order to explain it to her. It was difficult to convey my feelings to someone who has never been through what I'd experienced. "I feel like I have a chance at life, to really live. Before, I saw no purpose in doing anything because I saw no chance at life, no purpose in life, no hope. Life had no meaning because I was worthless. Now I feel like I do have a reason for being here. I do have a purpose. My presence is needed. My voice is heard. There's hope if I just do something," I said.

"Wow, Esmene. That's absolutely amazing. I mean, if we just look back a few weeks ago, your words were the total opposite of what you are saying to me right now. Do you see how the disorder lies to you? How even though you may not be feeling your best, you can't just listen to the lies depression tells you and give in? You have to use the skills you learned at Waterford to fight your way back. Listen to yourself right now. That's awesome." Nancy always was my biggest cheerleader. "Now, are you experiencing any agitation? Any nervousness, nervous energy, or insomnia? Nothing like that's going on, right?" she asked.

"No, nothing like that. Like I said I may stay up an extra half hour to an hour but then I go to bed. I sleep like I usually do and Kobe and I are up at five o'clock like always," I assured her.

"I can't believe you have your dog on a schedule. What if you wanted to sleep in one morning?"

"You know, on the rare mornings I oversleep, he does too. We have the same sleep patterns. It's weird that he's so in tune with me. He even takes naps with me."

"Really? That's interesting."

"Yeah. When it's nap time, he'll start barking and run over to the couch. When I lay down to take my nap, he lays beside the couch and naps with me. My kids think it's hilarious. And when it's bedtime, he barks and runs over to the steps."

"Isn't that something. Sounds like you and Kobe were meant to be together. Well, Esmene, it's so good to hear that mentally and emotionally you're doing so much better. I know your family will benefit from the changes as well. It's important that they see you being a participant in their lives when you can be. Your children may be adults but they still need you."

"Speaking of children," I said, "I'm concerned about Zeyonna. She's always been a messy little girl. Both my kids are. They never really learned to clean up after themselves because I was home and did the cleaning. I honestly thought she was going to be a hoarder. All of a sudden, she's turned into this neat freak. Every night I go to bed; and when I come downstairs the next morning, my house has been rearranged. Shoes are lined up perfectly on the shoe rack. Cabinets are organized.The counters are completely empty. I asked her why she was doing it and she said it was because seeing all the stuff everywhere was bothering her. It was all she could think about so she had to get rid of it. I'm concerned, Nancy. This has come on suddenly within the last four weeks. We both know this is OCD. I have OCD. I'm worried. What else might she have inherited from me?"

Nancy was silent for a moment. "I can see why you are concerned, Esmene. Zeyonna may be anxious and this is the only way she knows how to express it. She's been through a lot this year. She's missing out on the full college experience because of the pandemic. But she's missing out on the full experience because of the pandemic. That's a lot for a social young person to have to deal with. Also, a lot of her friends are probably leaving to go back to school. Anxiety could be the driving force behind all of this, not that she inherited anything from you. Don't look for trouble where there may not be any. You know what to look for. Talk to her about this change. Keep the communication flowing. Listen and hear what she's saying. You can teach her the same tools you learned to help her deal with any anxiety before it becomes a bigger issue. You can do this."

I inhaled deeply, taking in everything Nancy had said. It all made sense. Zeyonna had been through a lot and I noticed that she had been spending a lot of time with her three friends who were getting ready to go back to college. Maybe that's exactly what this was all about. My baby was anxious and probably sad about all the new changes in her life. "Maybe you're right Nancy. I never thought of it that way. She's got a lot going on in her world, a lot of adjustments she's been forced to make before she was ready. I need to be available to help her through it. It doesn't mean that there's anything more to it than that," I said.

"Right," Nancy agreed. "And if it turns out that there's something more, we can deal with it then. Don't make yourself anxious about something that hasn't happened yet. Deal with the here and now. Understood?"

"Understood."

"Alright Esmene. Our time's up. If you need any help with Zeyonna or anything at all, you know to reach out to me. If not, I'll see you next week."

Hunting the Road to November

It was dawn, five o'clock, my favorite time of the day. Even though I didn't have my job anymore, I still got up early. I liked having the time to myself, just me and the puppy. It was time I didn't have to have my mask on. I was free to feel whatever and however I was feeling. I didn't have to explain myself to anyone nor take into account the feelings of others. It was the only part of my day that I felt I was truly Esmene. Five o'clock, the golden hour.

So I was surprised to have my solace broken by my phone ringing. I knew it was Mom by the ringtone. "Good morning, Mother. To what do I owe the pleasure of this early morning interruption?" I teased as I took a sip of my coffee but I was really a bit nervous. Why would she be calling me so early in the morning?

I heard her sniffle and knew something was wrong. "Mom, what's wrong?" I asked, setting my coffee mug on the counter and turning to look out the kitchen window.

"Esme," she started tearfully, "Baby, I'm sorry. I have some terrible news," she cried.

My heart started hammering in my chest. Oh my God, had something happened to Dad? "Mom, is it Dad?" I asked hesitantly.

"No. No your Dad's fine. Esme, Angel's dead," she said, sobbing into the phone. I couldn't believe what I'd just heard. Angel was dead. Those were words I always desired to hear but would never dare admit it. But now, in this moment, when I received what I always wanted, I had absolutely no idea how to react. Angel was dead. Now what? "Esme, are you there?" My mother's hoarse voice came through the phone.

"How? How did he die?" I wondered. Did someone spill his blood? Was he violated, made to beg, cry and scream for mercy, only to be denied?

"No one knows. It's the first I heard of this. He hadn't been heard from for a few days, so his son went over to his apartment. He found him dead at the bottom of the stairs. It looks like he fell but no one knows what caused the fall. This is so horrible, him dying alone like that." She continued to cry.

Thus, the mighty Angel hath fallen and broken his scrawny neck. And now he would descend into the bottomless pit to spend an eternity with the rest of his fallen comrades in abuse. This was just too much, I thought. I had to get off the phone. I didn't know if I was about to cry with relief or giggle with glee. Crying, of course, was what my Mom would expect. Giggling would earn me a trip back to the hospital. Esmene, do not giggle I told myself. "Mom, I'm sorry you got such upsetting news. I just...I just need some time to process this. It's a little much this early in the morning. I never expected to get such news." Such glorious, glorious news, I thought with glee.

"Oh Esme, I understand and I'm sorry I had to tell you. I just wanted to let you know before you found out from someone else, like on Facebook. I know how close you two were and how much you loved your Uncle." I wanted to vomit because she was right, I did love my Uncle. But now he was my dead Uncle, found at the bottom of his steps like a dismantled Mr. Potato Head. Yes, Angel may have won our battles but I'm the one who survived.

"Yeah Mom, thank you. I'll call you later." I just hung up.

Uncle was dead. The man who taught me about the thin line between love and hate, who showed me the beauty in my pain, who took me to hell and then helped me navigate its walls, was dead. But Uncle had also taught me about the beauty of irony. It was November and today was my birthday. I continued to look out my window and it was not as dark as it was before the phone rang. I picked up my coffee mug and took another sip. Life was yet taking me down another road. I had traveled the path from death to life. I straddled the border between madness and sanity. I had driven through the tunnels of darkness into light. My travels had been many; but my journey was not over, for there were other roads ahead of me that I had yet to discover. I looked down at my wrist, at all the scars left behind by my own hands. My large blue-green veins made up the major roads in my life, while the faint lines made up the little side streets I had travelled down along the way. All those fine lines led me to today.

I hadn't realized up until that moment that I was crying. They weren't tears of sadness. They were tears of reflection and relief, that, despite all that I'd been through, I survived. I was here, standing in my kitchen, celebrating another birthday with another chance to get it right. The price for my freedom was a life, but not my life.

My family never gave up on me. I never gave up on me. But most importantly, God never gave up on me. Uncle had fallen and I was yet standing. And for the first time in a long time, I could truly say I was thankful to be alive.

Happy Birthday Esmene.

Made in the USA
Middletown, DE
25 February 2021

34256763R10156